THE COMPLETE IDIOT'S GUIDE® TO

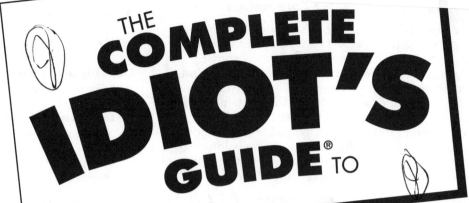

Finding Your Dream Job Online

by Julia A. Cardis

que®

A Division of Macmillan USA
201 West 103rd Street, Indianapolis, Indiana 46290

The Complete Idiot's Guide to Finding Your Dream Job Online

Copyright © 2000 by Que Corporation

International Standard Book Number: 0-7897-2326-3

Library of Congress Catalog Card Number: 00-100681

Printed in the United States of America

First Printing: May, 2000

02   01   00   4   3   2   1

Trademarks

Warning and Disclaimer

Associate Publisher
Greg Wiegand

Acquisitions Editors
Angelina Ward
Heather Kane

Development Editor
Sarah Robbins

Managing Editor
Thomas F. Hayes

Project Editor
Karen S. Shields

Copy Editor
Victoria Elzey

Indexer
Sandra Henselmeier

Proofreader
Maribeth Echard

Technical Editor
Harrison Neal

Illustrator
Judd Winick

Team Coordinator
Sharry Lee Gregory

Interior Designer
Nathan Clement

Cover Designer
Michael Freeland

Copywriter
Eric Borgert

Layout Technicians
Heather Hiatt Miller
Stacey Richwine-DeRome
Timothy Osborn
Mark Walchle

Contents at a Glance

Contents

16 Finding Industry-Specific Sites   229

17 Headhunters and Third-Party Recruiters   237

About the Author

Julia A. Cardis is an award-winning, independent professional writer and co-author of *The Complete Idiot's Guide to Planning a Trip Online*. She has also written about online business travel and wrote a Web development guide for small businesses. Julia has worked in health-care marketing and grant-writing, business-to-business advertising and marketing, as a content provider and Web marketer in a startup Web agency, and in the freelance market as a business writing consultant. She has written book reviews for Vault.com and contributes to other career-related Web sites.

Acknowledgments

Many thanks to Greg Wiegand and the folks at Macmillan USA for the opportunity to write another *Complete Idiot's Guide* and for their ongoing support, encouragement, and sound advice. Acquisitions editors Angelina Ward and Heather Kane deserve a hip-hoorah for their tireless efforts, and Sarah Robbins, development editor, gets a big pat on the back for helping me hammer out the structure and contents of the book and overseeing the project. Gracias to Sharry Lee Gregory for her gentle reminders and friendly support. Thanks to Harrison Neal, technical editor, for double-checking the how-tos and making sure the information in this book is accurate and as up-to-date as possible. Kudos to Victoria Elzey for a superb editing job and for watching my back side. Thanks also to Karen Shields for moving the manuscript and art through production, and to the Macmillan USA production team for turning out the fine-looking final product.

Special thanks to Kim Isaacs and Chandra Prasad, and all the other career experts who answered my questions, offered nuggets of wisdom, and helped me make sense of the seemingly endless stream of online career development information and job sites, and for making me believe that there is a dream job out there for everyone willing to make it happen!

Change Is Good...

It's sometimes hard to keep up with the Web. As you know, the Web is a constantly evolving animal, so please accept my apologies if a site listed in this book has changed addresses, dropped off the face of the Earth, or reinvented itself since I reviewed it for this book.

If we missed a site that you'd like to recommend for future editions of this book, please let us know:

The Complete Idiot's Guide to Finding Your Dream Job Online
Macmillan USA
201 West 103rd Street
Indianapolis, Indiana 46290-1097

What's on Your Mind?

As a reader of this book, you are our most important critic and commentator. We value your opinion and want to know what we're doing right, what we could do better, what areas you'd like to see us publish in, and any other words of wisdom you're willing to pass our way.

As an Associate Publisher for Que, I welcome your comments. You can fax, email, or write me directly to let me know what you did or didn't like about this book—as well as what we can do to make our books stronger.

Please note that I cannot help you with technical problems related to the topic of this book, and that due to the high volume of mail I receive, I might not be able to reply to every message.

When you write, please be sure to include this book's title and author as well as your name and phone or fax number. I will carefully review your comments and share them with the author and editors who worked on the book.

Fax: 317-581-4666

Email: consumer@mcp.com

Mail: Greg Wiegand
           Associate Publisher
           Que
           201 West 103rd Street
           Indianapolis, Indiana 46290 USA

Introduction

Boy oh boy, times sure have changed when it comes to looking for a new job or making a career move. We used to rely on newspaper classifieds, recruiters, headhunters, college placement offices, career advice books, and word-of-mouth to find jobs, make a career leap, or advance in our field of choice or even within our existing company. But now with the Internet and the World Wide Web at our disposal, locating the tools to help find a better job and advancing or redirecting our career has never been easier. The Web provides fast, free, convenient, and up-to-date resources and information—any time of the day or night.

But if you haven't looked for a job lately or haven't gone online to do your research or go job hunting, you'll be surprised and pleased to discover that now, more than ever before, your career opportunities are limited only by the choices you make. You choose whether you're going to get advanced training, whether you're going to look for a job that pays what you deserve, whether you're going to join that professional association your boss has been telling you about, whether you're going to learn HTML and build an online career portfolio for yourself. And, yes, you choose whether you're going to grow up and be a "Yes Man" the rest of your life.

That's right. In today's fast-paced world of work, also known as the "new economy," *you and only you* are in charge of your career destiny. If you think the ABC company you started with fresh out of college is the place you'll retire from, think again. In fact, most people will change jobs eight or nine times and change careers three times by the time they reach retirement, and the average length of employment is four and a half years.

With downsizing, restructuring, office politics, and all the other trials and tribulations of the modern work world, the days of lifetime tenures and job security are long gone. And the good news is that (even though this could change overnight) it is a job-seeker's market right now. Plus, the Web has opened up new opportunities in the shape of startups, dotcoms, telecommuting, advanced training, distance learning, consulting, freelancing, contract work, and other ways to redirect your career away from the traditional 9-to-5 office routine. Some experts even predict that over the next few years, more and more people will move from traditional office jobs to strictly contract or project work.

This book is about discovering your dream job—getting the job you *want*, not just another job. You'll have a much better chance of accomplishing this seemingly elusive goal by taking control of your career and the choices you make that determine the path you're on. After all, it's *your* path, isn't it? Why not invest as much time researching your job and career options as you would a buying a new house or making an investment.

So, let's get one thing straight. This book, although it does deal with online job sites, is not just about posting your résumé to a job bank and waiting for the calls to come in. In fact, if that's what you're hoping to hear, you had better look elsewhere for that bit of shortsighted advice. Your résumé is just one part of your job-hunting arsenal; emailing your résumé and/or posting it to a résumé database are not always the most effective ways to land your dream job.

Going online is a great way to learn everything you need to know about tapping into the incredible wealth of online career resources to market and position yourself ahead of the competition, and about acquiring the skills you need to move successfully through the job-search process—now or when the time is right to make a move.

The Web is an endless source of information for helping you make the most of your career. Hopefully, with these tools and information in hand, you can find the dream job that you know you've always wanted (and deserved).

How to Use This Book

I won't be offended if you don't read every page in this book. In fact, the book is designed for just about every type of job seeker—from college grads to high-dollar executives—so you might find there are some chapters that simply do not apply. Feel free to skip around to the chapters that deal with your needs and interests.

Job seekers generally fall into a few distinct categories. With this in mind, this book can be used by any of the following types of job hunter, at any level of experience:

➤ Those who need a job, and need it now!

➤ Those who know the days of 20-year tenures at the same company are long gone and are always on the lookout for new opportunities.

➤ Passive job seekers who want to go online to stay abreast of the latest trends, job growth markets, salary reviews, and hiring and firing trends and sort of wait for the perfect job to come their way.

➤ Others who use the Internet to stay connected—network with business associates, experts, and others who might come in handy when the next career move is being planned.

An important part of the book that every job hunter should read, though, is Part 1. This section of the book will orient you to today's high-tech recruiting and hiring trends, plus help you prepare for the online job search and help you develop a plan of action. Think of your career development as a long road trip. If you don't have a map or a destination in mind, you could spend your whole career meandering in the same circles, never really getting anywhere, always making the wrong turn. So, get a plan—your career road map—up-to-date with today's opportunities and your current interests. It'll be a much more pleasant ride!

Part 1: Throw Your Hat into the Ring: Preparing for Your Online Job Search provides you with an overview of the online career resource landscape so you know what tools and resources are at your disposal. You'll also learn about the dangers and pitfalls of online job hunting, such as getting caught looking for a job on company time. You'll also be brought up to speed on tips and tools to be a smarter and more efficient job searcher, and how to get organized to stay on top of your search efforts.

Part 2: Get a Charge out of Job Hunting: The Electronic Résumé and Cover Letter teaches you about the electronic résumé and what happens to your résumé after it's sent across the wires. You'll also get tips, samples, advice, and help revamping your résumé for today's new digital economy. Chapter 8, "Privacy, Distribution, and Access to Your Résumé," discusses résumé privacy and distribution issues and how to be sure your résumé doesn't fall into the wrong hands.

Part 3: Market Yourself: Tools and Techniques for Gaining the Competitive Edge takes you step-by-step to create a hi-tech online résumé and portfolio, how to network online to get the inside scoop on the "hidden job market," and how to research companies to knock 'em dead in the interview.

Part 4: Ready, Set...Hunt! The Online Job Site Landscape surveys the most popular (and populated) job sites, as well as starting points and gateway sites to lead you to the information you need—in a flash. You'll also get the scoop on regional job guides, niche industry job sites, how to work with headhunters and recruiters, and how to use company Web sites to land the job of your dreams.

Part 5: Resources for Every Type of Job Hunter has a little something for everyone, including students and college grads, entry-level workers, professionals making a career change, those currently unemployed, minorities, executives, and free agents, and entrepreneurs. If you're curious about Web-based free agent and entrepreneurial opportunities, be sure to read Chapter 24, "Just for Entrepreneurs and Free Agents."

At the back of the book, you'll also find a handy glossary of terms, as well as an appendix that provides a quick and easy overview of the features and functions of the major job sites.

Conventions Used in This Book

This book is full of insider tips and noteworthy sites, as well as advice and warnings you should know when you go online to find your dream job. There are four kinds of boxes in this book:

Site for Sore Eyes

Funny, resourceful, interesting, off-the-beaten-path sites to cheer you up along the way, or offer a fresh new perspective on the "world of work."

The Extra Mile

An extra effort can go a long way in advancing your career. Get advice on standing out from the competition and telling the prospective boss what (s)he really wants to hear.

Thanks for the Tip

Nibbles of advice and straight talk to keep you up to speed and in the game.

Techno Talk

Technical terms and job-hunting buzzwords you'll need to know.

Leaps and Assumptions

In writing this book, I assume you've been around the proverbial Internet block a few times. You either have access to or have your own computer (preferably, you have one at home, as job hunting on company time could cost you your job, but more about that later). You have good Web searching and navigation skills and you know how to use popular software programs such as Microsoft Word, which you'll need for the résumé part of your job search. I assume, too, that you're at least thinking about a new job or making a career move. Otherwise, why did you pick up this book?

If you're new to computers or the Web, here are some starting recommendations if you need a push in the right direction:

Internet and Web Help: *The Complete Idiot's Guide to the Internet, Sixth Edition*, Preston Gralla

Word Processing Help: *The Complete Idiot's Guide* series covers Microsoft Word, Office 95, Office 97, Office 98, and Office 2000. Please visit Macmillan USA's Web site at **www.mcp.com** for a complete list of titles.

Career Help: You'll find *Complete Idiot's Guides* for every aspect of career development:

The Complete Idiot's Guide to Changing Careers, William Charland, David E. Henderson, 1998

The Complete Idiot's Guide to Getting the Job You Want, Marc A. Dorio, Rosemary Maniscalco, 1998

The Complete Idiot's Guide to the Perfect Cover Letter, Susan Ireland, 1997

The Complete Idiot's Guide to the Perfect Interview, Marc A. Dorio, 1997

The Complete Idiot's Guide to the Perfect Résumé, Susan Ireland, 2000

The Complete Idiot's Guide to a Career in Computer Programming, Jesse Liberty, 1999

Internet Access Options: Try your local library or community center. Or bum some online time from a wired-up buddy. If you absolutely must do the online part of your job search at work, be sure to read Chapter 2, "It's a Jungle Out There: Job Hunters Beware!" and Chapter 8, "Privacy, Distribution, and Access to Your Résumé," before you make a move.

Part 1

Throw Your Hat into the Ring: Preparing for Your Online Job Search

Knowing what you want in a job or career is the first step to finding that dream job. This part of the book will help you prepare for the job hunt, from evaluating your skills and interests to determining your options and requirements, as well as gathering the tools you need to start the hunt. After all, if you think having an up-to-date résumé is all you need to land that dream job, you're mistaken. These days, it takes much more than skills to get a job. Research, planning, networking, and strategizing are equally important to position yourself favorably in the eyes of your potential employers.

You also learn about some of the pitfalls and dangers of online job hunting and how to avoid common mistakes to emerge as the hunter and not the hunted!

Chapter 1

Use the Web for Career Development: For a Job Now or Later

In This Chapter

➤ How to tap into the career development tools and resources on the Web

➤ How to compete in the "new economy"

➤ Where to get expert advice for your industry, experience level, and career interests

➤ Evaluating your job satisfaction, and knowing when it's time to make a change

➤ Determining salary requirements and assessing the costs associated with changing your job or career field

---

Career development is an ongoing process—and it really isn't something you should think about only when it's time to look for a new job. This book is about finding your dream job, right? If that's your mission, then you have to be proactive and stay in tune with the work world outside your office. You also have to be in tune with your skills and interests to find the job that's right for you.

After all, taking charge of your career destiny involves more than just updating your résumé when it comes time to look for another gig. To get the job you want—your dream job—you have to arm yourself with powerful self-marketing tools and be prepared with a well-stocked arsenal of job-hunting tools and information. You also have to decide the best plan of attack based on how fast and how far you're willing to go to get that elusive dream job.

Whether you're a college graduate, high-dollar executive, free agent, or someone looking to change jobs or careers altogether, the Web is an expansive and growing information hub for all your career-development needs, and it certainly goes beyond job-posting boards and résumé databases.

So, log on and take control of your career destiny. It's up to you, and you'll get out of it exactly what you put into it. This chapter is designed to introduce you to the resources and tools available online, and how to use those tools to help you find your dream job—now or down the road.

Career Tools, Resources, and Advice

The Web is not the be all and end all for job seekers. It's just one component of your career development strategy, but it is an excellent place to start gathering information, advice, tools, and resources.

By the way, I'm assuming you have a computer, or access to one, and that you know your way around the Internet and the Web. If not, you'll need to get up-to-speed to tap into the wealth of online career information. Plus, in this day and age, if you don't have basic computer and Web skills, I'm afraid to say you're at a disadvantage compared to your competitors—the same folks who are also looking for your dream job.

So, take it upon yourself to learn these valuable and increasingly required skills. To get started, try *The Complete Idiot's Guide to the Internet, 6th Edition* by Peter Kent (ISBN: 0-7897-2120-1), or go online to get help. A great starting point is Webmonkey (see Figure 1.1) at `hotwired.lycos.com/webmonkey/guides/`. But there are thousands of sites to help you navigate your way around the online world. Just go to a search engine such as Yahoo! (`www.yahoo.com`) or AltaVista (`www.altavista.com`) and do a keyword search using "beginning Web guides" and you'll have plenty of matches to choose from.

Welcome to the "New Economy"

What is the "new economy"? *Wired* magazine, the popular monthly mag that covers everything that is Internet, has put together "An Encyclopedia for the New Economy" (read it online at `hotwired.lycos.com/special/ene/`). When you reach the Web page, you will see the following manifesto:

"When we talk about the new economy, we're talking about a world in which people work with their brains instead of their hands. A world in which communications technology creates global competition—not just for running shoes and laptop computers, but also for bank loans and other services that can't be packed into a crate and shipped. A world in which innovation is more important than mass production. A world in which investment buys new concepts or the means to create them, rather than new machines. A world in which rapid change is a

constant. *A world at least as different from what came before it as the industrial age was from its agricultural predecessor. A world so different its emergence can only be described as a revolution... We are building it together, all of us, by the sum of our collective choices.*"

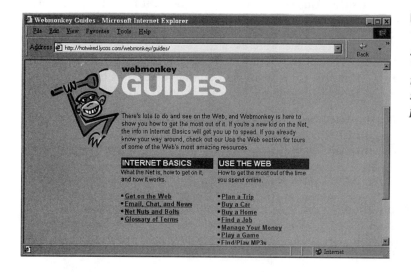

Figure 1.1

Wired's Webmonkey shows you the ways of the Web—even tips on using the Web in your job search. A great starting point for new users!

But what if your job or career has nothing to do with the "new economy"—the companies you want to work for probably don't even have Web access in the office. So what? A company that exists in today's economy is somehow touched by technology, the information revolution, the "new economy," and that means you, in turn, are touched by the radical changes taking place.

At the very least, what the new economy has to do with you and getting a job is that at no time before in the history of the world is it more important that you be skillful, smart, and up-to-speed with the tools available to you. It's never been easier to get the information and resources you need to find that dream job, and always keep in mind your competition is hot on your trail, looking for the same darned job!

In essence, whoever gets there first and makes the smartest, strongest impression wins. This is where the Web comes in.

"I Woke Up One Day and Realized I Hated My Job"

I've heard this over and over from job seekers (and coming from my own mouth, too) and it is quite a horrible realization when it hits you. It doesn't even have to be as bad as hating your job, but just knowing you want and deserve something better. I have one thing to say: Don't despair, and don't allow yourself settle for less. Not to wax poetic, but if you believe you want and deserve something better in your work life, you have the power to get it. You just have to make up your mind to do it.

I know, sometimes it's not that simple. Making a career move (or just getting a job now!) can be in response to a pending or sudden layoff, dissatisfaction with your current position or salary, and changes in the industry, or relocation. In these situations, time is not on your side. You have to get a job, and you have to get it now. Forget the dream job—you need any job. That's fine for now. But what about the next job? And the next? And the next?

Statistics show that the average tenure of a job is three years. Most people will change jobs more than 10 times in their lives, and change careers at least three times. If you're happy just bumbling along from job to job to job, good for you.

But hopefully, one day you'll decide it's high time you find your dream job. How do you do it? Sure, you can go to your college career placement office, the library, or a local bookstore and find hundreds, if not thousands, of books and other sources of information and career advice. You can even hire a professional career counselor to help you sort through your career development options.

But why leave the comforts of home or spend money on books or counselors when you can find career development tools and advice right at your fingertips? Take control of your work life the easiest way possible—by tapping in to the wonderful world of the Web.

Online Career Guidance

Sure, you can hire a professional career counselor to help you decide which career suits your skills and interests, and for some people this might not be a bad idea. But lucky for us, many of these experts have Web sites or write for career magazines and cover everything under the sun when it comes to career development.

The downside to career guidance counselors, or career coaches, is that everyone has their own ideas on how you should deal with your career options. A world of conflicting advice can leave your head spinning. But just like anything else, you might have to try on a few different pairs of shoes before you find the right fit. And try to not settle for the advice of just one person; try to get a second, third, or fourth opinion. Explore your options.

The world of work is changing at such a breakneck speed that those tried and true methods of yesteryear simply don't apply in today's business world. Traditional job search techniques still work for some people, but there is a new generation of career experts who take a totally different approach to coaching and advising you on how to survive in the "new economy."

Thanks for the Tip

Steer Clear of Dinosaurs

Some career "experts" haven't quite caught up with the online recruiting phenomenon, except that they've posted their tips and advice on their "career counselor" Web sites. If you're checking out an "expert," be leery of advice such as, "Résumés should be one page. No more. No less." That advice is old hat. The online job hunt is a different animal, so look for career experts who are up-to-date with today's trends, technologies, and techniques. To learn more about today's online recruiting trends, visit InterBizNet at www.interbiznet.com.

Career Magazines and Experts

Career magazines aren't just for human resource professionals or people getting started in the working world. Unless you're independently wealthy like me (ha!) and can coast by with little regard for an ongoing source of income, you need to approach your career as a lifelong journey. So, whether you're actively looking for a new job or just curious about your options when you do decide to make a change, you'll find plenty of articles and advice at various top-notch online career magazines.

Here, I've highlighted some of the most popular and valuable career magazines that you can access online. If you're looking for industry-specific publications, I'll get to those later in Chapter 16, "Finding Industry-Specific Sites." But for general career magazines and columnists, these are some sites you don't want to miss.

CareerMagazine (www.careermag.com)

CareerMagazine not only has a variety of articles and resources relating to the job search process, it's also one of the largest online employment services. The site features a magazine format and offers A–Z employment information for both job candidates and potential employers, including job listings, employer profiles, a résumé bank, a career forum for advice exchange, and a variety of articles relating to the job search process.

CareerMag.com pioneered the online employment magazine format and was one of the first Web sites solely dedicated to Internet recruitment services. CareerMag.com features include

➤ **Job Openings and Listings**—Search job postings by title, location, and skill levels in a wide range of industries and professions. Postings are updated every 42 days.

➤ **Résumé Bank**—Deposit your résumé and profile information into data banks for a six-month period. Let the recruiters and employers come to you.

➤ **Employer Profiles**—Information is power, and the more you know about an employer, the better equipped you are to succeed in getting a job with your target company. Although the information is provided by the companies themselves, you can get the company perspective on human resources philosophy and corporate culture.

➤ **Articles**—Get the scoop from nationally recognized experts and professionals on employment topics, human resources issues, and legal matters.

➤ **Message Boards**—Network, pose questions, and get answers from forum participants, and get insider advice on marketing and positioning yourself for a successful job hunt.

➤ **On Campus**—Stay up-to-date on corporate visits to university campuses nationwide.

➤ **Diversity**—Read up on Equal Employment Opportunity Issues, government rulings, and other issues affecting minorities in the workplace.

➤ **Recruiter's Directory**—Connect with the middleman—the recruiter who can connect you with employers that use outside services for finding new talent. Sometimes, this is your only foot in the door.

➤ **Relocation Resources**—In partnership with HomeFair (`www.homefair.com`), you can access handy relocation tools and resources such as salary calculators, moving calculators, city guides, and school reports.

Fast Company (`www.fastcompany.com`)

For all you movers and shakers, be sure to log on to Fast Company. This revolutionary think-machine aims to be the foremost handbook of the business revolution. According to Fast Company's positioning statement, the handbook covers "the changes under way in how companies create and compete, the new practices shaping how work gets done, and a showcase of the teams that are inventing the future and reinventing business."

Even if you don't consider yourself a mover and shaker today, oh boy, just you wait and see. Get a head start on your competition and woo potential employers with your knowledge of the changin' times. Fast Company can help you locate the tools, techniques, and the mindset you need to explore the "new economy."

Be sure to check out the Working Progress section (`www.fastcompany.com/career/`). Here, you can look for new jobs and learn new strategies for personal career management. The new-and-improved Working Progress career center has a job search function, featuring exclusive job listings, research reports, and user comments on fast companies.

What's a Fast Company?

According to the magazine's mission statement, "Fast companies come in all shapes, sizes, and forms, from high-tech high-flyers to bastions of the old regime trying to reinvent themselves. They can be local or global, big or small, young or old, the whole organization or just a renegade division. The difference is that their products and people always seem to have an edge on the competition. They get it—they're doing things differently and making a difference."

For a step-by-step approach to today's job hunt, no matter what your circumstances are, get the advice, tools, and information you need to find your dream job. Fast Company offers

➤ **Find Your Calling**—Why are you here? Is your job meaningful or just a way to while away the time? Think it's time to leave your job? Get on track to a more fulfilling career.

➤ **Search for a Job**—You've decided. For whatever reason, it's time for you to leave. Here's the help you need to find work at a fast company, including unique job listings from companies looking for people like you.

➤ **Build "Brand YOU"**—Even if you love your job, there's always the opportunity for something better around the corner. Take charge of your options and work on improving the brand called "YOU." This section goes beyond help with your résumé. Definitely not something you'll learn in college!

➤ **Make a Choice**—Time to decide. Should you stay or should you go now? If you stay, there will be trouble. If you go, it will be double. Enough of the clash. You've got an offer, maybe more. Should you take it? Which one should you take? How should you negotiate? What's the best way to leave without burning bridges? Find stories and advice on how to handle making the big leap.

➤ **Go Free Agent**—What will your mother say? It's a big decision to make, but more and more people are going free agent. If you're curious about this career option, before you declare your independence, get help with everything that goes along with free agency and entrepreneurialism, even advice on how to break it to your parents and peers.

➤ **Move On**—It's time to pick up and move. This section helps get you and all your stuff to where you're going.

And be sure to dig into the article archives for down-and-dirty practical guides such as "Your First 60 Days" and "35 Ways to Find a Job Online."

Wall Street Journal Careers (careers.wsj.com)

For all you executives, managers, and professionals, Careers.wsj.com is a gold mine for daily updates of news, features, and trends in the world of career development, whether you're looking for a new position or working to improve the job you have. Although you can look for a job here, the career resources are outstanding. The site's a little clunky, and takes more than enough time to download—even with a high-speed connection. But, it's worth the wait.

Don't despair, this site isn't just for high rollers. Career advice abounds for any level of job seeker, and there's a special section just for college students and recent grads. This site includes

➤ **Career Columnists**—Read from a selection of weekly columns from *The Wall Street Journal*, including Hal Lancaster's "Managing Your Career," Sue Shellenbarger's "Work & Family," and the Work Week column. Or, read through Deb Koen's Careers Q&A feature. There are tons of timely and informative articles.

➤ **Salaries & Profiles**—Are you getting paid what you're worth? Careers.wsj.com examines hiring demand and salary data in industries ranging from accounting to telecommunications. You also can read interviews with company hiring managers and executive recruiters to get the skinny on trends and career-related topics.

➤ **Job-Hunting Advice**—This is one of the best online sources of advice for job hunters, from résumé and cover letter writing, interviewing, networking, search strategies, Internet job hunting, responding to a job loss, and relocation guidance.

➤ **Succeeding at Work**—Career management is a big ball of wax, so tap into the brainpower of experts to get tips and advice on negotiating a better compensation package, getting ready for performance appraisals, surviving a discrimination lawsuit, or preventing a divorce from damaging your career.

➤ **Executive Recruiters**—To get the most out of working with recruiters, it's best to understand how their business works. Get the inside scoop here, and search Kennedy Information's Directory of Executive Recruiters database.

➤ **Working Globally**—Get advice on making the leap overseas and find out what happens when an expatriate tries coming back to the U.S. You can also connect with a database of international executive recruiters.

➤ **College Connection**—Maybe you learned everything you ever wanted to know about careers in college. It's doubtful, so gather up-to-date information and advice on how to move successfully from college to the real world.

➤ **Career Counseling**—Why try to find a career counselor in your hometown? Get telecounseled! It'll cost you, but there's no such thing as a free telecounsel, don't you know?

Work/Life Doesn't Have to Be a Juggling Act

This book is about finding your dream job. For some of us, we have more time to explore that option, and others, well, we need a job and we need it now. That's okay, but as you go about looking for a job, keep something in the back of your mind: No one ever lies on their deathbed and thinks, "Gee, I wish I'd spent more time at the office."

It's hard to be happy with material success when you don't have much else to be happy about—you've got no life outside work. Maybe you're not a workaholic, but you just don't feel connected to the work you do. That's to be expected, and unfortunately there are a lot of jobs that don't leave a lot of room for loving. Or even liking. It's just a job. At the end of the day, you go home and forget about it.

What about your dream job? Maybe not the next one, but somewhere down the road, you hope to find a job that makes you wake up early and that you're truly interested in for more than the money or prestige.

I'm not suggesting you halt your job hunt until you figure out what your dream job is. And I'm not suggesting you scrap your MBA and sign up for the Peace Corps or abandon your career plan entirely. That's on the verge of being ridiculous. All I'm suggesting is that, now, more than ever before, we workers of the world have options when it comes to choosing our life's work.

So, as you go about figuring out what kind of job you're looking for, and how you can find it using the information and resources on the Web, take a minute to think about your dream job—the job you know you want and deserve.

Be sure to read Chapter 20, "Just for Professionals Making a Career Change," for more on work/life balance and finding ways to bring meaning to your life through work, and to your work through living your life.

"I Still Haven't Found What I'm Looking For"

Come on, Bono! Haven't you figured out that you can't find it if you don't know what it is?! Remember in grade school when your teacher asked, "Little Johnny, what do you want to be when you grow up?" Stricken with fear and terror for not knowing, Johnny said he wanted to be a fireman. It was the first thing that popped into his head. So, for the next 12 years, Johnny studied to be a fireman, and then woke up one day and realized he liked starting fires. "What the heck am I doing in a fireman's uniform?" he asked himself.

Making a Life, Making a Living

Dr. Mark Albion was at the height of career success as a professor at the Harvard Business School. Although he enjoyed all the things that go along with a successful career—money, prestige, status—underneath it all, he was fundamentally unhappy. One day, he chucked it all to start on a new career path that took him down a road of successes, and failures. Through it all, he maintained the belief that to be truly happy in life, he had to "follow the love." Read his philosophy on work/life at www.makingalife.com.

Johnny set out to become the slickest and smoothest arsonist in town, but one day in prison, he realized that his newfound career path hadn't taken him where he wanted to be. He had to make some decisions and figure a few things out before he could answer the question: What do you want to be when you grow up?

But how can you know what you want to be when the jobs of tomorrow haven't even been invented yet? A smart job seeker realizes that career options and choices change quickly, and that exploring your options and interests is the first step to figuring out what you want to do with your life—today, and maybe tomorrow, too.

One way to get started on answering the question "What do you want to do?" is to take skills and interests assessment quizzes. You can do this online and in a short amount of time, bring focus to your job search, and go about it with more realistic expectations.

At some point in your career, you'll have to figure out what it is you're looking for. And when you find yourself asking, "What can I do?" turn that another notch and ask, "What do I want to do?" You'll be closer to finding your dream job that way.

The University of Waterloo Career Development Manual has a step-by-step guide to answering these critical career questions. Get started at www.adm.uwaterloo.ca/infocecs/CRC/docs/career-life.html. The content areas are pretty self-explanatory, but read the introduction to get a better understanding of the hows and whys of this handy career assessment tool.

Steps to Career/Life Planning Success:

➤ Step 1—"Self Assessment"

This section covers personality and attitudes, skills and achievements, knowledge and learning styles, values, interests, and your level of entrepreneurial spirit. Use these assessments to develop your personal career profile.

➤ Step 2—"Occupational Research"

Figure out what you want to do with your life by conducting an information search and informational interview, job shadowing, and gaining other hands-on experience. This section also covers trends in various occupations.

➤ Step 3—"Decision Making"

To help make career decisions, you first have to establish your objectives—personal and careerwise. Consider community service and lifelong learning when making decisions about your future, and then set up an action plan.

➤ Step 4—"Employment Contacts"

Now, it's time to look for work. Prepare your résumé and cover letters, and prepare for interviews.

➤ Step 5—"Work"

Learn how to evaluate job offers and negotiate your salary, and how to succeed at work.

➤ Step 6—"Career/Life Planning"

As your career develops, ongoing re-evaluation is necessary to stay focused and reach goals and objectives.

Are You Getting What You're Worth? Check Out Salary Surveys

Maybe you're looking for a new job because you know you're more valuable than what you're currently making, and the option of getting a raise or promotion is nonexistent. Or, after you get along in the job search process, you want to know how much to expect and ask for when the time comes for salary negotiation. You can go online to get advice and tools to answer those questions, too. Some companies charge a sometimes hefty fee to access their salary survey findings, but the following free online sources are good starting points:

➤ **Job Star (`www.jobstar.org/tools/salary/index.htm`)**—JobStar's Salary Surveys (see Figure 1.2) provides links and descriptions of more than 300 online salary surveys or summaries from several kinds of sources: general periodicals (*U. S. News & World Report, Working Woman*); local newspapers (*San Jose Mercury News*); trade and professional journals (*National Paralegal Reporter, Network*

World, Electronic Buyer's News); trade and professional associations (Health Physics Society, Society for Technical Communications); and recruiters or employment agencies (Source EDP, Franklin Search Group).

➤ **Wall Street Journal Careers** (`www.careers.wsj.com`)—Click the **Salaries and Profiles** link in the main navigation bar, and you are connected to in-depth reviews of hiring activity, salaries, and trends nationwide: Salary Data and Articles by Industry and Job; Regional Profiles; The Salary Calculator; Negotiating for More; Career Indicators; Hot Employment Issues; and Closing the Deal.

Figure 1.2

JobStar provides quick and easy tools to find out what you're worth based on your experience, location, and the going rate in the market.

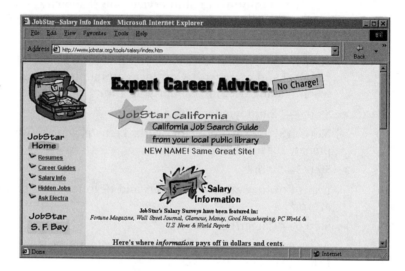

Relocation Tools for Smooth Moves

Say you're plain fed up with living in Podunkville. Or, maybe you have to move to a new area because your spouse landed a great job. Or, maybe you decided after a lifetime of battling seasonal depression that you must move to a more temperate climate. Or, maybe it's occurred to you that we live in a global economy and there are bountiful opportunities overseas.

Whatever your reason for picking up shop and moving, you can find plenty of tools and information online to help make the move a little less painful. You can also use relocation information to help you decide whether going from a $35,000-a-year job in a small town to a $38,000 job in a booming metropolis is a smart move or not.

For the skinny on relocation information, tools, and advice, be sure to read Chapter 15, "Regional Guides." A good starting point, though, is Relocation Central (`www.relocationcentral.com`).

Feds to the Rescue!

If you want to find out where the hot jobs are, take a look at the Occupational Outlook Handbook Quarterly from the Bureau of Labor Statistics (`stats.bls.gov/opub/ooq/ooqhome.htm`). This massive report includes reports on working conditions and information on the distribution of employment for an occupation among industries. In other words, you can find out what the forecast is in your field, and decide whether it's a good idea to stick with the typewriter repair business.

The report presents 1998 and projected 2008 employment data showing the distribution of total employment for more than 500 detailed occupations within more than 240 industries. The data can be searched by occupation or by industry.

After a Job Loss

It doesn't matter why or how you lost your job. It's gone. Bye-bye. Congratulations, though. Your new job is finding another job! For wisdom, insight, and encouragement during this difficult time, there are resources online to help you deal with the many issues surrounding unemployment, from emotional turmoil to explaining in your next interview what happened.

But that doesn't help the fact that you need income now. One option is to pick up a temporary job, although a word to the wise: You need to make time to job hunt, so look for assignments that offer flexibility to go on interviews or take a day off occasionally to focus exclusively on finding a job.

Whatever you do, don't hide under the blankets feeling sorry for yourself. Expect some bad days and down times, but it's important to stay positive. One thing you can do is volunteer at a local nonprofit organization. First, you might be able to learn new skills that you can add to your résumé. Second, you'll probably feel better about yourself. Third, you might just meet someone along the way who can point you in the direction of job leads.

For guidance and advice on dealing with a job loss, go online. One of the better starting points is About.com's Career Planning resources "Job Loss" section at `careerplanning.miningco.com/business/careerplanning/msub24.htm`.

One of the links to articles and features you'll find includes "Don't Let Emotional Turmoil Hold You Back," from *Career Magazine*, which helps you learn how to deal with the loss of a job so you can move forward. "Just Been Fired" offers practical advice for coping with a job loss. "Taming Workplace Monsters," also from *Career Magazine*, helps you prepare for an impending job loss.

For more practical matters, you can learn about severance pay issues, and find out how to determine whether you're eligible for unemployment compensation, including how to file a claim.

If you're currently unemployed, I know it won't make you feel better, but keep your chin up, buckaroo. You'll find something, even if it means you have to put your dream job on hold for a while. And that's okay. Be sure to read Chapter 21, "Just for the Currently Unemployed," for the full story on devising your job search strategy after a job loss.

Continuing Education and Training

You might discover after doing a skills and interests survey, or after scouring the want ads, that you just don't have the skills and training you need to land your dream job. Don't worry. There's a huge industry focused on continuing education and training. And these days, you can earn an advanced degree or get certified online. Distance learning programs are all the rage for busy professionals (and people stuck in the boonies), so go online to explore your resources and options.

A good starting point is your favorite search engine. Do a keyword search using "Microsoft certification" or "continuing education" or whatever specific words are related to the kind of education or training you need to continue on your lifelong journey of learning.

Here are some notable starting points:

➤ **Hungry Minds** (www.hungryminds.com) is a Web-based distance learning portal where students can choose from more than 37,000 Web-based classes on anything from Internet-related professional development topics to lifestyle and continuing education. Students can customize each course for their own personal learning experience. Course fees range depending on the complexity of the subject, but plenty of courses are absolutely free—and fun (see Figure 1.3). Even if you don't think you need additional training for your job and you're a life learner, this is an awesome site. Two thumbs up! Five stars!

➤ **Learn.com** (www.learn.com) provides Web-based courses and instruction in computers, automotive, business, foreign languages, and more.

➤ **LearnWell Web** (www.learn-well.com) links to online distance education courses and degree programs.

➤ **Web-Edu** (www.web-edu.com) offers courses in a variety of subjects, plus chat rooms and message boards to connect with teachers and fellow students.

Now, readers, as you venture out on the Web in search of your dream job, remember that to find your dream job, you first have to figure out what it is, and then you'll be able to spot it when you see it.

The next few chapters deal with the practical matters of job hunting, so with this philosophical part out of the way, get to work!

Figure 1.3

Hungry Minds is an awesome learning portal for anyone interested in expanding the mind. Partnerships with major universities put you in virtual classrooms, whereas other courses show you how to plan a bachelorette party or groom your dog.

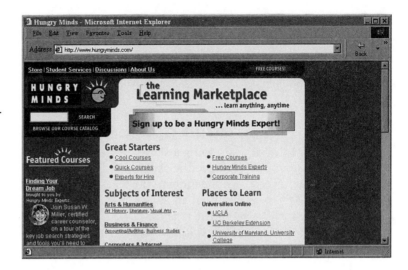

The Least You Need to Know

➤ You can go online to locate career resources, expert advice, and tools to help you figure out what direction to go on your career path.

➤ The "new economy" is a rapidly changing world of work that touches all parts of business and the way problems are solved.

➤ You can find out what the federal government has to say about growth industries and occupational outlooks.

➤ Skills and interests assessments are a good way to figure out not only what you can do, but what you want to do.

➤ Salary surveys and profiles can help you determine whether you're getting paid what you deserve, and help you prepare for salary-negotiation issues.

➤ If you need training or education to get the job of your dreams, there are online courses and other distance-learning opportunities for your life-learning needs.

Chapter 2

It's a Jungle Out There: Job Hunters Beware!

In This Chapter

➤ Precautionary measures before you put your name on the line online

➤ How to conduct your online job search and keep from getting caught or snitched on

➤ How to find out what your former employers are *really* saying to reference checkers

➤ Dig out those skeletons in your closet before your potential employer does

Life in the working world can be tough sometimes. It's not called the "rat race" for nothing you know. So, when the time comes to throw in the towel and look for a new job, be aware that things can go wrong—and I'm not talking about a blunder on your résumé or giving the wrong answer during an interview.

In a real-life hunting expedition, there are dangers and pitfalls—accidents with weapons, attack by prey, elemental dangers such as mosquitoes, quicksand, and snowstorms, or coming home empty-handed. And so, when you go online to job hunt, there are certain pitfalls and dangers you need to be aware of so that you emerge as the hunter and not the hunted.

I'm not trying to scare you away from the online job hunt. In fact, some things discussed in this chapter, such as background or credit checks, can happen whether you find your job lead online or not. The point is, the Internet itself has made tracking your online activity and gathering personal information about you much more accessible than in the past. So, what you'll gain from reading this chapter is an understanding of the ways potential employers and recruiters, as well as your current boss, can use today's technology to gather information about you.

You'll also learn how to be a discreet job seeker and protect your current position until you've found your next job.

Excuse Me, Ma'am, Your Résumé Is Showing

Posting your résumé on the Web opens up a can of worms when it comes to privacy and access issues. Many people think that the Internet is so vast that no one, much less their boss, would ever come across their résumé in a résumé bank or newsgroup. Think again. You can control to some degree who has access to your résumé in cyberspace, but there are very few guarantees you won't be found out if you're looking for a job while you're employed. Read on.

My buddy Rahul felt he wasn't getting paid what he was worth in his current position, so he thought he'd test the waters to see how many responses or offers he'd get by posting his résumé at a popular job site. Much to his surprise and dismay, his very own employer went to that very résumé bank looking for a new person. The boss conducted a keyword search, and up came Rahul's résumé with a posting date of two weeks prior.

Rahul's demise? He was first reprimanded, then taken off several sensitive projects, and was essentially given fewer and fewer responsibilities until he just couldn't take it anymore. Lucky for him, he got some inquiries from posting in the résumé database, but he did have a hard time explaining in interviews why he was leaving his current position. He also wondered what his boss would say when contacted for a reference.

Icky Spiders

Here's another danger of posting your résumé online. Even if you stopped your job search a long time ago and haven't posted your résumé on the Web in months, there's a chance that the database you posted to might be spidered to download your résumé to another job database. Some big job sites do this to beef up the number of résumés, and some headhunters, either manually or with spidering software, do this to add qualified candidates to their rolodexes, whether you want them to or not. Again, my point is not to scare you away from the Web—it can be an extremely useful tool in your job hunt—but you need to be aware of some dangers before you start your hunt.

Pesky, Pilfering Spiders

Spider technology works similar to the way a search engine does by scouring the Web for documents that have keyword matches and retrieving those document. Even if you post your résumé in a database that uses a firewall for protection against spidering, think twice before you hit "Send" and post your résumé for all to see—and all to pilfer.

Quick Tips for Résumé Privacy

Chapter 8, "Privacy, Distribution, and Access to Your Résumé," has plenty of tips and tricks to help you avoid these dangers, so be sure to read that chapter. If nothing else, follow these quick tips for résumé privacy and you'll decrease the dangers of putting your résumé out there in the vast reaches of cyberspace. Remember, in many companies, getting caught looking for a job is grounds for immediate dismissal, so approach your job search with a little bit of common sense.

Be Selective Where You Send Your Résumé

Unless you're desperate, a recent college grad, or a daring individual, don't post your résumé indiscriminately across the Web. It's not a very effective technique to begin with, and you increase your odds of getting nabbed later. Whatever you do, keep track of where you post. If you start getting calls or emails from headhunters or recruiters not associated with the banks you deposited your résumé to, you'll know it's been picked up and is in circulation, completely out of your control.

Use Candidate-Controlled Résumé Posting Sites

This means an interested employer contacts you via email (a special job-hunting-only account) with a job description, and if you're interested you can reply with a detailed résumé and short cover letter. You can also use a job agent (available at sites such as NationJob.com and CareerBuilder.com), which sends notifications of job openings to your email inbox.

Take Time to Read Privacy Policies or Make Phone Calls to Résumé Bank Administrators

Find out whether the database is accessible to third parties or spider technology. If this means you have to get on the horn and make a couple of phone calls to résumé database sites, do it. Ask who has access to the database—headhunters, recruiters, employers, anyone at all. Are résumés traded or sold to other databases? If the privacy policy isn't clearly stated or isn't easy to find, proceed with caution.

Find Out Whether You Can Remove Your Résumé After You've Landed a Job

Some job sites do not allow you this option, so think twice before posting at these sites. Also ask whether you have access to update your résumé in the event it sits there while you gain more experience, or simply change address or email.

Date Your Résumé

Date your résumé just in case it lands on your next boss's desk two years from now. On the other hand, if it lands on your current boss's desk next week, you have some explaining to do.

Beware of Sites Promoting Privacy

Some job sites give you the option of selecting companies that you don't want to allow access to your résumé, namely the company you work for. That's great if you work for one of the big companies on the list of forbidden eyes, but not so great if your boss decides to log on at home where the domain name identity would be the home ISP address rather than the "yourcompany.com" domain.

Don't Post Your Résumé to Newsgroups

Unless you're currently unemployed, I don't recommend posting your résumé to newsgroups, and even then be aware that your résumé will be in circulation long after you get a job. If you do have a job now, posting your résumé in a newsgroup is like playing with fire—you have no idea whether your co-workers visit job newsgroups, or whether your company's recruiters visit newsgroups to look for candidates. And after you post in a newsgroup, you run the risk of your résumé being recirculated around the Web, completely out of your control.

Conceal Your Identity with a Generic Résumé

This version of your résumé doesn't list your name or contact information, or any detail such as company names. If someone is truly interested in your credentials, they can contact you via a discreet, anonymous email address. Then, you decide whether to respond with your full-fledged résumé.

Oops—Getting Caught Looking for a Job on Company Time

We live a free and democratic society, so don't workers have certain privacy rights? In a word, no. Not when it comes to what you do on company time. Although we enjoy certain liberties and freedoms, those ideals are tossed to the ground the moment we enter our office buildings. Employers do have to protect themselves when it comes to what their employees do online and in the office. If a sexual harassment case arises, your employer can be held liable if they did nothing to prevent or stop threatening or inappropriate emails, for example, from being sent across company lines and equipment.

If you think the law is on your side when it comes to protecting your privacy in the workplace, it just isn't that way. Basically, anything you do at work is subject to monitoring, and anything you post to the Internet is considered public property, including personal information contained in your résumé.

Does Your Employer Monitor Your Online Activity?

Another friend of mine was fired on the spot for visiting a career-related site while at work. Did her boss walk in and see a big Monster.com logo flashing in her Web browser? No, a routine monitoring of employee Web logs revealed frequent visits to said job site. It was easy to track down the culprit, and without question or warning, the pink slip was signed, sealed, and delivered. Moral of the story? If you can at all avoid it, don't look for a job using company equipment or company time.

The American Management Association released a report stating that the share of major U.S. firms that check employee email messages has jumped to 27% from 15% in 1997, and overall electronic monitoring of communications and performance has increased to 45%—up 10% since 1997. You should know whether your company has a policy on this issue, as you were probably asked to sign an agreement saying you were aware that your activities could be subject to monitoring. If you're unsure about your company's policies, ask your supervisor or refer to your personnel handbook.

If you're a daring individual and you do decide to surf the Web for a new job while at work, at the very least keep an extra browser window open with a work-related site in the background. If someone walks in your office, just click the "work" window frame and it will override your job-hunting window (see Figure 2.1). Be sure the windows are about the same size so that the "secret" window can't be seen underneath the "work" window. Sinister, I know, but necessary nonetheless.

Figure 2.1

In the background, you can see the "work" window, which you should click on if your boss or a nosy co-worker walks in your office in the midst of your online job search.

Sneaky Don's Boss Page

Don and his fans love to one-up their bosses by surfing the Web on company time. If you're pretty sure your boss isn't sophisticated enough to review Web logs or monitor your online activity, surfing for jobs on company time can be accomplished with little danger. Get insider tips or download a phony spreadsheet from www.donsbosspage.com.

Free-Market Fascism: When Your Co-Workers Rat You Out

Remember that cubicle buddy who swore up and down he wouldn't tell a soul about your job search? Guess who's taking your place now that you've been fired for looking for another job? Welcome to the dog-eat-dog world of corporate America.

Although it's not a particularly popular method of keeping one ear to the ground, some employers are paying bonuses and giving out pats on the back to employees who snitch, discover another employee's résumé online, or hear through the grapevine that someone's on the hunt. In some human resources departments, there are full-time people whose sole purpose is to scour résumé banks, newsgroups, and message boards in an attempt to locate current employees' résumés. Yikes!

It's known as employee salvaging, and depending on your status in the eyes of your employer, you might be persuaded to stay (and possibly get a raise or promotion) or encouraged to pursue your opportunities elsewhere if your résumé is found in circulation on the Web.

Refrain from Venting About How Much You Hate Your Job (and Your Boss)

Another thing to keep in mind as you search for your next job is to keep your cool. If you're leaving because of personal differences with your boss or a co-worker, be careful about what you say to other people about these adversaries. And whatever you do, DO NOT send emails to anyone that say anything bad about people you work with.

In fact, a good rule of thumb is to never write anything in an email that you wouldn't write on a postcard. The danger is if you send one email to one co-worker complaining about your boss's incompetence and baldheadedness, for example, she might find it uproariously amusing and decide to forward it to another disgruntled co-worker who's "in the know." Then he sends it to the receptionist, who prints it out to take home and show her husband, but forgets to pick it up from the printer. Your boss visits the same printer to pick up a memo, and not only sees the email printout, but one by one, calls everyone in the email chain into his office to say, "Adios."

Quick Tips for the Discreet Job Seeker

There's a cliché that says the easiest time to find a new job is when you already have one. But the goal is to land a job without being found out, and to have the folks at your old job still think well of you even after you've left. Follow these tips before you set out on your job hunt.

Job Hunt on Your Time, Not Company Time

Besides the fact that many employers routinely monitor employee Web logs to be sure you're actually being productive at work, visiting a job site five times a day or going to a non–work-related Web site might win you some unwanted attention. If you can avoid it, don't spend time at work looking for another job! You're there to work, right? If you get caught, you could lose your job instantly. Then, you'll become desperate, and that's the worst way to be when you're looking for a job.

If you have no other options—such as your local library or your friend who has a home computer—at the very least stay late or go to the office when not many or any people are around. If other people have access to your work computer, especially, remember to delete your history log in your Web browser, and hope that the systems administrator doesn't have a grudge against you.

The Extra Mile

I'm Gonna Wash Those Sites Right Outta My Log

To remove visited sites from your history log, just select the sites you don't want someone else to see and drag them to your trash or recycling bin. This doesn't clear you from a networked Web activity log, but if you share your computer with other people, it's a good idea to delete visited job sites.

Set Up a Separate Account for Personal Email

If you absolutely must send résumés and cover letters during work time, set up a private, Web-based email account at JobMail (www.jobmail.net), Yahoo!, (www.yahoo.com), Hotmail (www.hotmail.com), or iVillage (www.ivillage.com). Figure 2.2 shows how to set up an account at HotMail. Although the systems administrator or Web log reviewer can see that you've visited these sites to access your email, they can't actually access your account without your password.

The Extra Mile

Always Log Off

Always remember to log out when you're done checking your email. If you're using a public terminal, such as a library or cybercafé, it's best to close your browser window, too, when finished. In fact, at work, just quit your browser application altogether to be on the safe side.

Resist the Urge to Brag

Especially if you're unhappy in your current position, the urge to share good news about your job hunt with your co-workers can be tempting, especially sharing the news with the same people whom you gripe with about work. Remember, though, your goal is to move on to the next job without burning any bridges, so force yourself to keep the good news to yourself until you've given your formal resignation.

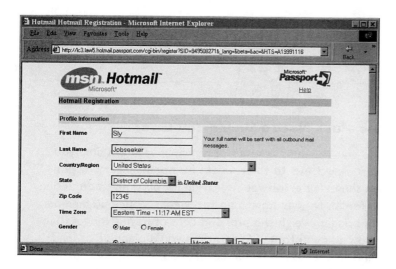

Figure 2.2

HotMail.com offers free Web-based email accounts for job seekers, or for all your nonwork email needs.

If you go around bragging about getting called for interviews and don't get an offer, not only will you look like a fool, you might end up coming across to your co-workers and managers as someone who can't be trusted. Are you about to fly the coop at a moment's notice? Who wants to get started on an important project with someone who everyone knows is "outta here"? Plus, you never know who's planning to move into your position when you leave, and they just might get the inspiration to move you out faster than you'd planned.

Watch What You Leave Lying Around Your Desk

You have one of those desk-size blotter pads and all over are little scribbles with dollar figures, phone numbers, and names followed by "VP Human Resources," or a note to yourself: "needs salary history with résumé." Co-workers don't mean to snoop. They just "happen to notice" things on your desk and around your office. And that could hurt you in the future if you decide to stay with the job you have. Be discreet and cover your tracks!

Don't Blow Off Your Responsibilities After You Get an Offer

After you've announced your resignation, the last weeks on a job are critical because employers tend to remember that time most vividly. Leave on good terms by working hard, tying up loose ends, and making the transition for the next sucker as smooth as possible. Hopefully, your boss and co-workers will be saddened to see you go, as you were a hard worker and a team player. When you leave, handle it in a discreet, professional manner—no boss could ask for more.

How Much Notice Should You Give?

The rule of thumb is to give the same amount of notice as vacation time you receive. Most employers expect two to three weeks for nonmanagement positions, but use common sense. If the job you're leaving for pays 30% more money, for example, you'd be foolish to give more than two weeks' notice. Remember, the goal is to not burn bridges. Weigh the pros and cons of staying longer than required, and if your boss asks you to stay longer than you'd planned, at least consider the request and talk to your new employer about extending your start date to a later time. Not only will you make your old boss happy, your new boss will respect your decision to honor your employer's request.

All Lips Are Sealed

If you're applying for jobs while you're still working, always state in your cover letter that your résumé is being submitted in confidence. After you've been asked for references, be sure to state in writing and in the interview that, "for obvious reasons, I'd prefer you not contact my current employer."

Make It Clear to Potential Employers That You're Job Hunting in Private

I read of another case of a recruiter calling on references (including the current boss) without the applicant knowing she was even being considered for the position. Granted, she had moved on to round two of the interviews, but was never asked whether it was okay to call her references that she provided at the end of the first interview.

One way to protect yourself from this happening is to state to the interviewer that you would prefer your current employer not be contacted, and to also include this in your cover letter. State it again if you're called for an interview. Most employers will honor this request, but just to be safe, be sure you tell them in writing and in person that you'd be jeopardizing your current position should your boss find out you're looking.

If you watch your P's and Q's while you search for a job when you already have one, you might have less to worry about when references checkers call your old boss. But if you're unsure what your former employer thinks about you, read on to find out how to discover what your old boss *really* says about you *before* potential employers start calling for a reference.

Career Sabotage: What Your Former Employers Really Say

So, you gave proper notice, tied up every possible loose end, had a nice going-away party, and moved on to your new job. Then, the time came again to look for yet another job, so you send out résumés, schedule interviews, and then find yourself sitting around wondering why you're not getting called back for second interviews. Your résumé was perfect. The interview was perfect. What's going on?

It could be a case of getting a bad rap from one of your former employers. Remember, even if you don't list your former employers on your personal reference sheet, they will be contacted to confirm that you are who you say you are and that you actually worked there.

Quick Tips for Reference Checks

Don't cross your fingers and hope your former employers are going to remember you as the stellar employer you were. Here are some things you can do to protect your good name and be sure your job hunt isn't being stalled by a bad or jumbled reference, or a bitter former employer.

Prescreen Your References

The most effective way to find out what your former boss really says about you is to hire an outside agency to perform a reference check on you, as if you were being screened for a real job opportunity.

One company that provides this service is Allison & Taylor, and you can visit them on the Web at www.myreferences.com (see Figure 2.3). Services range from $59 to $129, depending on the level of detail you require. The basic service asks your former employer to confirm dates of employment, salary, and title. The employer will also be asked whether you'd be considered for hire again and the reason why you left. Your "secret" reference checker also notes tone of voice, availability (were calls returned promptly, was the person accessible), willingness to participate, and other indicators that can mean the difference between your getting a call back with an offer or invitation for a second interview.

A former boss can say anything truthful about your performance, good or bad. However, most employers have a policy to only confirm dates of employment, final salary, and other limited information. But if prompted, some employers will really spill the beans, much in the same way a driver will speed if he thinks he won't get caught. The legal issue surrounding libel and defamation is a sticky one, and unless you can prove someone said something negative about you that is untrue, you don't have much of a case. What usually happens in a job hunt situation, though, is you never find out why you didn't get called back after your references were checked, much less what was said about you.

But there are steps you can take to be sure everything, including your reputation and track record, is in tip-top shape before you start sending out résumés. With the breakneck speed potentials of today's job search, you need to be prepared for the worst and hope for the best before you spend the time sending résumés and interviewing for that dream job.

Figure 2.3

MyReferences (myreferences.com) will contact your former employers and run a "pretend" reference check to find out what they could be saying to real potential employers or recruiters. Take a guided tour of the process to find out which level of service you require.

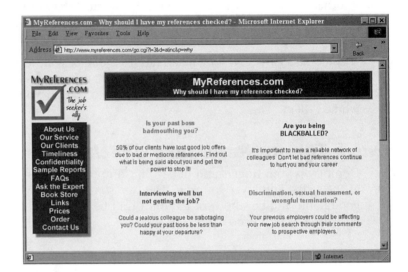

Get a Copy of Your Personnel File

You probably kept copies of your performance reviews and other pertinent information about your employment activities (and if you haven't, start a file and keep track of documents or incidents affecting your performance appraisal). And chances are you were never disciplined or "written up" without knowing about it. But just to be certain there are no black marks in your personnel record, get a copy of all the contents and read everything thoroughly to know beforehand what could be revealed to a potential employer.

Even if you don't work at a job anymore, you can usually request to see your file up to a year from the last date of employment and make copies of documents in your file that have your signature on them. You might also want to ask whether your former employer has a policy about the release of personnel records. Many companies limit the amount of information they disclose.

Under most state laws, most documents (except medical records) in your personnel file are not confidential and can be revealed by an employer.

Send a One-Page Fact Sheet to Your Personal References

Besides with your former employers, the references you supply will also be called upon by employers and recruiters to justify their decision to hire you. It would be a good idea to provide your friends and business associates with a one-page fact sheet that lists your job title, salary, term of employment, duties, awards, accomplishments, and, of course, your outstanding traits and qualities. Make it convenient and easy-to-access by sending your fact sheet to your references by email.

If there are discrepancies between the information you provide and what your references say, some employers consider this a red flag and might eliminate you from competition. Play it safe and provide your references with the information they need to give you a glowing reference.

Skeletons in Your Closet? Beware of the Background and Credit Check

This chapter is not intended to frighten you or dampen your job-hunting spirits. It's simply an eye-opener on issues you should be aware of before you endeavor to hunt. After all, if there's a flaw on your record or credit history, you might want to have that little problem taken care of before you send out résumés. Otherwise, you might find yourself sitting around wondering why no one's calling you for an interview. Worse, let's say you make it to the interview phase and your prescreening employment turns up a skeleton or two. The point is: Find out on your own what information employers look for, and what those sources have to say about you.

At ease, soldier. Not every person looking for a job or a promotion is subject to background checks other than verifying employment and calling your personal references. But in some industries and certain types of professions, it's commonplace for some type of background check to be performed prior to the job offer. Employers do screenings and background checks for two reasons: One is to be sure you're who and what you say you are; and two, to reduce the chances of a lawsuit if one day you fly off the handle, go postal, or decide it's high time to send a harassing email to a co-worker. It's called "negligent hiring" and employers more and more are using investigative agencies to check you out.

The Internet itself also accounts for the increase in background checks—the increasing availability and accessibility of computer databases containing millions of records of personal data. As the cost of searching these sources drops, employers are finding it more feasible to conduct background checks. It's alarming what they can find out, too, so read on to find out what areas of your private life are subject to investigation. You might be surprised to learn that many of the sources are public records created by good old Uncle Sam himself.

Lucky for you, though, you must give permission to a prospective employer to conduct a background check. That doesn't mean they can't find out stuff anyway, but for the most part, until you provide your Social Security number, most of the information isn't accessible. If you do find yourself in a position of approving a background check, these are some of the things employers can check out.

The Background Check

Oh, sure, you don't have anything to hide, right? Although some people aren't concerned about background investigations, why not go for 100% peace of mind by finding out for yourself what investigators might unearth when poking around in your personal history? In-depth background checks could uncover information that is irrelevant, taken out of context, or just plain wrong. A further concern is that the report might include information that is illegal to use for hiring purposes or which comes from questionable sources.

Nolo to the Rescue

Unless you're a lawyer (and thank heavens you're not, right?), from time to time you might need some general legal advice or some helpunderstanding legal terminology. Employment laws vary state to state, so go online to educate yourself about the laws regarding your right to privacy, the types of information your employer can release, and other things concerning public records and access to personal information about you. Be sure to visit www.nolo.com and click **Employment Law** to find what the laws are in your state regarding on-the-job legal issues. It's hailed by Yahoo! as "America's leading source of self-help legal information."

Background reports can range from a confirmation of your Social Security number to a highly detailed account of your history and acquaintances. Here are some of the pieces of information that might be included in a background check, many of which are public records created by government agencies.

➤ Driving records, including vehicle registration

➤ Credit records and credit card activity reports

➤ Air travel activity

➤ Criminal records

➤ Social Security number

➤ Education records

➤ Court records

➤ Workers' compensation

➤ Bankruptcy

➤ Character references

➤ Neighbor interviews

➤ Medical records and medical treatment history

➤ Property ownership

➤ Address history

➤ Employment verification

➤ Business associates and clients

➤ Telephone records

➤ Military service records

➤ State licensing records

"United, We Know More About You"

Some industries such as retail, trucking, or oil-rig companies have created a clearinghouse to exchange data about potential employees. The database has information provided by the member companies about their employees so when a jobseeker submits an application to another member company, that employer can check the clearinghouse for information on the applicant. If you had a bad experience with one company, you could be blacklisted with the other member companies for life!

Quick Tips for the Background Check

Before the background check begins, find out what an investigator could unearth about you. If there's a mistake, outright wrong information, or otherwise faulty information about you, finding out first gives you the opportunity to correct the problem before it interferes with your job search.

Order a Copy of Your Credit Report

If you're applying for a job that involves finances, such as investing or banking, an employer might conduct a credit check on you to be sure you can handle these money responsibilities in the real world, not just the work world. Other employers do credit checks just to see whether you're "responsible" in terms of managing your personal finances, and quite simply, because they can.

Thanks for the Tip

Turned Down

If you're turned down for credit or other negative decisions are made based on information contained in your credit report, you're entitled to a free copy of your report from the reporting agency.

If there's something on your credit report that you don't recognize or that you disagree with, dispute the information with the creditor or credit bureau before you have to explain it to the interviewer. There are plenty of places online to order your credit report. The fees are usually comparable to what you'd pay if you went the regular route and ordered one from the major credit reporting bureaus, but you'll get a report almost instantly online.

For an instant copy of your credit report, one place to check is QSpace (www.qspace.com). To find other online credit reporting services, perform a keyword search using "credit report."

Check Public Records Files

If you have an arrest record or have been involved in court cases, go to the county where this took place and inspect the files. Be sure the information is correct and up-to-date. Request a copy of your driving record from the Department of Motor Vehicles, especially if you are applying for a job that might involve driving.

Do Your Own Background Check

If you want to see what an employer's background check might uncover, hire a company that specializes in such reports to conduct one for you. That way, you can discover whether the databases of the information vendors contain erroneous or misleading information. Or, take matters into your hands and do your own background check.

For an alarming discovery into the types of background and other personal information available to you or an employer, be sure to visit HiTek Information Services at www.hitekinfo.com, the "ultimate Internet spy tool" (see Figure 2.4). For an annual access fee of $39.95, you get access to a massive amount of resources, tools, and insider reports, in addition to how to locate email addresses, home and business addresses, free resources that every online detective should know, private bulletin boards, where to find private investigators and the tools they use, or how to send email anonymously.

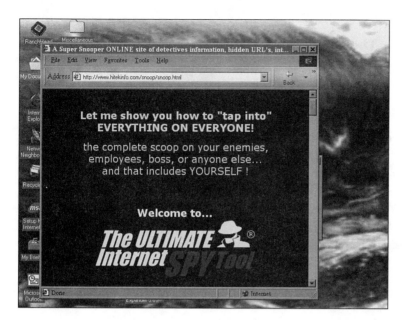

Figure 2.4

HiTek Info helps you become your own private investigator, plus shows you how to maintain your privacy online, be it email, newsgroup postings, or Web sites you visit. A must-see!

Read the Fine Print Carefully

When you sign a job application, you'll be asked to sign a consent form if a background check is conducted. Read this statement carefully and ask questions if the authorization statement is not clear. Unfortunately, job seekers are in an awkward position, because refusing to authorize a background check is a red flag and might jeopardize your chances of getting called back or being made an offer.

Forewarn Neighbors and Colleagues

Interviews with your acquaintances usually take place only if you're trying to land a job with the CIA, FBI, or some other high-level security position. But that's not always the case. Find out the extent of the background check and, if necessary, contact your associates, past and present, and let them know that they might be asked to provide information about you. This helps avoid suspicion and alerts you to possible problems.

Again, my paranoid readers, this chapter is intended to equip you with the information you need to be one step ahead in the job search process. You might not need to do your own background check or hire a private investigator, but you do need to be aware that with the power of the Internet, access to personal information about you is only a click away. Find out before they do, or correct misinformation before it interferes with your landing your dream job.

The Least You Need to Know

➤ Posting your résumé online can cause problems if your current employer stumbles across it, so exercise caution.

➤ Be discreet and keep your lips sealed to co-workers while you job hunt.

➤ Don't leave incriminating evidence on your desk—or desktop!

➤ Find out what your former employers really say before a reference checker does.

➤ Use the tools of the Web to perform your own background or credit check to be sure you have a clean record.

TEN-HUT!!!

Chapter 3

Getting Ready: Get Organized and Develop a Plan of Action

In This Chapter

➤ How the online job hunt works

➤ Devising a plan of attack based on how fast you need a job

➤ Using the Web as a powerful career research tool—not just the job posting boards

➤ Using tracking sheets and job-hunt organizers to manage your research findings and résumé-sending actions

➤ Getting ready to develop killer career documents

Hopefully by now, you've tapped into the career planning tools discussed in Chapter 1, and you're aware of some of the dangers and pitfalls of the online job hunt that I warned you about in Chapter 2. So, with that part behind you, it's now time to develop your plan of attack. The first step in coming up with an action plan to find your dream job is to understand how the online job search works, and which technique works best for your unique set of circumstances.

Believe me, there's more to the job hunt than searching the job banks and emailing your résumé. It takes a step-by-step process to be most effective, so be prepared to spend a little time looking for your dream job. After all, this is your job we're talking about, so before you start pounding the cyber pavement, figure out how you're going to approach the hunt and what tools you'll bring along.

How the Online Job Hunt Works

Don't start out thinking that the Web has simplified the job-hunting process to the point where all you have to do is have a killer résumé and nice blue suit and voilà!, there's your dream job. Although many job seekers have been wildly successful in finding a job at a job bank or by posting their résumé in a database, if you approach the Web as a hugely powerful research tool to help you find your dream job, you're definitely poised for success.

In fact, there's a chance that you might not find your dream job online at all. But using the Web as a research tool, you'll find the contacts, company information, and techniques to lead you to your dream job.

Here's a general overview of how any kind of job hunter can use the Web for locating a new job or for testing the waters when it comes time to go in for the kill. I'll explore each of these topics throughout the book, but just so you know what your options are, here's the skinny on how you can use the Web in your job search.

➤ **Log on to job posting sites**—There are literally thousands of Web sites that post millions of job openings. You're probably already familiar with some of the big names such as Monster.com or CareerPath.com. Problem is, with so many job sites, how do you know which one to use? Relax, you don't have to answer that question until you've figured out a few other things first, such as what kind of job you're looking for, and how and what your strategy is for finding said job.

Job-posting sites can be further broken down into regional or industry-specific (niche) sites. These might be the better choice for you if you have objectives in mind, such as finding a new job in a new town (or staying put) or when you want to look for a job in your area of expertise. Part 4 of this book, "Ready, Set...Hunt! The Online Job Site Landscape," details the various kinds of job sites and how to use the one that's right for you.

Some critics say online job sites are no better than classified ads, minus the ink-stained fingers. Others will shout to the heavens that these mega job sites are the wave of the future and anyone who skips this part of the online job search is missing the boat. Whatever the case might be, logging on to job-posting sites is just one of the many ways to use the Internet in your job search.

➤ **Deposit your résumé in a database**—Again, there are literally thousands of résumé posting sites, and many of the sites where you can view job openings also allow you to post your résumé for employers or recruiters to view. Different résumé databases have different policies on access and privacy, and I'll get into the nitty-gritty of that later, but you might find that instead of going out to look for jobs, you want one to find you. But before you make a deposit, be sure you're putting the best résumé out there. Part 2, "Get a Charge out of Job Hunting: The Electronic Résumé and Cover Letter," can help you with your résumé and cover letter. And be sure you don't get bitten by the privacy bug, so read through Part 2, which deals with electronic résumés, as well as issues regarding privacy, access, and distribution of your résumé.

➤ **Put a virtual job agent to work for you**—Job agents, or robots, scour the Web for jobs you're interested in and send matches to your email inbox. This is a particularly convenient tool if you don't want to visit job-posting sites over and over again looking for the right match. You'll learn more about job agents in Part 4.

➤ **Locate company Web site job postings**—Many companies use the Web as a recruitment tool by posting available positions on their home pages. Often, the jobs listed at a company site are the same postings you'll find in a job bank, but sometimes the openings can be found only at the company Web site. Once again, depending on your job-hunting technique, you might find that going straight to the source is the best way to find your dream job at your dream company.

You'll also need to locate company Web sites to do your research, so whether you've got a lead or are looking for an opportunity, you have to know how to get to the source. Chapter 18, "Go Straight to the Source," shows you the way.

➤ **Research target companies**—After you've found a job posting you want to respond to, you'd be a fool to fire off your résumé before doing your home-work first. NO JOB SEEKER SHOULD EVER APPLY FOR A JOB WITHOUT KNOWING AT LEAST BASIC INFORMA-TION ABOUT THE COMPANY FIRST! No exceptions, no way.

If you ask any employer or recruiter what they dislike most about online recruiting is the huge number of

No Penalty for Early Withdrawal

Before you deposit your résumé in a résumé bank (database), read the rules and regulations to find out whether you can withdraw your résumé after you've landed a job. Also, find out how long you can keep it there, and whether you can make changes or updates as you see fit.

Job Postings, Delivered to Your Inbox

Robot technology is a software application that enables you to complete a preferences and profile form, telling the robot (job scout) what types of postings you'd like to receive based on position title, salary range, geographic region, and other requirements. The scout then visits job-posting sites and finds matches based on your input, and delivers them to your email inbox.

résumés from unqualified or uninterested applicants. I'm telling you now, and I'll tell you many times throughout this book, that with the ease of access to company information made possible through the Web, you're shooting yourself

Site for Sore Eyes

Be Your Own James Bond

There are plenty of Web sites that provide detailed information you simply won't find at company Web sites. Hoover's (`www.hoovers.com`) and Vault.com (`www.vault.com`) can help you do in-depth research on some of the biggest companies—both U.S. and international.

in the foot by not equipping yourself with this knowledge. You're wasting your time and the employer's time, and that goes directly against what the Web is supposed to do—help us save time!

➤ **Participate in newsgroups**—Plenty of job seekers post their résumés in job-related newsgroups for the world to see. Others participate in newsgroups to get insider job leads or to stay up-to-date with industry trends and events. You also can develop networking contacts at newsgroups, so add that Internet feature to your job-search toolbox.

➤ **Establish or develop networking contacts**—Your networking contact might be a newsgroup participant who knows a lot about your target company (maybe they work there or know someone who does). Or, it could be your sorority sister who is now the manager at a company you might be interested in working for. It could be your cousin's neighbor who works at your target company's major competitor. My point? If you really want to increase your success in finding your dream job, networking is one of the most effective (but most often overlooked) tools in your job-hunting arsenal. Chapter 11, "It's Who You Know," is devoted entirely to networking, and every job seeker should read about the powerful advantages you'll gain if you learn to network effectively.

Although networking via email or newsgroups is a good way to establish contact or stay in touch with familiar members of your network community, nothing beats a conversation with a real human being. If the thought of having to talk to a human being gives you the willies, either get over it, or accept the fact that you are at a disadvantage in the online job search. If it helps, just remind yourself that your competitors probably aren't afraid of networking.

➤ **Connect with third-party recruiters and headhunters**—Many employers either have in-house recruiters or retain the services of a third-party recruiter to bring in new blood. Especially in executive searches or to fill positions in the high-tech field, recruiters are going to find you before you go out looking for them. For the rest of us, posting a résumé in a database is likely to lead to some type of interaction with recruiters or headhunters, so consider this in your options when devising your plan of attack. Chapter 17, "Headhunters and Third-Party Recruiters," discusses in detail the role of the recruiter and headhunter, so be sure to read that chapter before you start your search.

➤ **Stay up-to-date with industry trends and news**—One of the most powerful and effective tools in your job-hunting arsenal is information. That's right. When you're locating a target company or preparing your résumé and cover letter, demonstrating a strong knowledge of the industry or field you're searching in indicates to employers that you're interested in not only your job, but how industry trends and events can affect a company's bottom line. Also, knowing what's going on in your industry is like keeping your ear to the ground in terms of opportunities and threats.

Develop Your Job Hunting Tactics: Timesaving Tips and Tools to Be a Smarter Searcher

Again, the key to success in finding your dream job—online or otherwise—is research. The Web makes this easy; however, it can be time-consuming. But before you can prepare your top-notch self-marketing materials, you should do some research to know what employers are looking for.

After that research is complete, you can follow the steps outlined in this chapter to create not only the package, but the presentation and figuring out how to get your package in front of employers.

Don't spin your wheels and waste time looking for a job you don't want or can't get. If you haven't done a skills assessment or job-readiness evaluation, reconsider doing so. If you know what you want, though, and all you need is a way to go about getting it, read on.

So, first, decide on a plan of action based on your unique needs as a job seeker. And then, the real work begins.

Time to Decide: Are You an Active or Passive Job Seeker?

My guess is most of you consider yourselves to be active job seekers. Why else would you pick up this book? I'm here to tell you that even though you might be an active job seeker today, you should always be a passive job seeker—meaning, career development is an ongoing process. Sometimes, it involves getting a new job. Sometimes, it means you're trying to get a promotion within your existing company, or switch careers altogether. Maybe you have a bright idea and want to start your own business.

My point is, we can't predict the future, so you should always be on the lookout for opportunities regarding your career.

But to get started on finding your dream job, you first need to decide how to approach the hunt. Do you go for a midnight ambush? Do you come ashore inside the belly of a wooden horse? Do you wait for a headhunter to come a-knockin'?

Here are the most common game plans when it comes to finding a job using the Internet. Just because you use one technique today doesn't mean you can't switch gears and try a different approach down the road. But what you do need to do is have a road map in front of you so you don't get off track, and so you can make the most of your time on the online job-hunting expedition.

Fire Hose Technique

Maybe for you, getting *any job at all* is what your dreams are made of. Recently down-sized? Walked off the job out of disgust? Laid off? Fired? Can't get out of bed to go to the job you hate? Getting ready to graduate and can't face another day without at least some hope that there's a job out there for you? Unemployed for whatever reason? If you fit any of these descriptions, the "Fire Hose" technique is a good way to start.

The Fire Hose theory is if you spray enough water at enough cups, eventually you'll have a cup of tea. The downside to the Fire Hose technique is that it requires you to blast your résumé all over the Web for everyone and anyone to see—in turn, your privacy is compromised. You might also get so many responses (good or bad) that you can't handle the deluge. Or even worse, you might not get a single nibble, and what's that going to do to your self-esteem?

Either way, here's the plan of attack for you desperately-seeking-job-types. Try these techniques in any order:

➤ Post your résumé at the major résumé databases and mega job sites that accept résumés.

➤ Visit numerous mega job-posting sites such as Monster.com and CareerPath.com and search for jobs that interest you (and that you're qualified for). Send your résumé to as many job-posting contacts as you have time to research the company and customize your résumé for.

➤ Locate as many industry-specific job sites as you can find, and post your résumé to those that have résumé databases. Again, search for job listings you're qualified for, and research as many companies as you can, customize your résumé, and email to the contacts listed in the postings.

➤ Post your résumé in newsgroups related to jobs or specifically to your field.

➤ Blast your résumé to as many recruiters as you can find (see Figure 3.1).

➤ Let everyone you ever met know that you're looking for a job, and that includes your nagging aunt who can't understand why you're out of a job in the first place.

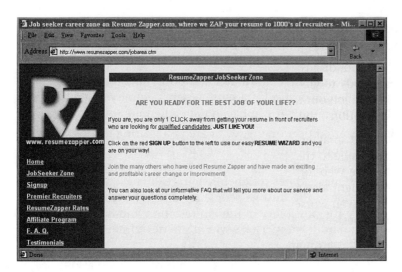

Figure 3.1

*ResumeZapper
(www.resumezapper.com)
zaps your résumé to thou-
sands of recruiters, placement firms, and search
companies for about $40.*

Selective, but Out There

So, you're not exactly out of a job, but you're just not into your job, either. Or, you've gotten wind of an impending layoff or change in management. Maybe you have the feeling your days are numbered, but you're not necessarily on red alert. Perhaps you're contemplating a move across the country or the globe, and you'll make the change if the right job comes along. Or, you know you're hot stuff and you want to feel out your options. In other words, you know a change is around the corner—you just don't know which corner. For you, I recommend the "Selective, but Out There" technique.

This plan of action offers more flexibility and options than the "Fire Hose" tech-nique, but still requires legwork, planning, and research. If you have time to explore your options in the job search, try these techniques as you go about finding your dream job. Heck, you might just discover along the way that to get the job you really, really want, you might have to take a class, get certified, or hone certain skills. But that's what the research is all about—finding out what it takes to get the dream job you know you deserve.

➤ Start researching and reviewing the Web sites of companies you'd love to work for. (If you don't know the answer to that yet, now's the time to start figuring it out.) See whether there are current job openings posted at these sites, and if you think you're qualified and ready to make a change sooner instead of later, go ahead and send your résumé. Be sure to state your search is confidential and that you're currently employed.

➤ Test the waters by posting your résumé to a small handful (two to four) of the major job sites and résumé databases, preferably ones that are candidate-controlled or have other privacy features. Better yet, I suggest posting an anony-mous résumé—one that doesn't list your name or the names of companies you've worked for, but lets employers, recruiters, and headhunters know enough to nibble on your bait. Include your job-search email address and wait to see what comes your way.

➤ Find industry-specific sites that accept résumés and post yours there. Also, review job postings and apply or just get a sense of what employers are looking for to start rehashing your résumé if you haven't already done so.

➤ If you haven't already started networking, what are you waiting for? Oftentimes, the best jobs go unadvertised. If time is on your side, really work the networking system to get the inside scoop on job openings or future openings. It's also a good idea to have an established network before you really need a job, so get started pronto. I think one of the reasons people are uncomfortable with networking is that you face the possibility of human rejection and have to ask for favors from people you hardly know. That's why it's better to start making friends before you need their help.

➤ Regularly visit your target company Web sites for job postings, and also to see what's new or whether any new press releases or new product announcements have been announced.

➤ Open the channel of communication with a select few third-party recruiters or headhunters. Chapter 17 discusses the pros and cons of working with these folks, so before you send your résumé to one, be sure you know what you're getting into.

➤ Stay current by reading up on industry news at online magazines that cover topics and events in your field. You can even subscribe to mailing lists or discussion forums that cover the news of the day in the industry you're fishing in.

The Extra Mile

Interview an Employee at Your Target Company

After you've done research on target companies, another way to help you figure out what your dream job might be is to ask current employees. Having someone explain their responsibilities and position might give you a more down-to-earth feel for the position, and whether you think you'd like it or not.

Come and Get Me

You're hot stuff and you know it. You don't have to go looking for jobs, but you still want to keep your options open and maybe have some job opportunities come your way via your job search email inbox. You're in a good position, but that's probably because you've got your career future on the brain even when you're perfectly happy in a job situation. You're smart for keeping one eye open!

If you're in high technology, you might not even have to think the words "new job." An employer or recruiter might already have an eye on you, so it's best to be prepared for possible offers.

Regardless of your field, the "Come and Get Me" approach leaves you lots of time and lots of options to explore. Hopefully someday, we'll all be in your position, so count your blessings and take a peek at what's out there:

➤ Start with industry-specific job posting sites and scan opportunities. Sign up for email notification of jobs that interest you and wait to see what comes your way.

➤ Just for kicks, check out the mega sites and see whether there's anything that fits your fancy. Again, sign up for email notification of jobs that match your requirements and interests.

➤ Keep up (or start) on your networking. Become an active member of discussion groups or message boards to meet people and share your experience and insight with others. Remember to keep a low profile, or at least don't allude to the fact that you might be looking for a job. The point here is establish yourself as an active and interested person in your industry. Here's a little secret: Some of the more savvy headhunters routinely monitor newsgroups and online communities to locate "intelligent" beings. They might just track you down if you prove yourself to be the hotshot you know you are.

➤ Spend some time researching third-party recruiters and headhunters that specialize in your field. Send them a confidential résumé (be sure to read Chapter 17 before you do this) to be put on file for the right opening.

➤ Relax, kick back, and see what happens.

Go for the Kill

You know what you want and you know how to get it. Ever since you were knee-high to a grasshopper (or since you learned how to recognize your dream company when you see it), you knew you HAD to get a job at ABC Corporation. And nothing is going to stop you. In fact, you'll wait patiently until it's time to go in for the kill.

If you've taken the career development bull by the horns, then you know that one of the best ways to get the job of your dreams is to locate a very select group of companies that suit your tastes. A job is a job, but a job in a good company is another experience altogether.

In fact, I hope that at some point in every person's career, they realize that the key to success and happiness is finding a career or a job that makes them wake up early. Stay late. Makes them dread Friday at 5 p.m. instead of Sunday evening. Well, you don't have to love your job, but the difference between a dream job and just another job is like night and day.

Forget the rest, you'll settle only for the best. Here's how to go for the kill:

➤ Research, research, research. The more you know about your target companies and industry, the better off you'll be.

➤ Visit those target companies' Web sites and review them thoroughly. Look for press releases, new product announcements, and a list of personnel or upper management. Print this directory of contacts.

➤ Do a power search and try to find those contacts or their names in newsgroups, discussion forums, or news reports.

➤ Go to Web sites that profile companies and see whether your target companies are featured there. You can gather information on stocks and tradings and other valuable information about the company. Some sites, such as Vault.com, provide insider interviews with people at these companies, but the odds are you'll have to do this on your own.

➤ Call or email one or two contacts at these companies. Ask for an information-gathering meeting. You can hint that you're looking for a job, but it's best to hold off on this. People will be more willing to spend time with you if they don't think there's an ulterior motive. Simply explain that you have followed their company (or them personally) and would like to ask questions on the industry or the company, its products, and the market. This is called an "informational interview." During this time, ask specifically whether there are any openings or anticipated positions opening up. Ask whether you can send your résumé. Most likely they will say yes, and they might even ask to see it right then, so be prepared.

➤ Follow up with a thank-you note. Chapter 4, "Don't Wait! Prepare for Calls and Emails to Start Rolling In!" provides samples of follow-up notes.

➤ Compose a killer, killer cover letter (which will be easy to do because you're packed to the gills with insider information on your target companies), and revise your résumé to reflect the individual needs of each target company. Email it to your inside contacts and follow up in a week or two with a phone call if you haven't heard back.

➤ Keep checking the company Web site postings. Hopefully, by now you're oh-so-close to landing an official interview.

The Plan Is in Place...Now Get Organized Before You Make a Move!

Now that you know what your options are in terms of your job hunting strategy, it's time to prepare and get organized before you put your plan into action. I'm the last person to be telling you how to organize your life, but I will tell you that the Web can yield some pretty amazing results in your job search (if you follow my other job-hunting advice, that is). So, it's important to stay on top of developments and responses, as well as the actions you've taken.

Create a Tracking Sheet and Job-Hunt File

If you're like me, if you don't write it down or print it out and file it, you can't keep track of what you did from one day to the next. When it comes to your job search, imagine the embarrassment of sending multiple résumés to the same company. You'll come across as disorganized and dimwitted, not to mention wasting your time. And that's what organization is all about: saving time.

Call it a job journal if you will. In fact, you could and should get a planner and jot down what you do from day to day (or week to week) in addition to the tracking sheet and job-hunt file you're going to set up.

First things first: the tracking sheet (see Figure 3.2). You can create a computer file (such as an Excel or a Word table) to track your efforts or make it by hand. Either way, your tracking sheet should have these column headers and look roughly like the one in the figure.

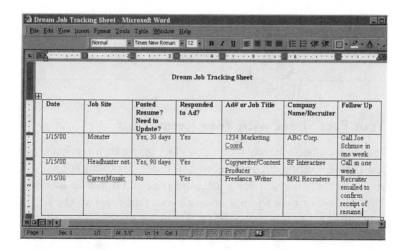

Figure 3.2

The job search tracking sheet will help you stay on top of your efforts, as well as follow-up activities.

In addition to the tracking sheet, print out all jobs postings you reply to and attach a copy of the cover letter and résumé you sent. Then, start a file or binder to store all your materials, including networking contact information and activity, as well as printouts of company research findings.

Complete a Job History and Accomplishments Worksheet

Take a sheet of paper or use a word processing program and create a chronological list of all the jobs you've had, with start and end dates. Include starting and ending salaries, title, and general duties. If you received and kept a copy of your job description, file this with the worksheet when you're done.

Now, forget about your daily tasks for a minute and think about your accomplishments. For example, "created and implemented incoming mail tracking system to expedite distribution of packages and letters," or "trained administrative staff on new intranet." Think of things that are above and beyond the call of duty, and if you can place a dollar value to these, make note of that. For example, "targeted six new clients and passed leads and research information to sales manager, resulting in $65,000 of account work for agency."

These are the things you'll be adding to your résumé, too, so think about your accomplishments in terms of how a potential employer views these achievements as transferable skills—things that you can do in your new job that affect the company's bottom line. Remember, an employer doesn't care what you can do. He cares what you can do for him! Which brings me to the next step.

Thanks for the Tip

Share Your Fact Sheet with Your References

The job history fact sheet will come in handy when you start going to interviews. Contact the people you plan on listing on your reference sheet, let them know (confidentially) that you're actively looking for a job, and that you'd like to list them as a reference. Then, email or mail them a copy of your fact sheet so they can speak accurately and eloquently about you when the reference checker calls.

Define Your Transferable Skills

Transferable skills involve doing something with people, data, or things. The more complex the function, the more specialized and valuable the skill. To determine your transferable skill set, take a sheet of paper or word processor and create column headings with these categories: people, data, things (machinery, equipment), communication, leadership, creativity. Under each heading start with *"I am good at...."* For example:

DATA

When dealing with data, I'm good at...

record keeping and filing

helping others retrieve information

compiling

researching

fact-checking

memorizing

paying attention to details

Better yet, go online and find a virtual transferable skills test. One of the better ones is available at `career-3.wustl.edu/cps/self/transfer.htm` at Washington University in St. Louis' Career Center (see Figure 3.3). The site has a Career Prep Series (CPS) Skills Search to help you identify your skills by taking Transferable, Self-Management, and Job-Content skills inventories. A must-see for any job seeker looking to gain the competitive advantage in the job search.

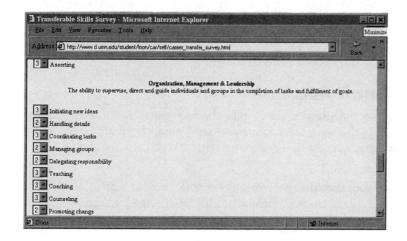

Figure 3.3

The Career Prep Series Skills tools help you identify career interests, job readiness, and define transferable skills.

Have a Basic Résumé and Cover Letter Ready

I'll talk about résumés and cover letters extensively in Part 2, but before you start your search, you need to have a basic résumé and cover letter ready to customize for each position you apply for, unless you're using the Fire Hose technique. In that situation, you might not have time to fire off 300 customized résumés, but if you have the time, always tailor your résumé to the job you're applying for.

If you haven't gotten around to thinking about your résumé, now is the time. You'll definitely need it before you go online to start your search. If you need help writing or revamping your résumé and cover letter for today's job market, be sure to read Chapter 6, "Get Help with Your Résumé Writing."

Develop a List of Keywords

Another thing to do now while you're preparing for the hunt is to develop a list of keywords that will be sprinkled throughout your résumé. Keywords are nouns that have to do with your industry, your skills, and your goals. One way to generate a list of keywords is to pay attention to the job descriptions contained in the job postings you find online. They're loaded with keywords employers are looking for in a candidate.

Here's an example of a keyword summary, but be sure to read Chapter 5, "Understanding the Electronic Résumé," for the skinny on keywords and how they can help you succeed in your electronic job search.

Web content development, project management, business-to-business marketing communications, client, deadline, detail, print and display advertising, negotiating skills, research, hard sell copy, direct marketing, consumer demographics, team player, Microsoft Word, Excel, Web applications, HTML basics, familiarity with Quark, analytical ability

This summary is a bit on the long side, but you won't have to include all these keywords in each résumé—remember, your goal is to tailor every résumé based on the job you're applying for. So, if you see a keyword in the position description that's not on your keyword list, add it. It might come in handy for another job, too.

Set Up a Special Email Account

Besides an increase in privacy while you job search, the nice thing about setting up a Web-based email account is that you can receive and send email from anywhere in the world, as long as you have access to a computer with a Web browser and an Internet connection.

I've found over the years, too, that using a work-based email account or an account through a local service provider can cause headaches if you change jobs, go away for the summer, go on vacation, or change Internet access providers.

Another benefit to having a job-search related email account is that you don't have to rely on your account at work to send and receive job search-related emails. Doing so not only increases your chances of getting nabbed by your current employer, but it sends a negative message to potential employers. It's almost the same as a guy two-timing his honey and borrowing honey's car to take his mistress out to a romantic dinner. Play it safe and get your own darned email account!

The downside to free Web-based email is that your inbox might become flooded with unsolicited emails (spams) from all sorts of characters. As the saying goes, there's no such thing as a free email account.

Although you can use your regular home account for the job search process, I think it's best to have a separate account devoted just to your job search email. Why? It's easier to track and separate your job search email from your personal email. It's that simple.

The Extra Mile

Choosing the Right Email Handle

When communicating with potential employers via email, you don't want an email handle such as cupiedoll@freeemail.com. Instead, choose a username that's more serious and professional, preferably some variation of your real name, such as j_doe@freeemail.com or tomwalters@freeemail.com. If you already have a free email account and need to change your username for the job search process, do so.

Here are just a few of the free Web-based email services out there. If you want to look for something different, just type in the keywords "free email account" at any search engine and you'll get a long list of services.

➤ *Hotmail.* The good folks at Microsoft Network make it quick and easy to sign up and access your free email account with Hotmail. Just go to www.hotmail.com and click **Sign Up for FREE Email** and you'll choose a username and password, and then fill out a brief registration form. Be sure to access your new account within 10 days, or else it won't be activated. You also need to check in every 60 days or the account gets closed.

Stop Junk Email Before It Starts!

One of the potential downsides of signing up for a free email account is junk mail, also known as spam. To limit access to your email address from fellow members who really want to help you "get out of debt" or "learn how to earn thousands of dollars without lifting a finger" (read: gimmick), uncheck the box that says you want to be entered in the member directory or any other Internet directory listings. You can also reduce the amount of direct email that comes your way by not signing up for the free subscription offers, or at least sign up only for those you have a strong interest in.

➤ *Yahoo! Mail.* Do you Yahoo!? Yahoo! Is another popular free email service. Just go to **www.yahoo.com** and click the **Check Email** icon or **Mail** link (you'll find both on the front page). The next page has a link that says **Sign Me Up!**, and by clicking this link you'll go to a page that asks pretty much the same information as Hotmail: name, gender, occupation, age, and whether you want to be listed in the People Search directory.

➤ *JobMail.* Signing up for an account at JobMail is pretty similar to Yahoo! and Hotmail. Go to **www.jobmail.net**, click **Sign Up**, choose a username and password, answer a few registration questions, and you're on your way to a new job search email account. This one even seems a bit more appropriate because the word "job" appears in your address. No guessing what this email is about!

Is JobMail any different from the preceding free email services? If you sign up for the more advanced features, you can use tools such as the Global Response folder, which can save you time when responding to many people with the same message. For example, your global response could be "Thanks for your interest. I have accepted an offer but thank you for contacting me about opportunities with your company" or something similar.

The Least You Need to Know

➤ The Web can yield an unruly amount of results in your job search—be prepared and organized before you begin.

➤ Before you start sending out résumés, decide on a game plan according to how quickly you need a job.

➤ You can use job agents to have positions delivered to your email inbox instead of visiting job-posting sites.

➤ The Web contains endless resources to help you research target companies, network, and get ahead of your competition.

➤ Setting up a Web-based email account offers added privacy and access from any Web-connected computer.

Don't Wait! Prepare for Calls and Emails to Start Rolling In!

In This Chapter

➤ Asking the right questions and getting the information you need during the prescreening phone interview

➤ Closing the call to get to the next step: the face-to-face interview

➤ Learning from rejection: what to do to get to a "yes"

➤ Interviewing FAQs: commonly asked questions by interviewers and job seekers

➤ Follow-up note samples to say thanks, no thanks, and even thanks for turning me down!

Even before you get down to the nitty-gritty of résumé and cover letter preparation, company and job research, and actually putting your job hunting plan into action, there are a few loose ends you should tie up before you venture out on your online job hunt. The Web can really speed things up when it comes to getting responses to your job hunt activity, so you'd best be prepared.

Especially if you're going for a rapid response tactic such as the "Fire Hose" technique talked about in Chapter 3, it's quite possible you will get responses from recruiters and employers within a single day of putting your job hunt plan to work! You want a job fast, but *that* fast!?!?

You all know the Boy Scout motto, so I won't repeat it here. This chapter will help you get ready for the results of your job search efforts, from interview preparation, prescreening by phone, and how to say yes, no thank you, and other follow-up communications. I'll also teach you how to deal positively with rejection—the biggest fear of all job hunters. Plus, you get a list the most commonly asked interview questions to help start formulating responses, plus a FAQ list for you to ask the interviewer.

Prescreening by Phone

You put your job-hunting strategy to work and now your phone is ringing off the hook. Maybe, maybe not. But before the calls come in, take some time to prepare for the prescreening questions and answers that both you and the recruiter or employer will bring up in the first round of calls. The person who calls might be a third-party recruiter, an inhouse recruiter, a personnel jockey, or possibly the person you'd be working for.

From the employer's perspective, prescreening by phone is their chance to determine whether you really live up to the hard-sell claims on your résumé, but really it's their chance to see whether you seem like a good candidate for the position. And they try to do that in about five or ten minutes. When hundreds of résumés roll in, it makes sense to weed out the candidates as soon as possible.

From your perspective, this is your chance to get answers to questions that were probably not answered in the job description or unearthed in your company research. Another goal here is to gather more information, and based on what you find out, to decide whether you want to try to move on to the next stage of the game: the first interview. Here are some tips on getting the most from your prescreening calls.

Thanks for the Tip

Attitude Adjustment

When communicating with employers and recruiters by phone, keep an upbeat, positive attitude, but don't go overboard, as in "OH MY GOD! I can't believe you called!"

Getting Organized

Remember that job hunting folder and tracking sheet I told you about in Chapter 3? It's time to pull it out and keep it close to the phone. This source of information is going to help you stay focused and organized during the prescreening session and be able to respond quickly to questions from the caller. But there is one more form (see Figure 4.1) to help you get the most out of your prescreening call.

For every call you get (or if you're communicating via email), be sure to gather the following information from the caller. Keep all your notes in a notebook that you can keep handy near the phone or the computer.

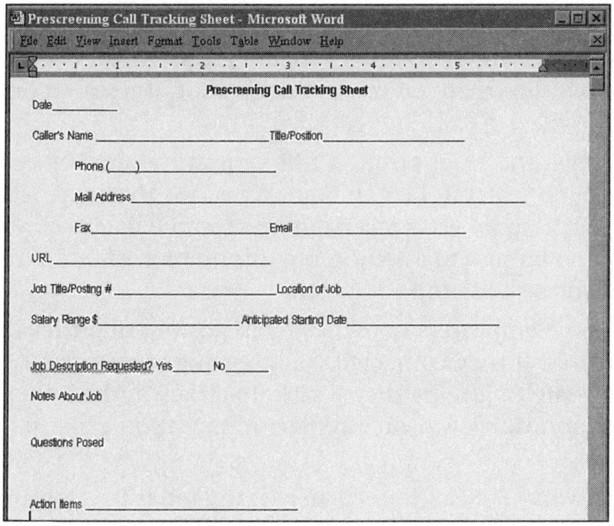
Prescreening Call Tracking Sheet - Microsoft Word

File Edit View Insert Format Tools Table Window Help

Prescreening Call Tracking Sheet

Date________

Caller's Name ______________________ Title/Position__________________

Phone (___)_______________

Mail Address____

Fax______________________ Email__________________

URL______________________

Job Title/Posting #________________ Location of Job__________________

Salary Range $________________ Anticipated Starting Date________________

Job Description Requested? Yes_____ No_____

Notes About Job

Questions Posed

Action Items ______________________

Figure 4.1

This Prescreening Call sheet will help you cover the important conversation points and gather critical information for follow-up and keeping track of incoming calls.

Details and Tips for the Prescreening Call Sheet

Employers and recruiters don't have all day to chit chat with you, but you do need to try to get as many questions answered as possible during the preliminary call to help you prepare for the next phase: the face-to-face interview. Here's the "why" and "what" information to get during your prescreening call.

- **Date** Enough said. If you have a lot of follow-up action items, though, this can help prioritize things to do based on the order in which the calls came in. Remember, the online job hunt can move quickly, so you need to take action to stay in the running.
- **Caller's Name** Ask for the correct spelling, especially the last name, even if you think you know how to spell it. As Ms. Cardis, I get miffed when I get a letter addressed to Ms. Carter or Ms. Curtis.
- **Caller's Title or Position** Did you speak with a recruiter, manager, human resources rep, or so on? You'll need to know this so you can refer to the person in your follow-up notes. You also need to know the person's position so you can ask the right questions at the right time.
- **Contact Information** You might be asked to mail or fax a print version of your résumé or send your electronic résumé and cover letter (again!) to a different person from your original contact. People do lose things, you know! Be sure to ask what kind of résumé you should send—scannable, plain-text, or formatted.
- **URL** If you're dealing with a recruiter or employer who found your résumé at a résumé bank, you'll want to do research on the company to prepare for a possible interview, or to determine whether you're interested in the company at all.

If the person calling is a company you applied to directly, don't ask for the URL. You should already know it, and if you don't, figure it out on your own. You don't want to send a message that you haven't done a lot of research on the company.

➤ **Job Title**   Be sure to get the exact position title or posting number so you can locate this in your job search folder and quickly access the cover letter and résumé you sent. If your résumé was picked out of a résumé database, you won't have a file on the job, so be sure to ask for more information about job requirements, such as experience, skills, and education.

➤ **Location of Job**   Some employers state in the job posting that they do not cover relocation expenses. If they contacted you knowing you live halfway across the country, it's safe to assume they'll pick up airfare and hotel expenses if they decide to offer an interview. Don't ask about relocation expenses at this point, though.

You might also want to end the call immediately if the job is in a location you won't consider—unless the money is right.

Thanks for the Tip

To Move or Not to Move?

Always state on your cover letter (and résumé if you're depositing it in a résumé bank) whether you're willing to relocate. Recruiters and employers alike get tired of tracking down candidates who aren't interested in making a move. It wastes your time, too, so eliminate yourself from positions that you're not willing to consider.

➤ **Salary Range**   If the caller is a headhunter or recruiter, they'll likely tell you this right off the bat. If you're talking to an employer, they might bring up the salary issue if they think, based on your experience and past titles, that the starting salary is too low. They don't want to waste their time or yours, but unless they bring it up, it's not a good idea to ask at this point.

➤ **Job Description Request**   Do this only when you've been invited to an interview. Some recruiters and employers might think this is asking a lot, but it's worth requesting. Just say, "Would it be possible for you to fax or email me a copy of the official job description? I think it would help me identify areas in which I can really contribute to the company." So ask. If they can't do it, they'll tell you. Sometimes, an official job description doesn't exist because the position is still in the development stages.

If they say they'll fax you a copy and you don't have a fax machine, Kinko's and many office supply or copy shops will let you receive faxes at their number for a price based on number of pages. Have these numbers ready just in case. You can also receive faxes via your email inbox through services such as Jfax.com (www.jfax.com).

Thanks for the Tip

Get Faxes and Voice Mail in Your Inbox

Jfax.com Free Fax *Plus* assigns you a single number that acts as both your fax and voice mail number. Both faxes and voice mail messages are attached to an email and automatically delivered to your email address. Visit them at www.jfax.com. To send faxes, too, it's only $2.95 a month. Otherwise, it's free to receive.

➤ **Details About the Job Not Provided in the Posting** If you're talking to a third-party recruiter, ask what they think the employer's problems or needs are to determine how you might be able to help solve those problems. If you're talking to the employer, ask whether there's anything specific on your résumé that they see as a solution to problems or challenges the company faces.

➤ **Anticipated Starting Date of Job** Do they need you yesterday? Next month? Sometimes, you can't wait two months to start a job, and sometimes you can't start when they need you. You also need to buy some time to see what other leads come your way, so don't always jump on the first train that comes to the station.

➤ **Questions Posed** Did the caller ask about specific skills or experience; why you're leaving your current position; why you want the job; why they should hire you? This will come in handy if you're asked to send a detailed cover letter and résumé, or come in for an interview. You can assume that the questions asked in the prescreening are indicators of the employer's needs and requirements, and that they'll come up again. This gives you the chance to prepare responses to specific needs or interests of the employer.

➤ **Action Items** The caller might ask for a salary history or a detailed cover letter and résumé. Or, you need to follow up with a quick email thanking them for contacting you and restating your interest in interviewing, a no-thank-you letter, or a confirmation of the date and time of the interview. See the quick and easy follow-up note samples at the end of the chapter.

Closing the Call

Unfortunately, you'll have to think fast to decide whether or not to pursue the next step: the interview. If you're interested in pursuing further discussions, be sure to end the conversation on an upbeat note. State your interest in the position. Here are some killer call-closers to move you along in the process.

➤ "Wouldn't you agree this sounds like a good fit? I'd like to set up a time to come in and talk details. When can you meet?"

➤ "From what you've described, this sounds like a good match with my skills and interests. I'd like to meet for an interview to talk about how I can contribute to the company's objectives. Can we set up a time to meet?"

If you're not interested for whatever reason (you'll be expected to travel 75% of the time, or your first assignment is in a part of the country you won't consider living in, the salary is too low, or so on), you should also state this at the conclusion of the prescreening call. Here are some tactful ways of saying, "No thank you."

➤ "I appreciate your interest in my application, but I don't think this is the right direction for me at this time. Good luck in your search."

➤ "Based on what you've told me, I don't think this is the best match with my skills and interests at this time. I would, however, appreciate your keeping my résumé on file, and if a position that matches my skills opens up, please contact me."

➤ "The salary range you quoted is less than what I'm looking for. Although your benefits package sounds exceptional, I do have to consider income, so I must respectfully decline your invitation to interview."

The Dreaded "R" Word: Rejection

The prescreening call is the employer's chance to find out more about you and to ask specific questions about what you can bring to the table. Although you might meet the requirements outlined in the job posting, the employer might decide you simply aren't the right fit. So, be prepared for rejection right off the bat—when the interviewer says, "Ya know what? I think you have a lot to offer, but we were looking for someone with more experience in handling premature gorillas. I will keep your résumé on file, though. Thank you for your time."

Yes, rejection is a tough pill to swallow. However, if you approach it as a *learning experience*, you can pick up clues and cues from the interviewer as to what you need to do to be successful the next time around, or with the next interviewer calling about a similar position.

"Thanks for Turnin' Me Down"

Well, I wouldn't use those exact words, but a good reason to send a thank-you-for-turning-me-down letter is because you don't know what can happen down the road. A similar position that fits your skills more closely might open up. The "other" candidate might turn down the offer to interview or decline the job offer. The person interviewing you might move to another company and have a match for you there. Send a brief email to your contact, and you'll likely be remembered for your graciousness and good sportsmanlike conduct. See the section "Samples of Quick and Easy Follow-Up Notes" at the end of this chapter for an example of a "thanks for the rejection" note follow-up.

What If the Phone Doesn't Ring at All?

So, you did your research, put your plan of attack into action, and you wait...and wait...and the phone doesn't ring. What went wrong? If you're just not getting the response you expect, take a look at your career documents. Did you include keywords on your résumé? Are there spelling errors? Did you target your career objective? Did you include correct contact information?

The answer could be a simple one, so don't throw in the towel if your first attempt at the online job hunt doesn't bring in the results you're expecting.

Re-evaluate your strategy. Review your materials. And if necessary, start over.

Preparing for the Interview

The interview can induce sweaty palms for any job seeker, but if you prepare for the questions and approach the situation as an information-sharing experience, you'll be much more relaxed and confident. Besides preparing for the questions, take time now to get samples or a portfolio together. Be sure to read Chapter 9, "Hi-Fi Online Portfolios," for the scoop on high-impact presentations—both online and in hand.

But to get you started thinking about your witty and hard-hitting responses to the most commonly asked interview questions, read on.

FAQs—By the Interviewer and for the Interviewer

There's no time like the present to prepare for the first interview, but it's hard to prepare when you stop to realize that there are hundreds of different interview styles, not to mention thousands of possible questions that could be asked. However, there are standard questions that usually come up in one form or another in interviews, so knowing beforehand what to expect will give you a chance to prepare a clever response.

There are some great places online to prepare for the interview. Most of the major job sites such as Monster.com (www.monster.com) and Career Mosaic (www.careermosaic.com) offer sample questions and timely tips and advice on how to prepare for interviews. Another site you won't want to miss is Job Interview Network (www.job-interview.net), which has a question bank, an interview success guide, and links to job interview tips, questions, and answers for specific careers or jobs.

For an insider's opinion from real job seekers, JobReviews.com (www.jobreviews.com) collects interview reviews about interviews at specific companies, and features chat rooms and message boards where you can meet and get advice and tips from both career experts and job seekers.

After the interview (the same day if possible), send a quick note or email thanking the interviewer for meeting with you (see Figure 4.6 in the section "Samples of Quick and Easy Follow-Up Notes"). If you're interested in the position, restate this in your note. If you're not interested, just thank them for their time (see Figure 4.7 in the samples section later in this chapter).

When to Provide Salary Information and References

The salary issue is a sticky one, but you'll find plenty of advice online to fit your unique situation. Depending on the demand for your type of skills, your experience level, and the type of job you're applying for, the point at which you should provide your salary history will vary. After the salary door is open, it's hard to close until you know what to expect and what to ask for. Don't back yourself into a corner by stating a figure that is too high or too low. Provide your salary history only when asked, and expect to be asked at any time during the interview.

To find help online for handling the salary question in interviews, you can visit Monster.com's Negotiation Coach at midcareer.monster.com/experts/negotiation (see Figure 4.2). You can also go to your favorite search engine and do a keyword search using salary negotiation advice, plus college grad, or executive, or whatever your level of experience is. The rules vary, so get advice that's suited to your unique needs.

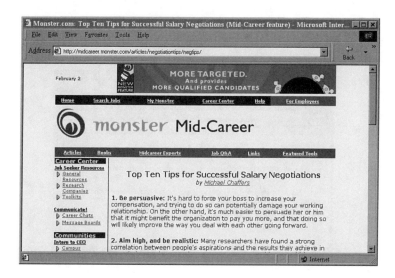

Figure 4.2

Monster.com's Negotiation expert can point you in the right direction when it comes to asking for and getting the best salary offer. Read the advice articles or post a question to the Negotiation Expert forum.

As far as references go, do not send them with your résumé. Take a sheet with you to the first interview, and provide them on request. I've heard horror stories of people providing references too early, and losing the job lead to the very people on the list. Why? Because chances are the people on your list are folks you've worked with—people who are equally or better qualified for the job themselves.

Samples of Quick and Easy Follow-Up Notes

These follow-up notes cover saying thank you, no thank you, and thanks for turnin' me down, in a polite and professional manner. You can prepare notes ahead of time and customize them for accordingly after the action begins.

The note in Figure 4.3 includes a summary of what took place in the prescreening interview. It shows your enthusiasm for the opportunity to interview, as well as demonstrating your ability and willingness to follow through.

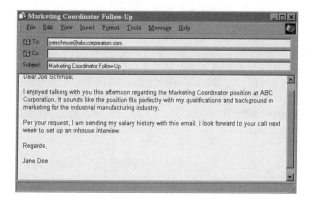

Figure 4.3

After the prescreening interview or first interview, send a brief note of thanks, and include any requested information, if applicable.

Send a "thanks but no thanks" note (see Figure 4.4) if you want to be considered for future opportunities, and just to say thanks for the interest.

Figure 4.4

This sample note is a gracious way to turn down an offer to interview, but demonstrates your appreciation for being considered.

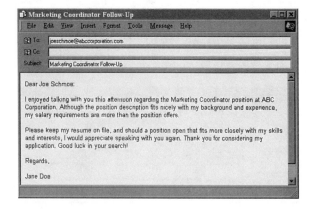

Even if you're rejected during the prescreening phase, don't give up hope. You never know when a more suitable position will open up, and because not many people bother with this type of note, you'll stand out as a good sport! Figure 4.5 can help you get started writing this type of note.

Figure 4.5

Here is a simple, brief note that says thank you and please keep my résumé on file if a more suitable position opens up. You never know whether the "other" candidate will work out!

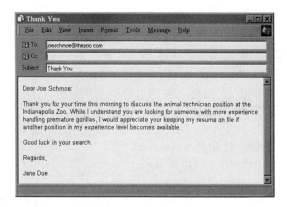

Always, always, always send a follow-up note after an interview. This is your chance to restate your interest in the position, and remind the employer why you're the right person for the job (see Figure 4.6). If you decide after you leave the interview that you don't want to pursue the opportunity further, be courteous and let the employer know and explain why (see Figure 4.7). They might call back and say, "If salary is the only issue, perhaps we can renegotiate."

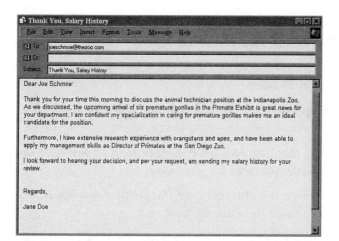

Figure 4.6

Send a brief thank you and a summary of why you're the right person for the job—if you're still interested.

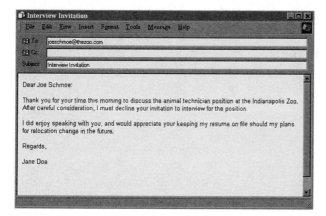

Figure 4.7

Thanks, but no thanks, might lead to renegotiation if the employer really wants to bring you on the team. If there's no way you'd consider any offer, make that clear, tactfully and quickly.

Again, the key to moving successfully through the job search process is being prepared. By going online to do a bulk of your research and legwork, you can save time and get up-to-date advice from industry experts who deal with the ever-changing face of careers and recruitment.

Follow the Boy Scouts' advice, and you'll gain confidence as well as a stronger understanding of what it takes to find and land your dream job.

The Least You Need to Know

➤ Prepare for prescreening calls before you send out your résumé—the phone could start ringing within 24 hours!

➤ Ask specific questions up front to determine whether you should pursue leads and opportunities.

➤ Gather information, put together your interview portfolio (if you have one), and do more research while you wait for responses.

➤ Practice interviewing with a friend to get over the preinterview jitters and walk with confidence through the interrogation.

➤ Know what questions to ask the interviewer to position yourself as the ideal candidate.

➤ Go online to get the latest advice concerning salary negotiation and when to provide your salary history.

Part 2

Get a Charge out of Job Hunting: The Electronic Résumé and Cover Letter

The résumé is a fundamental tool in your job-hunting arsenal, but it's a different animal in the online world. In this section, you learn about the different types of electronic documents and how to format them for the Web, such as résumés, cover letters, and other job-hunting and networking communications. You also learn that employers are more interested in what you can do for them rather than what you've done in the past, so your résumé is a document that you'll tailor to tell the story your target employer wants to read.

The electronic résumé provides an ideal way for employers to scan, store, and search databases for the perfect candidates. As more and more employers look to the Web as a new recruitment tool, you need to find out what employers are looking for when they go online to find new talent and how to be sure your résumé doesn't get lost in the vast reaches of cyberspace.

Chapter 5

Understanding the Electronic Résumé

In This Chapter

➤ Why you need a résumé

➤ How to answer the question every employer wants to know: "What can you do for me?"

➤ Deciding on a chronological or functional résumé

➤ How to write keyword and skills summaries

➤ What not to put on your résumé

➤ Getting free help and advice online, and what to know before you spend money on software or a professional résumé writer

No one I know enjoys writing or updating résumés. It's one of the more agonizing parts of job hunting, but you simply can't avoid it. The résumé is the cornerstone of the career document package, and it's probably the most important selling tool in getting an employer's attention other than direct contact, through a recruiter or head-hunter, or by networking. Even then, you need to have a résumé (preferably several versions of a résumé) on hand when you look for a job.

Your résumé has to work hard and sell fast—like a billboard—especially if you're playing the craps game of online job sites and résumé databases. I'm not suggesting online job sites and résumé databases won't help you find a job—I think there are more effective ways to go about finding your dream job, but any way you slice it, you still need to have a killer résumé.

In a word, your résumé has to be perfect. And I'm not just talking about typos, spelling, and grammar. Your résumé has to communicate as quickly and effectively as possible why the employer should pick up the phone and call you to find out more.

This chapter will show you how to write a knock-'em dead résumé—what to include, what to keep out, and how to create a hard-selling self-marketing tool that will get attention and invitations to interviews.

So, if you find yourself suffering from "writer's block" or just know that you can't or don't want to suffer the pain of résumé writing, don't worry. Help is available. There's plenty of free online advice, plus résumé-writing software and wizards. Or, you can hire a professional résumé writer to write your killer résumé for you.

This chapter takes you through the résumé-writing process, step-by-step, to show you how to create a résumé that lands an interview so you can answer the one question on the minds of every employer: "What can you do for me?" Or, if you do decide to get professional résumé help, I'll tell you what to look for, how much you should expect to pay, and how and why you should avoid the cookie-cutter approach that some résumé "experts" offer.

A Little Background on the Purpose of the Résumé

In the business world, cover letters and résumés are part and parcel of the job-hunting game. Employers need summary information and details about you, and both you and the employer have been led to believe that the only way to present this vital information is with a résumé. So, why do so many résumés land in the trash? Because most résumés are about the people who write them and all the great things they've done in the past for all those "other" employers. It's all about me, me, me—me and my experience. Well, that's just lovely. But, guess what? The employer doesn't care.

The Love Letter Résumé?

Imagine meeting a new Romeo or Juliet and sending a love letter detailing all the great things you did for your *former* loves—reasons why you think this new Romeo or Juliet should fall in love with you. Do you think that's going to inspire feelings of devotion, or any interest at all? Probably not.

But what if you wrote a love letter that spoke to what you were going to do based on Romeo or Juliet's personal needs and interests? "I am going to make you a crown of yellow roses, just like the ones you sing about from your balcony every night." Or, "I'm going to take you away from all this madness because we both know your family is dysfunctional and it's killing you inside."

Let me put it this way: If you approach your résumé as a chronicle of your qualifications and your future ability to do the job, rather than a chronicle of what you did before, your résumé has a much better chance of being read with interest. And that's what you want.

Self-Marketing 101

Here's another clever metaphor to ponder as you work up a sweat thinking about redoing your résumé. Every marketer knows that the most effective forms of advertising are ads that speak to the consumer's needs and interests. These marketers know that they have to answer one question on the minds of consumers: "What's in it for me?" Good ads are benefit-oriented (it will make you look 30 years younger) rather than feature-oriented (this age-defying lotion has ancient, secret ingredients). Who cares what's in it? I need to get rid of these wrinkles!

Those basic marketing concepts apply to you and your résumé, too. Instead of focusing on your features (your experience), focus on your benefits (your qualifications.) Here's an example of the difference between experience and qualifications:

➤ Experience: Administered resident and family satisfaction survey
➤ Qualification: Increased occupancy by developing a word-of-mouth and family referral program in response to findings from resident and family satisfaction surveys

The message here is simple: Rethink the way your résumé works to represent you. Instead of focusing on you and your experience, focus on meeting the needs of the employer. You do this by knowing the industry, the employer, and either finding out exactly what the employer's problems or challenges are, or by making educated assumptions about the needs of most employers in your industry. Preferably, you'll do the former and not the latter, but either way, for your résumé to make the "hard sell," you have to answer the question, "What's in it for me?"

Résumé Blasphemy!!

Nick Corcodilos, author of *Ask the Headhunter* and outspoken career expert at the Ask the Headhunter Web site (www.asktheheadhunter.com), doesn't like résumés. Not one bit. He sees them as static documents that don't communicate who you are and that only tell the employer what you did before, rather than offer solutions that meet your target employer's current needs or problems. Who cares what you did two years ago if you can't convince the employer you can do the job now? He has a point.

So, Nick invented the "Working Résumé." It lists no credentials. No education or prior employers. What it *does* include is a clear understanding of your target employer's business and the problems and challenges the employer faces. It has a plan describing how you would do the work that needs to be done, and an estimate of what or how much you could add to the bottom line. As Nick describes it, the Working Résumé "requires you to *do* the job, not just apply for it."

The Headhunter Speaks!

For an aggressive, yet irreverent and refreshing, approach to how to get a job, visit Ask the Headhunter at www.asktheheadhunter.com. Nick Corcodilos answers every question posed at his ATH message board, so if you have a burning question for the man with all the answers, ask away. Coming from someone whose livelihood is based on successfully matching employers and candidates, it's good food for thought.

Nick's theory is based on the assumption that you have targeted and thoroughly researched the one employer that could offer you a "dream job." Talk about putting all your eggs in one basket—but when you think about his approach, it makes sense. After all, "If it's the job worth wanting, it's worth doing," he says.

I'm not suggesting you chuck the more traditional résumé. I'm just giving you food for thought: What Nick is getting at is that to land your dream job, you have to convince the employer to give it to you. Merely wanting it and demonstrating that you've been able to do jobs like it in the past leaves it to the employer to convince himself that you can do this job, too. That's not his job. It's yours.

Think about the theory of the Working Résumé, but don't scrap your résumé. To get to the point where you can sit down and convince the employer you're the right person for the job, you have to plant the seed of interest with your résumé. From there, love will blossom.

Remember, your dream job is not going to find you, and certainly scattering a half-baked résumé out across cyberspace is not going to produce a dream job for you, either. To find it, you have to work hard, and you have to know what it is you want. Otherwise, your résumé could end up in the big pile of "blah" résumés that employers don't ever read.

Now that you know how the résumé works, it's time to get down to business. The rest of the chapter deals with the contents of your résumé, but we'll get into formatting for the electronic world in Chapter 6, "Get Help with Your Résumé Writing," including how to format plain text, rich text, scannable, and traditional printed résumés.

First Things First—Choose Your Format

There are a handful of basic résumé formats: reverse chronological, functional (or skills) résumé, and curriculum vitaes (CVs). A CV is used primarily for academia-related jobs, and is the European term for résumé. Here's a quick overview of chronogical and functional résumés, and when to use which one.

The Chronological Résumé

A reverse chronological résumé lists your positions and qualifications, usually from college through to the present time. I answer the "how far back should I go?" question later in the chapter, but you should go back as far as your experience relates to the job you're trying to get. That doesn't mean you should have chunks of time missing if you worked at a job that's unrelated to the position at hand, but don't spend a lot of time or space on unrelated or outdated experience.

Most people use the chronological résumé, and it's the preferred format by most employers.

Thanks for the Tip

THANKS!!

Formatting Versus Format?

Don't get confused by the word "format" when it comes to your résumé. The formatting of your résumé can be in plain text, rich text, and HTML. The format of your résumé can be chronological, functional, or curriculum vitae.

The Functional Résumé

The functional, or skills, résumé has headers such as "Management Experience" or "Customer Service Skills," and then has bullet points supporting the header. The functional résumé is often used by folks with limited on-the-job experience, "job hoppers," and people re-entering the workforce. As such, functional résumés are usually considered red flags to employers, and also a bit of an annoyance. They require the employer to "construct" who you are and where you've been. Use the functional résumé as a last resort, and always be sure to include some kind of chronological summary of your experience.

Next Things Next: What to Write

Depending on what field you're in and what level of experience you're at, the guts of your résumé will vary. The nuts and bolts, however, remain the same. Nearly every résumé contains some variation of the following: contact information, objective statement, skills and keyword summary, work experience, and education summary—and they usually appear in that order.

Contact Information

Your contact information includes your name, address, nonwork phone number, and email. If you're posting your résumé to a database, you can leave out your address and even a phone number. If an employer is impressed by your skills and experience, they'll email you. For details on how to format your address block, read Chapter 6.

The Objective Statement

The objective statement is a quick and hard-selling line stating why you're sending your résumé. It's not just the title of the kind of position you're looking for, as in "Production Assistant." Here's an objective statement that states your qualifications, and what you can bring to the employer's table: "To be a member of a team that benefits from my five years of experience managing projects, negotiating with vendors, and controlling costs and schedules to complete projects on time and on budget."

Skills Summary

Make it easy on employers by providing a super-fast paragraph or bulleted summary of why you're the right person for the job. Here's an example of a good skills summary:

Deadline-oriented communications expert with six years in both client- and agency-side marketing with a proven track record in direct response advertising.

Or, for the bulleted list style:

➤ Award-winning copywriter and communicator

➤ Deadline- and goal-driven team leader

➤ Thorough understanding of business-to-business marketing communications and direct response advertising

Keyword Summary

The keyword summary lists industry buzzwords and nouns that an employer might use as search criteria to home in on qualified applicants. You can develop a list of keywords by reviewing job descriptions, reading industry trade publications, and generally staying aware of current trends and hot topics.

Here's an example of a keyword-search-friendly summary:

Technical writer. Advertising copywriter. Business-to-business marketing communications. Direct response. Direct mail. Display advertising. Brochures. Product development. Packaging. Press releases. Web content development. Brand identity. Market penetration. Demographics. Project management.

Work Experience

Self-explanatory. Your work experience lists the names of employers, dates of tenure, and your title. Under each heading is a summary of qualifications that are relevant to the job you're applying for. For example, if you worked for a business-to-business advertising agency and you're applying to a consumer advertising agency, you can play down or leave out items such as product brochures, technical specification sheets, channel marketing, and so on.

Education Summary

Your education summary lists the institution or course title, dates you attended, degree or certification, and area of study. You don't have to put your GPA—but many college grads who are fixated on this know that if you don't list it on your résumé, it's going to come up in an interview. Follow your instincts. If your GPA stinks, don't include it.

Thanks for the Tip

Your Job Description

Although you should never line-list your job duties and tasks on your résumé, a job description can help you get started developing a list of qualifications and skills you gained on the job. Dig it out when it's time to update your résumé. It's incredible how much you forget what you "do" at your job.

How Long Should It Be?

Get out your ruler: Your résumé should be exactly one and 1/16 of a page in length. No more, no less. No, I'm just kidding. I'm making fun of all those experts who tell you the résumé should be a certain length, usually one page and one page only. That's a myth! Your résumé should be only as long as needed to include pertinent skills and experience.

Plus, in this day of the digital domain, if an employer prints out your plain text electronic résumé, they aren't going to freak out if it's more than a page long. They will, however, freak out and throw it away if you include stuff that has nothing to do with the task at hand: how your qualifications meet the job requirements and how you can benefit the employer.

A good rule of thumb is the "1/3 screen rule." No matter how long your résumé is, try to put the most important information in the top third. I don't know why, but there's a theory circulating that people don't like to scroll down to read—if you capture someone's attention right away, they'll scroll.

What to Leave Out

Here's a laundry list of things to leave out of your résumé. Remember to make room for the juicy stuff, such as why you're the best candidate for the job.

To Live, You Must Laugh

I follow that advice whenever possible, so here's a little something to lighten the load while you agonize over your résumé. This condensed list of résumé blunders was compiled by *Fortune* magazine, taken from real résumés from real people, just like you!

"I have lurnt Word Perfect 6.0, computor and spreadsheat progroms."

"Received a plague for Salesperson of the Year."

"You will want me to be Head Honcho in no time."

"Am a perfectionist and rarely if if ever forget details."

"Marital status: single. Unmarried. Unengaged. Uninvolved. No commitments."

"I have an excellent track record, although I am not a horse."

"Personal interests: donating blood. Fourteen gallons so far."

"Instrumental in ruining entire operation for a Midwest chain store."

"Note: Please don't misconstrue my 14 jobs as 'job-hopping.' I have never quit a job."

"Reason for leaving last job: They insisted that all employees get to work by 8:45 every morning. Could not work under those conditions."

"Finished eighth in my class of ten."

"References: None. I've left a path of destruction behind me."

How Far Back Should You Go?

Of course, everything you've ever done is important. We know that, but employers don't care. Limit the amount of information on jobs to no more than 10 to 15 years ago, unless the experience directly relates to the job you're applying for.

Chuck the Irrelevant Skills and Experience

This part is easy: For every item on your résumé, ask yourself, "Will this help me get the job?" If the answer is no, toss it.

Reasons for Leaving Previous Jobs

Don't open the door of suspicion and give the employer a reason to throw your résumé away—an employer will ask this question during the interview.

Personal Information

That's great that you love needlepoint—it's good to have a life outside work. But unless you're applying for a Head Needlepointer position, employers don't care. Your personal interests and activities don't answer the question, "What can you do for me?" Unless you plan on needlepointing a nice hankie for your boss's Christmas gift, even then, don't spoil the surprise by listing your hobbies on your résumé. Save room for the important information—what you can do at work.

Don't include a photo. Don't indicate your age, weight, race, gender, religious beliefs, sexual preference, marital status, number of dependents, medical conditions, or anything that's not directly related to your ability to perform the job. Again, employers don't care. Plus, if you list personal information such as race, age, or religious background, you open up a big can of worms in terms of Equal Opportunity Employment. If you don't get hired or interviewed based on lack of skills or qualifications, employers fear you might try to say you didn't get hired because you were discriminated against.

For safety's sake, don't include your Social Security number, licensing or certification numbers, or any other personal information—especially if you're planning on posting your résumé at a database. In fact, I recommend not even including your street address in résumés posted to the Web. For a few gentle reminders on online privacy, be sure to read Chapter 8, "Privacy, Distribution, and Access to Your Résumé."

Redundant Information

You don't have to say things such as "References Available upon Request." Employers assume you'll provide references when they ask for them, so you're just wasting space. And don't include your references with your résumé, either—if your résumé falls into the hands of a wiley recruiter, your references might seem more attractive than you.

Salary History and Desired Pay

Even if the ad says to include a salary history, don't put it on your résumé or cover letter. Send it as a separate part of the package. Whenever possible, avoid the salary issue until you're in a better position to negotiate.

Date of Availability

Don't worry about this until it becomes an issue during the interview.

Go Online for Free Advice

I am not a résumé expert or a professional résumé writer, and I am not about to say which résumé expert is right and which is wrong. I am, however, a Web research guru, and I have located a handful of sites that provide you with free and timely advice on résumés. Here are my favorites.

College Grad Résumés, Cover Letters, and More (`www.collegegrad.com/resumes/index.shtml`)

The hardest résumé to write is the first one. You're sitting there thinking, "I've done nothing with my life! All I've ever done is go to school." Precisely. But don't despair. College Grad helps you figure out, step-by-step, how to turn seemingly worthless experience and education into marketable selling tools for a variety of job fields (see Figure 5.1).

Figure 5.1

College Grad's résumé section takes you step-by-step to help you figure out how to build a résumé and other tips to get you started on your career path.

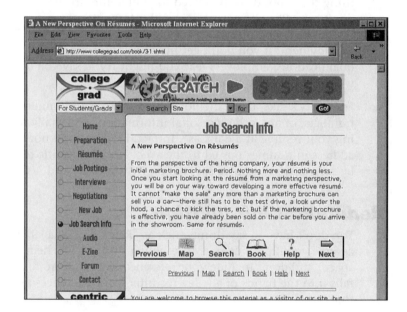

Monster.com's Résumé Expert (`content.monster.com/resume/samples/resumes/index.stm`)

Monster.com's Résumé Expert, Kim Isaacs, offers a custom résumé makeover to three Monster users each month. The "before" and "after" résumés of the lucky winners are posted on the site. You also get insider advice on the "extra touch" to make your résumé stand out from the pack. Learn about techniques and formats, and check out samples to get started. You can also pose questions at the Résumé message board, or ask Kim for specific advice on your résumé. (Be sure to follow directions before using the message board.)

Other columns and features include How to Convert Your Résumé to ASCII Format; Common Résumé Blunders; Tips for Creating a Scannable Résumé; FAQ: Applying for Jobs Online; You Just Scanned My Résumé!; How to Take Care of Weaknesses on Your Résumé; Résumé Faux Pas; Action Phrases and Power Verbs; and Résumé Rx.

JobStar (`jobstar.org/tools/resume/index.htm`)

Hands down, JobStar is an excellent career resource site. The résumé tips and advice are equally impressive, so be sure to check it out and pay special attention to the columns and advice of Mary Ellen Mort. Other notable features include Yana Parker's and Clara Horvath's expert knowledge of résumés—traditional and electronic. Yana Parker is the author of the popular *Damn Good Résumé Guide* series and has her own Web site at www.damngood.com. Clara is a librarian with an attitude and is an expert on the electronic job search process. Besides the free advice of said résumé gurus, JobStar provides lots of links to other résumé sites.

Using Résumé Software and Wizards

Although résumé writing software and wizards can help you jump-start the process of pounding out a résumé, be sure to customize your résumé and cover letter content based on your unique skills. Employers who receive a lot of résumés know a cookie-cutter résumé when they see one, so if you do have to use software and wizard cheat sheets, take care to cover up the evidence.

Ready-to-Go Résumés by Yana Parker

Ready-to-Go Résumés was rated "the best of the bunch" and "the best value" by New York *Times* reviewers in the summer of 1999. Ready-to-Go Résumés is a set of three disks containing résumé templates that you pull up and customize with your personal statistics and experience. You also get guidelines for choosing formats and the Résumé Clinic, which has answers to common résumé dilemmas, such as lack of experience, gaps in work history due to babies, unemployment, or other circumstances. The maker of Ready-to-Go also writes *Damn Good Résumés*, and maintains a Web site at www.damngood.com.

RésuméMaker Deluxe 7.0

RésuméMaker covers all the bases when it comes to the job search process. Besides the fill-in-the-blank Guided Résumés feature, you get Résumé Caster, which blasts your résumé into cyberville, and Job Finder, which does a meta search of the major job posting sites to find positions matching your criteria. A cool feature is the contact manager function (see Figure 5.2), which helps you stay on top of the who, what, where, and when of the job search process.

There's also a Career Planner function to help you figure out basic career planning decisions, sample cover letters, salary negotiations, and interviewing. One-stop job search tool? Perhaps, but don't rely on any one tool or technique (especially the blast-the-résumé-across-the-Web approach) and expect to get results.

Figure 5.2

RésuméMaker's contact manager can help you stay focused and organized during your job search.

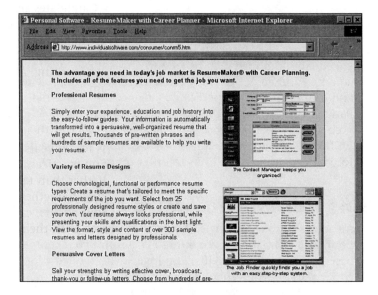

The Hired Gun: Working with a Professional

If I wanted to, I could hang a sign outside my door and open up shop as a professional résumé writer. I've got no training and no proof of being an expert except that I call myself one. Unfortunately, a lot of people do this, so proceed with caution when you decide to hire a professional résumé writer.

Here are things to look for, but don't settle for claims and membership in résumé-writing associations. Get samples, ask for references, and interview your résumé expert before you hand over any cash. This is your future, after all. Don't put blind faith in "experts" who can't back up that claim!

Certification

There are two certifications that professional résumé writers can earn:

➤ *Certified Professional Résumé Writer (CPRW)*. This credential is issued by the Professional Association of Résumé Writers (PARW). To earn a CPRW designation, the résumé writer must pass a rigorous test of knowledge of résumé writing, proofreading, and the employment field. Testing involves the résumé writer preparing a fictitious résumé and cover letter to be judged by professional résumé writers.

➤ *Nationally Certified Résumé Writer (NCRW)*. The National Résumé Writers' Association (NRWA) certifies résumé writers who pass a three-part exam measuring skills in résumé writing (grammar, punctuation, layout/design, proofreading, and electronic document preparation). Candidates also have to provide a written résumé, cover letter, and scannable résumé that meets the "standards of excellence" developed by NRWA's Certification Commission. Candidates who pass the exam must then earn continuing education credits, to stay up-to-date in the constantly changing field of résumé writing. About fifty percent of résumé writers fail the certification exam.

Years of Experience

Just because someone's been in the business for 20 years doesn't mean they're up to speed with today's recruiting and hiring practices. On the other hand, you don't want to be someone's Frankenstein. Rather than taking a résumé writer's "word for it," get samples and judge for yourself whether the person has the right stuff. Better yet, get the names of three or four clients, call them or email them, and ask them how they did in their job search with their professionally written résumé.

How Much Will It Cost?

Résumé writing fees are based on how long it takes to gather information through consultations, interviews, and research, plus preparing the document and proofreading sessions to finalize the project. Because of the amount of time and expertise involved, a professionally prepared résumé is an investment in your career and future. My observation has been that a professionally written résumé costs from $100 to $300, depending on the types of services you require.

Take a look at the "before and after" résumés in Figures 5.3 and 5.4. Kim Isaacs of Résumé Systems (www.resumesystems.com) and the Résumé Expert at Monster.com provided these samples to illustrate the value of getting a professional résumé makeover.

There are no "flat fees" for professional résumé services, because individual projects differ in complexity and time requirements. A résumé for a college grad with limited work history and experience will usually be less than a résumé for a high-roller executive with a 25-year work history.

STACY MARKS
15 Elm Street
San Diego, California 55555
(222) 333-2323
stacymarks@resumepower.com

OBJECTIVE-Seeking a challenging position with a growing company which will utilize my experience and talents.

EDUCATION
Bachelor of Business Administration in Accounting, 1995
San Diego University

Master of Business Administration in Finance, Fall 2000 completion
California University
Member - Beta Gamma Sigma National Honor Society
Maintain 4.0 GPA

SUMMARY
• Proven communicator. Effectively advise and counsel clients and contribute as an integral team player. Co-chair on a variety of intercompany meetings.
• Professional with established track record as a top producer in high stress, volume environments. Twice awarded Advanced Oil Victory Award for Professional Achievements.
• Computer literate. Spreadsheet programs including Excel, Research systems including Bloomberg and Internet sites, Word, MS Access, Lawson, SAP R/3,Crystal Reports and SQL. Adaptable to any system/application. Train new users on systems and applications.
• Research, observe and analyze client requirements to accurately determine financial and business options.
• Motivated and competitive. Enjoy and adapt to new business and learning experiences.

EXPERIENCE
ADVANCED OIL COMPANY, San Diego, California
1998 to Present-Financial Accountant/Analyst
• Selected "Power User" for corporate wide SAP R/3 implementation. Responsible for configuration, system testing, and training end users on new system.
• Discovered irregularities in various systems processing, coordinated with Treasury to reconcile and correct $5 million error in cash.
• Developed & implemented automated journal entry system across several departments, decreased time spent on monthly journal entries.
• Analyze financial statement accounts for corporate operations. Maintain accounts for corporate financial reporting and budget analysis. Responsible for cash accounts in excess of $1 million.
• Prepare corporate reports required for governmental filings including EDGAR and PEDRO.
• Prepare entries and adjustments to corporate financial statements for reporting purposes.
• Prepare month end closing and adjusting entries for financial reporting purposes.
• Serve as liaison between various corporate and business units regarding accounting issues and procedures, including foreign operations. Advise Canadian subsidiaries on financial issues.
• Serve as key departmental advisor on systems related problems and operations. Including Lawson, Excel and MS Office.
• Recognized for independent/team building contributions, troubleshooting and effective customer relations skills.

THE RICHMOND INSURANCE COMPANY, San Diego, California
1996 to 1998 - Bond Underwriter
Broad-based financial/management analysis involving direct client services and special project assistance.
• Analyze & evaluate financial statements and management teams for sole proprietorships, partnerships, S and C corporations, non-profit and subsidiary entities.
• Organize and conduct meetings with client owners, officers and board of directors to discuss credit and financial requirements.
• Customize and prepare client financial information to computerized underwriting system and spreadsheet programs.
• Market products to clients and maintain professional relationships with respective agents.
• Report directly, and work closely with the department manager to accomplish special company/client projects.
• Handle complex questions and inquiries from clients and advise on appropriate recourse and options.

Figure 5.3

The "before" résumé has an unclear objective statement and lengthy bulleted lists—a résumé has to make a strong impression quickly.

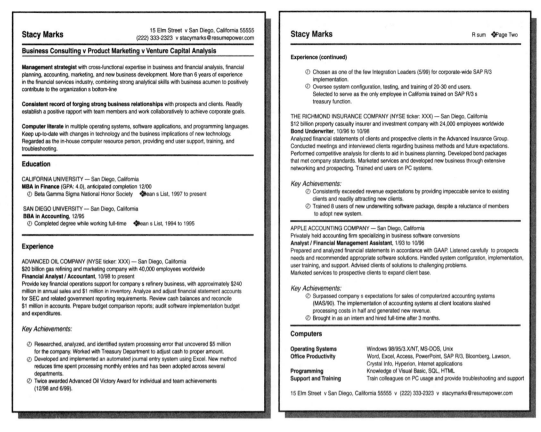

Stacy Marks 15 Elm Street v San Diego, California 55555
(222) 333-2323 v stacymarks@resumepower.com

Business Consulting v Product Marketing v Venture Capital Analysis

Management strategist with cross-functional expertise in business and financial analysis, financial planning, accounting, marketing, and new business development. More than 6 years of experience in the financial services industry, combining strong analytical skills with business acumen to positively contribute to the organization s bottom-line.

Consistent record of forging strong business relationships with prospects and clients. Readily establish a positive rapport with team members and work collaboratively to achieve corporate goals.

Computer literate in multiple operating systems, software applications, and programming languages. Keep up-to-date with changes in technology and the business implications of new technology. Regarded as the in-house computer resource person, providing end user support, training, and troubleshooting.

Education

CALIFORNIA UNIVERSITY — San Diego, California
MBA in Finance (GPA: 4.0), anticipated completion 12/00
- Beta Gamma Sigma National Honor Society Dean s List, 1997 to present

SAN DIEGO UNIVERSITY — San Diego, California
BBA in Accounting, 12/95
- Completed degree while working full-time Dean s List, 1994 to 1995

Experience

ADVANCED OIL COMPANY (NYSE ticker: XXX) — San Diego, California
$20 billion gas refining and marketing company with 40,000 employees worldwide
Financial Analyst / Accountant, 10/98 to present
Provide key financial operations support for company s refinery business, with approximately $240 million in annual sales and $1 million in inventory. Analyze and adjust financial statement accounts for SEC and related government reporting requirements. Review cash balances and reconcile $1 million in accounts. Prepare budget comparison reports; audit software implementation budget and expenditures.

Key Achievements:
- Researched, analyzed, and identified system processing error that uncovered $5 million for the company. Worked with Treasury Department to adjust cash to proper amount.
- Developed and implemented an automated journal entry system using Excel. New method reduces time spent processing monthly entries and has been adopted across several departments.
- Twice awarded Advanced Oil Victory Award for individual and team achievements (12/98 and 6/99).

Stacy Marks R sum Page Two

Experience (continued)

- Chosen as one of the few Integration Leaders (5/99) for corporate-wide SAP R/3 implementation.
- Oversee system configuration, testing, and training of 20-30 end users. Selected to serve as the only employee in California trained on SAP R/3 s treasury function.

THE RICHMOND INSURANCE COMPANY (NYSE ticker: XXX) — San Diego, California
$12 billion property casualty insurer and investment company with 24,000 employees worldwide
Bond Underwriter, 10/96 to 10/98
Analyzed financial statements of clients and prospective clients in the Advanced Insurance Group. Conducted meetings and interviewed clients regarding business methods and future expectations. Performed competitive analysis for clients to aid in business planning. Developed bond packages that met company standards. Marketed services and developed new business through extensive networking and prospecting. Trained end users on PC systems.

Key Achievements:
- Consistently exceeded revenue expectations by providing impeccable service to existing clients and readily attracting new clients.
- Trained 8 users of new underwriting software package, despite a reluctance of members to adopt new system.

APPLE ACCOUNTING COMPANY — San Diego, California
Privately held accounting firm specializing in business software conversions
Analyst / Financial Management Assistant, 1/93 to 10/96
Prepared and analyzed financial statements in accordance with GAAP. Listened carefully to prospects needs and recommended appropriate software solutions. Handled system configuration, implementation, user training, and support. Advised clients of solutions to challenging problems. Marketed services to prospective clients to expand client base.

Key Achievements:
- Surpassed company s expectations for sales of computerized accounting systems (MAS/90). The implementation of accounting systems at client locations slashed processing costs in half and generated new revenue.
- Brought in as an intern and hired full-time after 3 months.

Computers

Operating Systems	Windows 98/95/3.X/NT, MS-DOS, Unix
Office Productivity	Word, Excel, Access, PowerPoint, SAP R/3, Bloomberg, Lawson, Crystal Info, Hyperion, Internet applications
Programming	Knowledge of Visual Basic, SQL, HTML
Support and Training	Train colleagues on PC usage and provide troubleshooting and support

15 Elm Street v San Diego, California 55555 v (222) 333-2323 v stacymarks@resumepower.com

Figure 5.4

The "after" résumé has a hard-hitting skills summary and easy-to-read experience and achievements categories.

Thanks for the Tip

THANKS!!

Concerned About Price?

Consider the price of *not* having a winning résumé: wasted time, lost opportunities, and diminished self-esteem and confidence. If you're not confident of your abilities to produce a winning résumé, invest in professional résumé services to give yourself a chance to succeed.

Avoid Cookie-Cutter Résumé Services

Steer clear of résumé writers who offer flat-rate services. This usually means your résumé won't be customized based on your particular needs and experience, or that very little time will be spent with you discussing your needs as a job seeker.

The Least You Need to Know

➤ Employers don't care what you did before—they want to know what you can do for them in the future.

➤ Your résumé is the first step in getting to a face-to-face meeting with employers, so don't blow it with typos or spelling errors, or by including the wrong information.

➤ There is an endless amount of conflicting advice about résumés—go online to get the most up-to-date tips and techniques.

➤ Résumé software and wizards take you step-by-step through building your résumé, but beware of the cookie-cutter end result.

➤ Anyone can call themselves a professional résumé writer, so know what to look for and what questions to ask.

Chapter 6

Get Help with Your Résumé Writing

In This Chapter

➤ The four types of résumés: formatted, plain-text, scannable, and Web résumés

➤ How to format each type of résumé, and how to avoid common errors and mishaps

➤ How to use your résumé with online forms and applications

Life was so simple, uncomplicated, back in the days when all you had to worry about regarding your résumé was writing it and debating over what kind of paper to print it on—heavy-bond ivory or slate gray?

These days, thanks to the high-speed online job hunt, you now need a variety of résumés in order to respond to job postings. But don't worry—it's a matter of a few simple formatting techniques, and I take you step-by-step on how to format your résumé for electronic transmission. I also show you how to prepare your résumé for scanners, and a few quick tips on making a Web résumé.

The Many Faces of the Electronic Résumé

As I promised, even though you now have to have different formats of your résumé, converting from the traditional, fancy formatted résumé is a simple process. This section covers the different types of résumés, and how to format your existing document for electronic transmission across the digital domain.

In a nutshell, there are four different types of résumés:

➤ *Plain-text.*   No frills, no nothing. Just the facts, ma'am. It's got to be the ugliest résumé out there, but making a plain-text résumé is simple, and it's the preferred format for online job hunting.

➤ *Scannable paper résumés.*   Lots of large companies use scanning technology to process the large number of résumés that come their way via snail mail (U.S. postal service) and fax machines.

➤ *Formatted electronic or paper résumés.*   Before the days of desktop publishing, job seekers either had to hire the services of a professional typesetter or do résumés on a typewriter. Not anymore. Anyone with a word processing program and a printer can make their very own résumé. Electronic résumés as attachments are usually Microsoft Word documents. You should never send your résumé as an attachment to your email unless you're instructed to do so.

From time to time, an employer might ask to see your "official" résumé—in other words, a non–plain-text résumé. This is when the fancy-schmancy paper résumé comes into play.

➤ *Web résumés.*   One way to impress a potential employer, or to provide additional information to what you include on your plain-text résumé, is to build and post a Web résumé. It's easy to do, and if done properly, you can really stand out from the competition.

ASCII and You Shall Receivey

Plain-text or ASCII (pronounced "ask-ey") résumés are no-frills documents that all computers can read and understand. Even though they don't look good—plain-text résumés have no bold, italics, underlines, bullets, or any "frills"—they're the safest bet when it comes to transmitting your résumé across the Internet.

Techno Talk

ASCII

ASCII is the American Standard Code for Information Interchange—a standard system for encoding letters of the alphabet, digits, and symbols that can be read by any computer. Generally, any keys you see on your keyboard are safe for ASCII format.

You'll use a plain-text résumé when you email your résumé to an employer, when you post your résumé to a database or an employer's Web site, and when you complete an online application. As a safe bet, if you're asked to email or otherwise electronically transmit your résumé, plain-text is the way to go.

Formatting Your Plain-Text Résumé

If you already composed your résumé after reading Chapter 5, "Understanding the Electronic Résumé," you're in good shape. If you're starting from scratch, skip to step 2. After setting up the document layout (these steps apply to popular word processing programs such as Microsoft Word or WordPerfect), begin entering your text.

1. Just open your existing résumé document, choose **Select All** from the **Edit** pull-down menu (or **Ctrl+A** for Windows or **Cmd+A** for Macintosh). Then, select **Copy** (or **Ctrl+C** for Windows or **Cmd+C** for Macintosh) from the same **Edit** pull-down menu.

2. Open a new document and set the **Margins** at 1.75 inches on the left and right, or allow for 60 characters (including spaces) to fit across the width of the document. Because most electronic screens use this as the default width, setting your résumé margins at this size will prevent goofy line breaks and spacing problems.

3. If you're working with an existing résumé, just paste (in the **Edit** pull-down menu, select **Paste** or **Ctrl+V** for Windows and **Cmd+V** for Macintosh) your existing résumé text into your new document window. Change the font to **Times New Roman** or **Courier** and the font size to 10- or 12-point type.

4. Format the résumé text using ALL CAPS for headers, and use hyphens in place of bullets or to set off a new line of items. Figures 6.1 and 6.2 are samples of plain-text résumés, and show various formatting options in terms of section headers and line breaks. Be sure the text is left-justified and avoid using any tabs. If you need to indent or create space between headers, use the spacebar. And be sure to put parentheses around your area code, and use hyphens, as in (123) 456-7890.

5. Save the document as a text file. In Microsoft Word or WordPerfect, for example, go into the **File** menu and choose **Save As**. Give the file a name—for example, abccorp or something more generic if it's going to be used as the résumé from which you'll customize other versions, such as firstres. Then, at the bottom of this menu, you'll see **Save File Type As** or **File Type** and choose **Text Only with Line Breaks** from the pull-down menu.

6. Close the document. You'll probably get a message box telling you that you'll lose formatting, and a question if you want to continue with the Save. Click **OK** or **Yes** and close the document.

7. Reopen the document to fix spacing problems—using your spacebar only—or to add hard returns between sections or jobs. Close the document again, and open it one last time to check spacing and formatting.

8. Email the résumé to yourself to make sure it transmits across the digital domain and looks okay upon arrival in your email inbox.

If you want to take a shortcut and you've got an existing résumé, you can skip the entire process and simply follow steps 5 through 8, but make sure your margins, font, and font size are set at the recommended settings.

Proofread 'Til Your Eyes Bleed

Before you email your plain-text résumé (or any career document, for that matter), run a spell check and always, always, always be sure to print out the document and proofread very carefully. Then get a second and third set of eyes to look things over. It's especially important with plain-text résumés, as the document is so bland and boring, it's much easier to miss typos or other blunders.

MARYANNE WALKER
15 West 52nd Street, Apt. 3K
Brooklyn, New York 55555
Home: (333) 555-2222
Cellular: (777) 555-3333
maryanne.walker@somewhere.com

===
SALES PROFESSIONAL
Software / Information Technology / Finance
===

* Top-producing sales expert with 10 years of experience maximizing sales within highly competitive markets.

* Unique combination of knowledge of retail sales and information technology; expertise in providing technical and systems support. Computer literate - knowledge of Word, Excel, Outlook, and Windows NT/98.

* Establish genuine rapport with prospects and clients. Utilize comprehensive product knowledge, familiarity with diverse cultures and personalities, and enthusiastic personality to quickly map out client needs and recommend appropriate solutions. Earn clients' trust by consistently proving that their needs are paramount.

* Confident, articulate, and professional speaking abilities. Team leader and team player.

* Combine patience, determination, and persistence to troubleshoot client issues and ensure 100% satisfaction.

===
EXPERIENCE
===

MAJOR INVESTMENT COMPANY - New York, New York
FINANCIAL REPRESENTATIVE / TECHNOLOGY SPECIALIST, 19XX to present
Promoted to highly visible position with multibillion-dollar Wall Street Investment Division based on ability to prospect, negotiate and close deals, and forecast and track business activities. Serve high-net-worth clients, including CEOs of Fortune 500 companies. Build relationships and drive business through new account, portfolio review, and MAPS prospecting. Provide information on brokerage services, including stock trades, mutual funds, estate planning, life insurance, fixed income securities, and variable annuities. Develop asset allocation strategies to maximize investor return while minimizing risk.

-- Achievements include:

* Established relations with institutional clients for the first time on a large scale; successfully landed ABC Company account, resulting in over $200 million in additional assets. Act as main contact person for account.

* By providing excellent service and follow-up, generate a high number of referrals and repeat business.

* Regularly featured in New York / New Jersey sales highlights publication for outstanding sales achievements.

* Ranked in top third of peer group, which includes 145 representatives.

* Regarded as in-house systems expert; provide hardware and software troubleshooting for LAN-based system.

MUTUAL FUND SALES REPRESENTATIVE, 19XX to 19XX
Sold mutual funds using Major Investment Company's proprietary sales profiling techniques. Provided clients with trade, account information, and account maintenance services.

-- Achievements include:

* Consistently met or exceeded sales expectations while maintaining a high level of customer satisfaction.

* Ranked 12 out of 260 (September 19XX), 31st in nation for accounts YTD, and 28th in conversions.

ABC MEDICAL SUPPLY - Brooklyn, New York
Sales Representative, 19XX to 19XX
Sold medical supplies to doctors and health care facilities;
built solid customer base.

===
EDUCATION & LICENSURE
===

UNIVERSITY OF TAMPA - Tampa, Florida
Bachelor of Arts - Psychology, 19XX
- Dean's List
- Founded and led Debate Team - qualified for statefinals, 19XX
- Semester abroad in Rome

LICENSES: Series 7, Series 6, Series 63, New York State Life

Figure 6.1

A plain-text résumé formatted with all caps for headers and nifty section dividers.

Pasting Your Résumé into an Email Message

More often than not, you'll be submitting your résumé as part of an email message. Usually, the email consists of a quick cover letter (see Chapter 7, "The E-Cover Letter") and your plain-text résumé pasted into the body of the email message (not as an attachment), after your closing line.

To copy and paste your résumé into the body of an email message, simply open the résumé file and select **Copy** from the **Edit** menu. Start an email message, and then paste the résumé into that message simply by selecting **Paste** from the **Edit** menu. If you don't have an Edit menu, just use a keyboard shortcut to paste: in Windows, **Ctrl+V**, and in Macintosh, **Cmd+V**.

That's it! Compose your cover letter and include the job title or posting number in the subject header. Before you send off the email, though, email the résumé to yourself first to see how it looks and to make sure the line breaks and spacing are in order. Don't forget to print it out to proofread and check for errors.

Keyboard Shortcut

To save steps and quickly accomplish repetitive tasks, use keyboard shortcuts. A shortcut involves holding down a key such as command, option, or control, and typing a letter. For example, in Microsoft Word, pressing **Ctrl+A** selects all the text on the screen, instead of dragging your mouse across all the text to highlight it for editing.

Scannable Résumés

To manage the enormous amounts of paper résumés received at larger companies, electronic scanners are used to scan and store your résumé information in a résumé database. When an employer needs to fill a position, they'll run a keyword search of the résumé database and look for résumés that contain the skills, experience, and keywords the employer requires.

The problem with this type of paper résumé is that there's a fine line between a scannable document and documents that get rejected by the scanner as unreadable. For example, if you put your area code in parentheses, as in (765), some scanning technology won't read that as your phone number. If the rest of your document makes it through the scan, but they can't read your phone number, you're in trouble. Instead, just use dashes, as in 123-456-7890—without the parentheses, the characters are distinctive and recognizable to the scanner.

Scannable résumés are as simple and plain as a plain-text résumé: no bullets, no underline, italic, bold, fancy fonts, or columns, as seen in Figure 6.2. You'll use a scannable résumé when you're asked to send a paper résumé to an employer. Even in this case, a plain, scannable résumé is a safer bet than a fancy-schmancy formatted résumé with pretty fonts and design if you're asked to fax your résumé.

Figure 6.2

Another sample of a plain-text résumé. No frills, but readable by any computer or scanner.

Judith Gordon
1515 Elm Street
Philadelphia, PA 55555
215-555-5555
JGordon@ResumePower.com

Professional Goal:

Entry-level position in international business
... Building Global Relationships
... Consumer Banking
... Trading

Qualifications:

Highly motivated business professional with a strong interest and educational background in global business, banking, and trading. Special interest in Mexico, Central America, South America, and Europe (available to relocate, U.S. or abroad). Solid work ethic and initiative demonstrated by earning international business degree while holding a demanding job.

Outstanding communication, persuasive, and presentation skills. Bilingual in English and Spanish. Innate ability to bridge the gap between disparate cultures and business philosophies. Establish genuine rapport with colleagues and work collaboratively to achieve business goals. Produce high quality work and meet deadlines while juggling multiple assignments. Quick learner, highly adaptable, and flexible.

Education:

PHILADELPHIA COLLEGE - Philadelphia, PA
B.S.B.A.
- Major in International Business,
Minor in Spanish, January 2000
- District 8 AACO-STW Merchant Marine
Scholarship (1993 to 2000)

Relevant Courses:

- International Finance
- International Business
- Business Management
- Economic Development
- Creative Marketing
- International Marketing
- International Economics
- Business Calculus

To create a scannable résumé using your plain-text résumé as a basis, open the plain-text résumé and **Save As** a different filename, such as scanres.doc or any variation so you know what the file is. As far as formatting is concerned, you can increase the font size of your name and other headers. Otherwise, you're pretty limited on adding any other design elements. Don't use bullets, underline, or italic, and stick with traditional fonts such as Times New Roman, Courier, Palatino, or Helvetica.

Print your scannable résumé onto bright white paper for the best contrast possible and definitely avoid colored or tinted paper, or fancy paper with flecks or other textured surfaces. If you're faxing your résumé, set the fax settings to "fine print." If you're mailing your résumé, don't staple your cover letter or anything else to the résumé, and don't fold the documents. Send your application documents in a flat 9"×12" envelope.

However, if you're dealing with a small company, you can bet that no scanners or résumé-tracking software is being used. If nothing else, ask what format is preferred when you get the call asking you to send in a paper résumé. Employers will tell you exactly what they need, so don't try to guess. A company Web site might even provide detailed instructions on preferred document formatting—a good example is the CIA Web site (www.cia.gov).

OCR

Scanners use a technology called OCR, or Optical Character Recognition. This allows the recognition of printed or written characters (such as handwritten addresses on an envelope) to be scanned character-by-character and then translated to ASCII or plain text for use in data processing, such as résumé-tracking software.

Formatted Electronic Résumés

From time to time, you'll come across a job site or employer site that accepts formatted résumés as attachments to your email cover letter. A formatted résumé simply means that you can use a variety of fonts, underlines, bullets, tabs, special characters, headers, and even color text if you so choose.

The most common form of a formatted résumé is a Microsoft Word document, but unless this application is the specified document type, don't assume that all companies use Microsoft Word, which is required to open and view a Word document. And whatever you do, don't send anything as an attachment unless you're asked to or the directions on how to apply say you can do so. Attached documents can carry viruses, and many employers will otherwise not take the extra step to open your résumé attachment.

To create a formatted résumé, start from scratch using a word processing program (Microsoft Word is probably a safe bet) or open your plain-text résumé and **Save As** a new name (frmtres1.doc, for example) so you don't save over your plain-text résumé. Then, change the file type from text only to a Word Document.

To format your résumé, use any style elements, fonts, vertical lines, columns, boxes—whatever you want. Just don't go overboard and use too many fonts or formatting tricks. If you've never "designed" a formatted résumé before, or the concepts of good design are foreign to you, check out this article by Roger C. Parker, "Ten Rules of Good Design," at designrefresher.i-us.com/article1.html. Figure 6.3 is a sample of a formatted résumé.

Figure 6.3

The formatted résumé, which is sent as an attachment to an email cover letter, is sent usually by request and when you know the person on the receiving end uses the same word processing software that the document was created in.

CRAIG LAWRENCE
15-15 55th Road, Apt. 5 • Staten Island, NY 55555
(555) 555-1515 • Cellular: (555) 555-1111 • E-mail: craig@xxx.com

CONCIERGE 1 HALLMAN 1 DOORMAN
Perfect Security Background / Bondable / New York State Driver's License
Highly motivated and dedicated professional with over 10 years of experience as a concierge and doorman. Provide courteous and efficient service to tenants and guests. Demonstrated record of exceptional reliability and perfect attendance. Resourceful and knowledgeable about travel and entertainment services in the New York metropolitan area. Strong interpersonal skills and positive work ethic; keep a neat, clean, and professional appearance. Excellent common sense, judgment, and decision-making abilities. Computer literate in Windows 98, Internet programs, and Microsoft Works.

PROFESSIONAL EXPERIENCE
PARK HOUSE REALTY COMPANY – New York, NY
Concierge, 19XX to 19XX
• Served as concierge at 555 East 32nd Street, a prestigious co-op apartment building housing celebrities, high-ranking dignitaries, and top corporate executives.
• Took over management responsibilities of superintendent in his absence.
• Directly supervised team of lobby workers and doormen. Trained new staff members.
• Earned a reputation for going above and beyond concierge responsibilities to ensure satisfaction of residents and visitors.
• Regarded by tenants, guests, managers, board members, and colleagues as the consummate professional, committed to providing impeccable service.
• Maintained the highest emphasis on safety and security at all times; monitored traffic and deliveries in and out of building.
• Handled telephone communications; reserved cars, limousines, and taxis.

ABC REAL ESTATE COMPANY – New York, NY
Doorman, 19XX to 19XX
• Provided doorman services at 222 West 92nd Street, a luxury residential building with 400 apartments and 1,000 residents.
• Greeted tenants and guests in a friendly and courteous manner; provided tenants with a clean and safe environment.
• Hailed taxis and assisted with luggage and packages as needed.
• Monitored the building's arrivals and departures.

ACTION CAR, INC. – New York, NY
Owner / Operator, 19XX to 19XX
• Provided limousine services on order of 25 calls per day.

NYC TAXI – New York, NY
Owner / Operator, 19XX to 19XX

EDUCATION
ABC MECHANICAL ENGINEERING COLLEGE – London, England
Mechanical engineering courses, 19XX to 19XX

Web Résumé

It's actually pretty easy to make a Web résumé. Many word processing programs such as Microsoft Word offer the option to save your document in HTML (Hypertext Markup Language). After you've formatted your résumé using Word style and formatting tools, simply **Save As** an HTML document. It's really that simple.

You can send your HTML résumé as an attachment to an email message, which the employer can open using any Web browser, or you can publish your "Websumé" at a host site. I'll give you the details on Web résumés in Chapter 9, "Hi-Fi Online Portfolios," so if you think you want to go the extra mile and create a knock-'em-dead online résumé, be sure to read that chapter.

Open the Word-turned-HTML document and make changes or add hyperlinks to your email address, or to company URLs, or subpages of your résumé that contain more detailed information about your skills and expertise.

To add a hyperlink in Word, highlight the text, email address, or Web address you want to add a link to and go into the **Insert** menu. Click **Add a Hyperlink** and type in the address you want to link to in the **Link to File or URL** field—for example: `mailto:miriam@aol.com`. That will add in a hyperlink for the email address in the Web version of your document, as seen in Figure 6.4.

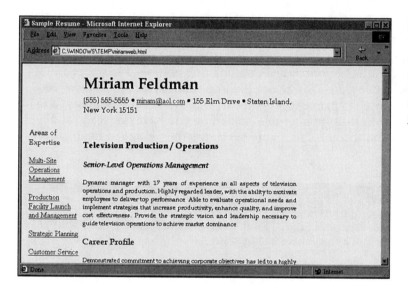

Figure 6.4

Turn your Microsoft Word résumé into a Web page, and add links to your email address, former employers, or Web-based projects or associations.

To see what your Web résumé looks like, you can open the HTML document in your Web browser by going into the browser's **File** menu and selecting **Open File**. Locate the résumé file and open it. Voilà! It's your Websumé!

To learn more about formatting your résumé as an HTML document and how to use HTML editors, read Chapter 9. Chapter 9 will show you where to post your HTML résumé, and how to build a multipage site that showcases your skills, samples, and accomplishments.

Tripod Free Résumé Hosting

For a quick and easy start on building and hosting your very own personal Web page and online résumé, visit Tripod at `www.tripod.lycos.com`. Besides point-and-click résumé wizards, you can learn everything about building your personal Web page—from beginning to advanced help.

Online Résumé Forms

If you plan on using the mega job sites to look for and apply to jobs, most of the sites have résumé databases that allow you to complete an online profile and résumé to use when applying for jobs found at the site. Many of the sites even let you create different versions of your résumé so that if you don't have a specific job title in mind, you can create a new résumé for different positions. You can usually edit your résumé after it's been posted, too.

More and more employers are providing online forms for you to complete, too, rather than just taking emailed résumés. The procedure is similar to what you'll find at the major job sites and résumé posting databases.

The job sites differ in the type of information that is asked for, but generally speaking, you'll fill in your contact information, a résumé title of desired job category, a skills summary or objective statement, relocation information, and other assorted items such as whether you're eligible to work in the U.S. There's almost always a field for you to copy/paste your plain-text résumé, so be sure you have one ready and proofed before you log on to a job site. Figure 6.5 shows the résumé form at Hotjobs.com.

Figure 6.5

Hotjobs.com has a résumé upload form that lets you copy and paste your existing résumé into an input field.

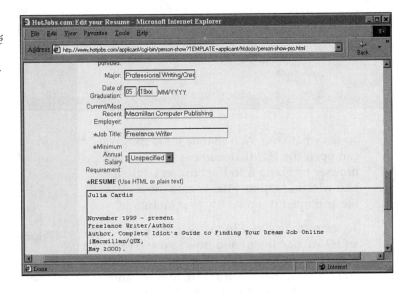

So, you see, the many faces of the electronic résumé aren't that strange at all. Really, the hardest part of résumés is customizing them for each job you apply for. Trust me on this one. Employers are turned off by job seekers who don't take the time to tailor the résumé content and objective statement to fit the job description and requirements. Don't be lazy! Take the time to do it right, and you'll ultimately reap the rewards of your hard work.

The Least You Need to Know

➤ There are four résumé formats for the online job hunt—plain-text, formatted (electronic and paper), scannable, and the optional Web résumé.

➤ A majority of the time, you'll simply copy and paste your résumé into the body of an email message.

➤ You'll also need a plain-text version of your résumé to complete online applications or upload your résumé to a job site résumé database.

➤ A Web résumé is a good way to demonstrate your Web-savviness and to flesh out a shorter version of the résumé you email or fax to an employer.

Chapter 7

The E-Cover Letter

In This Chapter

➤ How the electronic cover letter differs from traditional cover letters

➤ What happens to your cover letter after it's received

➤ Killer e-cover letter samples

➤ Common cover letter blunders and how to avoid them

➤ Step-by-step formatting of your cover letter for email transmission

➤ Where to get help writing your cover letter online

A résumé without a cover letter is like a sandwich without bread, and yes, there are a lot of different types of bread: croissants, wraps, buns, pita, toast, rolls, even crackers. Usually, the sandwich ingredients and whom it's being served to determine the type of bread you'll use.

Before you get up and go make a tasty snack, you should know there have been some big changes in the length, style, and contents of your cover letter—depending on what type of job you're applying for and your level of experience, as well as what stage of communication and level of contact you're in. For example, if you're sending your résumé to a networking contact or "cold-emailing" a company about job opportunities, the length of the cover letter will be much shorter than the "detailed" version you're asked to send with your "detailed" résumé.

You're thinking, "Great. There's no simple answer." Hey, I never said the job search was easy, did I?

Don't worry. This chapter explains the evolution of the cover letter and gives samples and guidelines on when to send what type of e-cover letter, as well as how to format your letter for online transmission. There's also a section on common cover letter blunders and how to avoid them, so get your thinking cap on and get ready to compose and format a killer electronic cover letter.

The New Rules of the Online Job Hunt and the Role of the Electronic Cover Letter

The electronic cover letter is a different slice of bread from the cover letter you might have worked with up to this point. In fact, with scanning technology and résumé databases, there's a good chance your cover letter might never be seen by human eyes. What?!?!?

Companies that use the Internet as a recruiting tool have specific goals in mind: to save time, save money, and reach a wider pool of qualified candidates. All these factors have changed how the cover letter works and how employers manage the documents associated with hiring. Think about it: A hiring director posts a job opening at Monster.com or CareerPath.com, as well as in several newspapers. Soon the email inbox, regular mailbox, and fax machine are bombarded with résumés and cover letters. Not many companies have the time or person power to go through each one by hand.

Instead, employers are taking advantage of other technologies to manage the paperwork: Oftentimes, those résumés are sent directly to a searchable database or scanner, and then deposited in a tracking program to locate candidates best suited for the position. If an employer doesn't immediately discard your cover letter, it's put in a different file from your résumé. If they really want to track it down, they will, but essentially it is expected that everything they need to know about you is contained in your résumé.

Even employers that don't use scanning or résumé-tracking software don't want to spend the time reading a lengthy cover letter. Remember, they're using the Internet to save time, so be sure everything they need to know is in the real meat of your self-marketing package: the résumé. But don't dismiss the cover letter as an unimportant part of your job search. You might very well respond to online job postings that require the old-fashioned print résumé and cover letter. Just be aware that the rules have changed a bit.

If No One Reads It, Do I Need to Write One?

Good question. Why should you rack your brain trying to compose a killer cover letter if no one reads it anyway? Because *you don't know* whether it will ever reach human eyes. All I'm saying is there's a good chance that if the company you're sending to uses scanning technology or résumé-tracking software, the cover letter is usually discarded or otherwise separated from your résumé.

So, yes, you still need to write a killer cover letter, but the length of the letter is what's changed in the online job search, and that doesn't mean you can skip this part of the self-marketing package. You still need to write cover letters and résumés that are customized for each position and that answer the question employers really want to know: What can you do for me?

Can't Believe No One Reads Cover Letters Anymore?

The world is full of conflicting advice, isn't it? If you're skeptical about the reality of the changing face of online recruiting, I won't be offended if you disregard my advice to send a short cover letter in place of the traditional three- to five-paragraph rule. The worst thing that will happen is no one will read the whole letter.

Follow your instincts, and exercise some common sense. If you're applying to a major corporation, assume they're using résumé-tracking software or scanning technology. If you're applying to a small company or a Ma and Pa operation, go ahead and send a traditional cover letter if it makes you feel better.

My point is, we use the Internet to save time, and a common complaint about cover letters from employers is that they're too long. If an employer is really interested in a detailed cover letter, they'll ask for one.

Electronic Cover Letter Samples

Using the Internet to recruit new blood is designed to help employers save time, so your cover letter has even less time and space to make a statement. If an employer wants a more detailed cover letter and résumé, they'll ask for it. If you're only researching job options and plan on sending your résumé via mail or fax, stick to the more traditional rules of the game.

Whether you're sending a one-, three-, or seven-paragraph cover letter, every word in it needs to work hard. Here are some samples and descriptions of the three variations of the electronic cover letter and when to send which type.

The Short Cover Letter

The short cover letter has just the facts, ma'am. It opens and closes quickly and is the most common version of the electronic cover letter. Typically, an interested employer will contact you based on the contents of your résumé, but if they want a more detailed letter that highlights your qualifications for the position, they'll request it.

Sample 1 (see Figure 7.1) is an example of the type of cover letter to send in response to a job posting at an online job board. It contains just the essential ingredients.

Figure 7.1

Sample 1: Responding to an Online Job Bank Posting

This brief, one-paragraph cover letter has just the basics: job posting number, where the job was posted, job title, and contact information. This length of your electronic cover letter is fine for an initial response to online job posting.

To: joeschmoe@abccorp.com
cc:
bcc: janedoe@email.com
Subject: Monster.com Posting #1234

Dear Joe Schmoe:
Following is my résumé sent in response to the January 4, 2000, posting at Monster.com, Marketing Coordinator (Posting #1234), at ABC Corporation. I found the description to be an excellent match with my education and professional experience. I look forward to speaking with you soon regarding this opportunity.

Regards,
Jane Doe
(123) 456-7890
janedoe@email.com

(paste résumé here)

Another situation that calls for the short electronic cover letter is Sample 2 (see Figure 7.2), sent in response to a company Web site job posting. Again, the idea is to save time, so employers don't want to wade through a full-blown cover letter.

Figure 7.2

Sample 2: Responding to a Company Web Site Job Posting

This cover letter indicates that you have researched the company and are interested in not only a job there, but in the company itself.

To: joeschmoe@abccorp.com
cc:
bcc: janedoe@email.com
Subject: Marketing Coordinator Position

Dear Joe Schmoe:
I visited the ABC Corporation Web site on Monday, January 3, 2000, and was pleased to see there is a Marketing Coordinator position available. Following is my résumé, which highlights my seven years of experience in healthcare marketing and public relations, and demonstrates the contributions I can make at ABC. I look forward to arranging a time when we can meet to discuss this opportunity.

Regards,
Jane Doe
(123) 456-7890
janedoe@email.com

(paste résumé here)

Sample 3 (see Figure 7.3) is an appropriate length for a "cold" email inquiry, considering you're sending your résumé unsolicited. You can't expect an employer to spend the time reading a long cover letter from someone they don't know, and for a job that might or might not exist, so keep it short and sweet!

To: joeschmoe@abccorp.com
cc:
bcc: janedoe@email.com
Subject: Copywriter Position

Dear Joe Schmoe:
I visited the ABC Corporation Web site and was impressed with your online portfolio, as well as your client roster, and can see that ABC Corporation lives up to its reputation as a top-notch marketing services agency. I feel my ten years of proven copywriting experience in business-to-business marketing would be an excellent match with your company's projects and clientele. While I am currently employed at a similar agency in the Midwest, my mid-range plans call for relocation to the East Coast. Although I did not see any copywriter positions posted in the "Jobs" section, I would like to discuss future opportunities with you, and have included my résumé for your review. I look forward to discussing possible openings with you.

Regards,
Jane Doe
(123) 456-7890
janedoe@email.com

(paste résumé here)

Figure 7.3

Sample 3: "Cold" Email Inquiry

The job seeker has done her research and indicates her familiarity with the company, as well as including a compliment. This is a good way to ignite interest in an employer, especially a nonimmediate-need inquiry. This requires consistent follow-up, however.

The Medium Cover Letter

The more experience you have or the higher-level position you're applying for, you'll need to explain why you're the right person for the job. In this case, your cover letter should open quickly, but then go into detail on your related experience and tell the employer exactly what you can contribute to the position. The theory is fewer people respond to these job postings, so the employer is willing to spend more time with the cover letter.

You might also be asked by a headhunter or third-party recruiter to send a cover letter with your résumé explaining in detail what you can bring to the position. In this situation, the employer is expecting (and looking forward to) learning more about you.

The Extra Mile

Include Your Contact Information

In the event your letter and résumé get separated, be sure to repeat your name, phone number, and position applying for somewhere in your cover letter—either at the top near the salutation, or at the end after your signature. Be sure to put parentheses around your area code, as in (317), so scanning technology knows to read this as a phone number.

Sample 4 (see Figure 7.4) is a cover letter and résumé sent via a networking contact lead. First, you need to warm up to the employer by dropping a name and then indicate that this person has already given you some background on the employer's needs. Then, you can explain how you can best meet those needs.

Figure 7.4

Sample 4: Cover Letter and Résumé Sent via Networking Contact Lead

Note the appropriate name-dropping right off the bat. This is essentially an endorsement from a colleague or associate, which holds the interest of the reader, all the way to your résumé. Also note the elaboration of accomplishments are directly related to the needs of the employer.

> To: joeschmoe@sleepymeadowsvilla.com
> cc:
> bcc: janedoe@email.com
> Subject: Marketing Assistant Position
>
> Dear Joe Schmoe:
> I spoke with John Smith last week at the Annual Healthcare Associates Planning meeting and he suggested I send my résumé to you to be considered for the Marketing Assistant position that recently became available at Sleepy Meadows.
>
> As you will see in my résumé, I have six years' experience as Marketing Coordinator at Pine Mills, a 259-bed long term facility in the Chicago suburbs. Mr. Smith mentioned that you are in the early stages of developing a Family Council program, so you will be pleased to know that I successfully developed and directed a similar program at Pine Mills, and also coordinated and publicized the home's Speaker's Bureau program.
>
> With a proven track record in healthcare marketing and an insider's understanding of family and resident relations, I feel I have significant contributions to make to Sleepy Meadows' marketing and public relations efforts.
>
> I will contact you next week to arrange a meeting time to discuss the Marketing Assistant position and how my skills and experience apply to the position requirements. Thank you for your time and for your consideration of my résumé.
>
> Regards,
> Jane Doe
> (123) 456-7890
> janedoe@email.com
>
> (paste résumé here)

If you've already met or talked with the employer, as in Sample 5 (see Figure 7.5), the first cover letter and résumé sent by request should tell your story in greater detail than you can accomplish with your résumé. Remember, this is by request, so expect that the letter will be read from start to finish. You can even go as long as five to seven paragraphs, if necessary, but this length should suffice.

Figure 7.5

Sample 5: First Cover Letter and Résumé Sent by Request

Right away remind the reader that he has requested your résumé. Then, the writer elaborates on specific accomplishments related to the employer's needs.

To: joeschmoe@abccorporation.com
cc:
bcc: janedoe@email.com
Subject: Media Director Position

Dear Joe Schmoe:
I enjoyed speaking with you at the Chamber of Commerce After Hours function at the Radisson last week. Per your request, I am sending my résumé for your review.

After learning about the job requirements and position description for Media Director, I am confident that my ten years in public relations and media planning will prove to be a valuable asset to your company.

My résumé highlights my accomplishments working on the Riverfront Development Project and how my relationships with key media contacts proved to be valuable in garnering public approval for the project through positive portrayal in both broadcast and print media. Moreover, my board of directors position and ongoing volunteer activity with the United Way keeps me in touch with the community and the area's key decision makers.

I will contact you at your office next Monday, January 10, to arrange a time to meet. I look forward to discussing in more detail how I can contribute to ABC's public relations activities and challenges.

Regards,
Jane Doe
(123) 456-7890
janedoe@email.com

(paste résumé here)

The Long E-Cover Letter

The long cover letter is similar to the traditional cover letter in terms of length and purpose. The long cover letter, which is about five to seven paragraphs long, is most often sent by high-level applicants who may have already met with the employer and have been asked to submit your formal, detailed résumé and cover letter package. At this point, you know in greater detail what the employer is looking for, so your cover letter should speak to those issues. Sample 6 (see Figure 7.6) is an example of the long cover letter, sent in response to the employer's request for a detailed cover letter and résumé. You can bet your bottom dollar that every word of this letter will be read, so be sure you tell a compelling story. This letter usually weighs heavily in the employer's decision to hire you, so make it work.

Figure 7.6

Sample 6: Sent in Response to Employer's Request for a Detailed Cover Letter and Résumé

More experienced job seekers or high-level executives will be asked for detailed résumés, including a longer cover letter that summarizes the writer's many years of experience, and how this can be of direct benefit to the employer.

To: joeschmoe@midtownsuntimes.com
cc:
bcc: janedoe@email.com
Subject: Media Director Position

Jane Doe
1234 Main Street
Anytown, USA 12345
(123)456-7890
janedoe@email.com

Dear Joe Schmoe:
Thank you for inviting me to interview for the Editor-in-Chief position at the Midtown Sun Times. I look forward to discussing how my 18 years of experience in journalism and editorial work can benefit your paper's position as the top-rated print news source in Midtown.

At your request, included with this email is my detailed résumé, which outlines my responsibilities and accomplishments as city desk editor, entertainment editor, and editor-in-chief at the Johnstown Daily and New City Times. You will see that I have the editorial and management skills required at a paper of your circulation, as well as the ability to manage a diverse team of staff reporters, assistant editors, and publishers.

In addition to my work in journalism, I have been an ongoing contributing editor at several university periodicals, most notably the Journal of Foreign Publications Quarterly. I was selected from a candidate pool of 150 editors to provide my expertise in cross-cultural communications, and how new media impacts global access to news and information.

I was particularly interested in your description of the Editor-in-Chief's responsibilities associated with the paper's efforts to expand its online readership. Having worked with teams ranging from three to 23 members, I have a solid understanding of what it takes to direct and manage large projects. And as you are aware, there are many editors, but few with the broad range of experience I have gained in my many years of journalism, new media, and academic writing experience.

I look forward to our meeting January 18.

Regards,
Jane Doe

(paste résumé here)

What Needs to Be Included?

The components of a cover letter are pretty basic: The salutation, opening line, message, and closing comments. If you operate under the assumption that your letter and résumé might get separated, be sure to include the most important information in your résumé. It's what employers really look at, after all. But the medium or long cover letter gives you the chance to elaborate on the important points in your résumé. Be sure to read "Common Cover Letter Faux Pas and Fix Ups" and "Composing and Formatting Your Electronic Cover Letter" later in this chapter for tips on content for the medium and long letters; the short letter includes the job position, where you saw the ad, and a strong closing line.

Thanks for the Tip

Dear Mr. Phil Daly:

A standard salutation, right? Yes, but Phil happens to be Philomena, and SHE might be annoyed at being addressed as a mister, just as Ms. Pat Daly might be miffed when HE reads the opening to your cover letter. Play it safe and address all your correspondences to the person's full name, such as *Dear Phil Daly:* until you've confirmed the person's gender. Hopefully, you won't be communicating with someone like Androgynous Pat from "Saturday Night Live" fame, but if you do, just use the full name in case you can't figure out whether to use Mr., Mrs., Ms., or Miss.

Common Cover Letter Faux Pas and Fix-Ups

This section covers the most common mistakes with cover letters—both electronic and paper. Don't worry—you get suggestions to correct or altogether avoid these costly mistakes.

1. **Unrelated career goals or experience.**

   If you've followed my advice on finding your dream job, you won't be prone to this blunder. So many applicants (especially college grads, unemployed folks, and misdirected job seekers) apply to jobs they're not qualified for or interested in. Not only are you wasting your time, you're wasting the time of hiring managers and recruiters. Here's an example of what not to do: "Although my career ambition is to be an entertainer, I am seeking a more stable source of income and feel a job in customer service would help sharpen my people skills while I wait for a casting call-back."

   Take the time to tailor your résumé and cover letter for each job you apply for, research the company, and always remember that employers aren't at all interested in your career goals and ambitions. They want to know what's in it for them. Your cover letter and résumé must communicate this quickly and effectively. Here's an example of a good objective statement: "I have a proven track record in customer service and client relations and am confident of my ability to make a long-term contribution to upholding your commitment to service-oriented technical support."

2. **Form letters or mass emailing of your résumé.**

   Every e-cover letter you send should be personalized, and when possible, addressed to an individual rather than a generic title such as "Dear Sir or Madam." If the job posting does not give an individual's name, go to the company Web site and look for a personnel directory. If you can't find that, look for a phone number and call to find out the name of the person who will read your email. If the ad specifically states "No phone calls, please," don't be a pest. Use "Dear Hiring Director" or "Dear Human Resources."

   Again, tailor each cover letter and demonstrate your interest in the specific industry and your familiarity with the company. I heard of one goofball who photocopied hundreds of form cover letters and left the company name and job title blank. When he found a position he thought looked interesting, he penciled in the name and job title. What a dork! I heard of another horror story of a young whippersnapper who put the contact names of five different employers in the to: section of his email message.

   Although using samples to get started composing your letter is a good idea, you need to add a touch of your personality to each letter as well.

3. **Clichés, anecdotes, and informal tone.**

   Even if you know the person you're emailing your résumé to, make the letter serious and professional and use standard business format. If this person has to forward your materials to another set of eyes, it will come across as unprofessional if your salutation reads something like, "Hey Girlfriend!" Also, don't get sappy, personal, or cheesy. Avoid clichés such as, "I type faster than a speeding bullet," or "I nearly hit the ceiling when I saw this job posting! It's the perfect job for me!"

   Rather, stick with a professional tone and avoid obvious comparisons, washed-up clichés, and an under- or overly enthusiastic tone. Refer to the cover letter samples in this chapter for style, tone, and phrasing.

   Remember, though, your cover letter represents your personality. If you know you don't want to get calls from stuffy, stiff employers, use a more relaxed tone. Just don't get chummy, and if you choose to use an informal tone be sure you don't come across as disinterested or blasé. I have a friend who responded to a job posting that read something like, "Our administrative assistant's got a bun in the oven…send your résumé to Joe, the Bottle Washer." My buddy signed his cover letter, "Robb, the Boy Wonder." He got the job.

4. **Desperation or admitted shortcomings.**

   Again, college grads and unemployed job seekers are most prone to these blunders. Avoid comments like, "I am eager to start as I've been looking for work for eight months," or "I'll be waiting with bated breath for the phone to ring." If you're confident that you can do the job, but lack more than one major requirement, don't draw attention by saying things such as, "I may not meet all the requirements, but I'm a fast learner and I have always wanted to find out what it's like to be a department manager."

You should come across as determined, not desperate. And always focus on your valuable skills, relevant experience, and detailed knowledge of the company. If you really aren't qualified, however, don't apply for the job. It's that simple.

5. **Misrepresentation and outright lying.**

   Call it what you like: straight up bs-ing, embellishment, or exaggeration. Employers call it "grounds for dismissal" after the "little white lie" is uncovered. Here's an example of a slight exaggeration of a real skill: "thorough knowledge of C++" when all the person really did was take a class that covered the language over a one-week period. Don't take credit for things you didn't do, and don't make it sound like you did more than you actually did. First of all, you might be called on to apply your "expertise." Second, if your misrepresentation is discovered, you could lose your job.

   If you have a skill or accomplishment, state it truthfully. It may not seem like much to you, but your goal in finding a new job is to develop skills and experience. We all have to start somewhere, right?

6. **Including photos, hobbies, personal information, race, or religious affiliation.**

   Unless your age, weight, height, marital status, religious beliefs, hobbies, or looks are directly related to the position or job requirements, don't list these qualities on your résumé or cover letter. First of all, indicating these things causes headaches for human resource folks because it makes them susceptible to claims of discrimination if they don't hire you or call you for an interview. Some minority job seekers are at an advantage, however, when applying to companies that seek a diverse workforce. But don't state, "I'm an Asian American female with a slight physical disability."

   If you have leadership or work-related experience with a club or organization that indicates your minority status, then state, "As president of the Students with Disabilities Club, I spearheaded a campaign to increase membership of fellow Asian-American students." Many minorities, however, prefer to be considered solely on the basis of their skills and experience and don't reveal a minority status in their self-marketing materials at all. It's entirely up to you.

7. **Stating personal preferences or making demands.**

   Keep in mind getting a job is not about you. It's about what you can do for the employer. Don't get pushy or presumptuous with comments like, "While I prefer to work independently, I have worked with teams in the past and am willing to do so for this position." Another thing that pushes the buttons of employers are comments like, "I would like to meet next Tuesday before noon to discuss in detail my qualifications for this position."

   Be polite and demonstrate your ability to meet the needs of the employer. It's okay to indicate that you will follow up with a phone call to arrange a meeting time, but don't make demands based on your preferences or availability.

8. **Typos, spelling errors, and grammatical or pronoun errors.**

   You'll get plenty of warnings about proofreading your materials for typos, spelling errors, and grammatical mistakes. Another thing to avoid is writing your cover letter in the third person. It comes across as if someone is writing for you and about you, rather than you communicating your own abilities and contributions you can make. Don't refer to yourself, as in, "Jane Doe is an award-winning journalist with 18 years in the field."

   Instead, "I am an accomplished, award-winning journalist with 18 years' experience in editing, writing, and reporting."

Composing and Formatting Your Cover Letter for Email

If you've already tooled around with saving your résumé as an ASCII or plain text document to send as part of your email message, this part is a cake walk. I suggest working on the draft version of your cover letter in a word processing program rather than composing directly in your email program. First, you don't have to worry about accidentally clicking **Send**, and you'll have the opportunity to organize and save copies of the various versions of your email cover letter.

To compose your cover letter using a word processing program:

1. Open your word processing program (such as Microsoft Word, AppleWorks, or Corel WordPerfect) and create a new document.

2. **Save** the document before you begin typing, just in case. For the first version, save it as a covdraft.doc or something that indicates the file is a draft version and not something you plan on sending. Repeat this step and **Save As** with a recognizable filename each time you revise your cover letter. Create a folder, too, to organize and manage the different versions of your cover letters.

3. Type your name, email address, phone number with the area code in parentheses, and job title or posting number you're responding to, if applicable. You can also put this information in the signature area of your email (see both styles in the "Samples" section), but I'm going with the scroll-down rule: People don't like to scroll, so make darned certain the most important information appears in the top third of the page. Personally, I don't know why people don't like to scroll down, but research shows busy people want the information super fast, and if they have to go looking for it, you might be out of luck.

4. Begin composing your letter, starting with the salutation. Unless you know the individual personally or the ad instructs you to send your résumé to the attention of *Ms. So and So*, always use the full name. Put a colon at the end of your salutation (as in *Dear Phil Daly*:).

5. In the first sentence, identify the source of the job you're applying for and a posting number if there is one. If you saw the ad at a company Web site, indicate the title and date you saw the posting. Or, if you were given the lead by a networking contact, drop names off the bat.

6. If you're responding to a posting in a job bank, keep it short—about one paragraph and a strong closing line. Always be sure the keywords in the job description are listed somewhere in your résumé, too. If this means you have to make a slight revision to your résumé for each job you apply for, do it. If you were asked to send a cover letter and résumé or have significant experience in your field (8-12 years), write about three paragraphs, and focus on your qualifications and accomplishments in regard to the requirements outlined in the job posting. If you were asked to send a detailed cover letter and résumé or are applying for a very high-level position, write about five to seven paragraphs—be as brief as possible, but highlight important accomplishments in relation to the requirements for the job and what you have learned from the employer up to this point.

7. After you have finished composing the body of your letter, write a brief closing sentence that states what action you will take next. Again, see "Sample E-Cover Letters" for ideas and examples. Then, sign off with *Sincerely,* or *Regards,* or another appropriate closer, press **Return** or **Enter** twice, and type your name. Run a quick spell check, but don't rely on this as your only proofing mechanism.

8. **Save** the document again. Then, go back into the File menu and select **Save As**. At this point, you'll save the document in ASCII or Text Only format and choose a new filename for the plain version, preferably something that identifies the job posting or company, as in `cl_ascii_exxon_sysadm.doc`.

9. Click **Save** again, close the document, reopen it, and print it out. I find it much easier to read and proof a hard copy versus reading on the monitor, but you can check the plain style format for line breaks and spacing before you print for proofing. Make any necessary adjustments and **Save** again.

When you're ready to send your résumé and cover letter, simply open your word processing program and find the file.

1. Select/highlight the entire letter and go into the **Edit** menu or use a keyboard shortcut to **Copy** the selected text.

2. Open your email program, start a new message, and place your cursor at the top of the message screen. Select **Paste** from the **Edit** menu or use a keyboard shortcut to paste your cover letter plain text into your email document.

3. Press **Return** or **Enter** four times after the last line of your cover letter and paste your résumé (that's also saved as plain text or ASCII) into the email message.

115

Before You Press Send...

➤ Email the message to yourself first to double-check line spacing and breaks, and to be sure it transmits as plain text. You get one shot and one shot only to make a first impression, so double checking the appearance and format is good measure.

➤ Print the message for review and proofing.

I personally find it much easier to read and proof a hard copy than directly on my computer screen. Again, this might seem time-consuming and tedious, but your objective is to get noticed for your accomplishments and abilities, not for your blunders.

➤ Read the letter out loud.

This is a tried and true writer's technique. Oftentimes, you'll catch awkward phrasing or wordy sentences. Remember, every part of your self-marketing package is an indicator of your general abilities. Poor communication skills, cluttered thoughts, incomplete sentences, or any other blunder in your written communications will probably be held against you.

➤ Proofread until your eyes bleed.

You'll have to do this with your résumé and any other written communications, so get used to it. Try to have a second set of eyes read your materials, too, and don't rely on your grammar and spell check to catch all your mistakes. You've seen it happen before—"I will contact you next weed to set up an interview." Word processors are smart, but they won't always catch wrong words that are spelled correctly, so play it safe and proofread very, very carefully. If you're not the world's best writer, speller, or grammarian, hire a professional or ask a friend whose abilities you can count on to proof it for you.

➤ Be sure you've followed directions.

Most employers don't want to receive résumés or cover letters as attachments. But if the job posting says to send your résumé as an attachment, do so. If the ad says to include a salary history in your cover letter, do so. Oftentimes, this is used to eliminate applicants who are out of the compensation target range, so include a range of your annual salary for each job listed on your résumé. Do not include references with your letter and résumé. Rather, the employer will ask for these (hopefully) at the end of your first interview.

➤ You're ready to send.

After you've completed the previous steps and you're 100% sure your cover letter (and résumé) is error-free and speaks directly to the job you're applying for, it's time to send your email. First, type the job position or posting number in the **Subject** box of your email message. Next, double check that you've pasted both your cover letter and résumé into the body of your outgoing message. (I'm not trying to be petty. I personally emailed a résumé and cover letter and forgot to paste my résumé in the email.)

For good measure and to help keep track of your job search efforts, blind carbon copy (bcc:) the email to yourself (see Figure 7.7). "Blind carbon copy" (bcc:) means the person you're sending correspondence to doesn't know that you or other people are getting copies of the same document.

This is used primarily as a CYA (cover your arse) technique. For example, your supervisor sends you a memo outlining your duties and responsibilities while she's on vacation. To cover her arse and ensure the work gets done, she may blind carbon copy the memo to her boss so this person can monitor your progress while she's away. The reason she didn't just carbon copy the memo to her boss for you to see is so you don't feel like she doesn't trust you. But bcc: is also useful during your job search to help you keep track of emailed résumés or other email exchanges dealing with your job hunt.

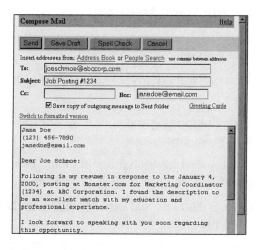

Figure 7.7

You can use the bcc: field in your outgoing emails to send yourself a copy of the letters you send for your job search. It's just another way of tracking your activity.

Online Resources for Help with Your Cover Letter

For help writing the medium and long cover letter, be sure to check out these sites. Although you'll have a doozy of a time finding online advice that deals specifically with electronic cover letters, these experts offer solid advice when it comes to writing traditional cover letters, which will come in handy, as you should have a print version of your résumé and cover letter available at all times.

➤ *CareerLab* (`www.careerlab.com/letters/`)   With a slew of top site awards and recommendations and accolades all over the Web for this site, you can bet there's help for you here. Or, take a peek at more than 200 samples of cover letters for any occasion, from cold inquiries to saying yes or no to a job offer.

➤ *JobStar* (jobstar.org/tools/resume/cletters.htm)   Formerly JobSmart California, this site has changed its name and formed alliances with big names such as *Wall Street Journal*'s Career column to continue bringing job seekers the tools and resources necessary to succeed in the job hunt. Besides a slew of cover letter samples, JobStar provides you with links, recommended reading, and advice from seasoned experts.

The previous sites are good starting points. Most of the major job sites have career resource sections, so do a keyword search for "cover letters" or look in sections dealing with résumés. These two are often grouped together, as they should be!

The Least You Need to Know

➤ Companies that use résumé databases and scanning technology oftentimes separate your cover letter from your résumé.

➤ Hiring managers and employers prefer short cover letters, and usually read your résumé first anyway.

➤ Depending on the source of the job posting and your level of experience, the length of your cover letter varies greatly.

➤ Your cover letter should be customized for each job and should demonstrate knowledge of the company and how you can benefit the employer.

➤ Typos, grammatical errors, spelling mistakes, and other blunders could land your cover letter and résumé in the trash.

Chapter 8

Privacy, Distribution, and Access to Your Résumé

In This Chapter

➤ Keeping your résumé hidden from prying eyes and Internet spies

➤ When to use a public or private résumé database

➤ How to protect yourself from identity thieves

➤ What not to include on your electronic résumé

So, you've composed a killer résumé, you've got your job hunting plan nailed down, and now you're ready to trek out to the want-ad jungle—the online job site and résumé bank scene.

In Chapter 2, "It's a Jungle Out There: Job Hunters Beware!," we covered a variety of things that can go wrong when you go online to search for a job, such as your co-workers ratting you out or your boss receiving your résumé from an unaware or irresponsible recruiter. That chapter had quick tips on résumé privacy, but this chapter goes into more detail on what you can do to protect your résumé from prying eyes, and which type of job seeker needs to be most concerned about access and distribution issues.

Who Needs to Worry About Résumé Privacy?

Essentially, anyone who posts their résumé to a public database or newsgroup is at risk when it comes to privacy issues. Not only can your résumé be spidered and deposited into another database without your consent or knowledge, an identity thief can take your name, credentials, and work history and pretend to be you. In a twisted way, that's sort of flattering—to think that someone is so impressed with who you are and what you've done that they want to be you!

Spiders, and Untangling from Their Webs

A spider is a program that scours the Web on its own, returning indexes of Web pages and documents (résumés) it finds and depositing them into another database. How do you get untangled from its web? You don't. You usually don't know your résumé has been picked up until you start getting calls from recruiters saying, "I saw your résumé at such-and-such site," but you know you didn't put it there.

But it's not flattering when you sit around and wonder why you're not getting called back for second interviews. If your online persona has been tainted by an identity thief or passed around like a rag doll to every résumé database on the Web, you might never fully recover from the damage that can de done—creditwise, credibility-wise, and identitywise.

Before you do anything cyber-related with your electronic résumé, take some time to know what to look for at each site, and what questions to ask if the privacy and access policies aren't clearly stated. Most of the major job and résumé posting sites make this information clear from the get-go, but if you're using a regional job site, an industry-specific job site, or emailing your résumé to a recruiter's database, privacy issues aren't always as much of a priority, or as easy to read.

For a quick overview of select general and industry-specific résumé databases, Margaret Dikel at The Riley Guide (www.dbm.com/jobguide/résumés/html#res) has assembled a list specifying which databases allow public access to résumés with side notes on whether confidentiality options are available (see Figure 8.1).

High-level executives and those in high-demand positions usually won't have to post a résumé in a database, much less respond to an online job posting. Chances are, you've already got recruiters and headhunters banging down your door. Even so, the executive-level and high-tech résumé databases usually offer added protection, given the credentials and high dollars at stake.

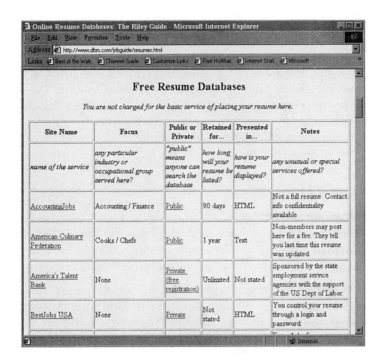

Figure 8.1

The Riley Guide's "Online Résumé Databases" chart shows whom the database is targeted for, whether it's public or private, how long your résumé is posted, what format it's presented in, and miscellaneous notes about the database.

Job seekers with limited experience or who are undecided on a career field might want to experiment with posting a résumé at a database to keep the job hunt rolling, and to see what kind of offers or leads come in. And that's fine. Just be cautious as you go about blasting or sprinkling your résumé across the Internet—it could fall into the wrong hands and cause you years of grief. Here are some tips for online résumé privacy, and controlling who has access to your résumé.

Post Only at Password-Protected, Private Databases

One way to have control over résumé privacy is to post at private databases that allow access only to registered, prescreened employers and recruiters. You can (and should) ask for a list of qualified employers and recruiters, and also ask whether those companies and recruiters share your résumé with other nonregistered employers or recruiters, or whether the database itself is shared with or spidered by other résumé databases.

In this day and age of cross-marketing partnerships and agreements, sending your résumé to one database might mean its online partner also has access to your résumé. Now, it doesn't seem so private, does it?

Maximum Protection: Post Only at Candidate-Controlled Databases

But even a password-protected database doesn't guarantee your complete privacy. For full résumé privacy, you also need to be able to decide who gets your résumé. The best privacy protection comes through using a candidate-controlled résumé database. In this type of private résumé database, you have to give permission as to when and whether you want to release your résumé, and to which employer. Your résumé goes directly to the employer, not to another database.

Beware of "Vapor Openings"

Also known as "blind ads," recruiters post bogus job openings to gather résumés that they turn around and sell to other recruiters, or to add to their own résumé stockpile. When an employer calls a recruiter and asks, "How many résumés do you have on file?" the recruiter can beef up the numbers by counting all those swiped résumés.

When you respond to an online ad that doesn't list a company name and get a call back, first find out whether the recruiter is inhouse or third-party. Inhouse recruiters are on staff at the company posting the ad, but a third-party recruiter works for an agency whose job is to find qualified candidates. Always ask for the name of the company the recruiter represents, as well as the job title. If the recruiter doesn't give an exact name, the ad is probably a fake. Just say "no, thank you" and hang up.

There's another reason recruiters post vapor ads—to not only fill current positions, but to collect as many résumés as possible so that when a client calls with a job that needs to be filled, the recruiter can access the ever-growing database of résumés collected through phony ads. You might get called months after your résumé has been vaporized by a recruiter!

Set Up Password Protection for Your Home Page

If you're planning on using a Web-based portfolio and résumé to showcase your skills and talents, find an Internet access provider or hosting service that allows and can help you set up password protection for your résumé and personal Web site. This way, when a recruiter or employer asks for more information or to see your body of work, you can distribute the password only to those who ask to see it.

Use a Job Agent

A job agent, available at sites such as NationJob.com (see Figure 8.2) and CareerBuilder.com, sends notifications of job openings to your email inbox. All you have to do is complete a profile of job titles you're interested in and enter keywords to control the number of matches you get. Not only do you not have to post your résumé to a database, you don't even have to go out looking for a job—the jobs come to you!

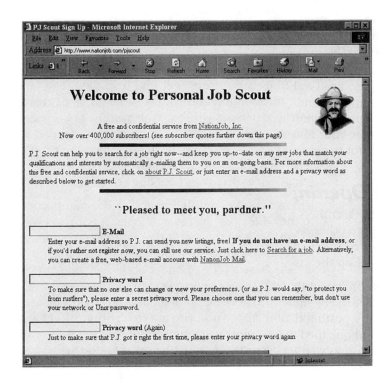

Figure 8.2

Personal job agent P.J. Scout will scour job postings and deliver matches based on your skills, interests, and experience.

Removing Your Résumé After You Land a Job

Most résumé databases are very clear on how long your résumé will be kept on the database, ranging from 30 days to forever. Obviously, you don't want your résumé posted forever—just until you land your job! Ask about being able to access your résumé to remove it, or to update as needed.

Updated Résumés Rise to the Top

Some employers and recruiters search for the freshest résumés, so be sure to post at a database that allows you to go in and update your résumé whenever you want. Each time your changes are saved, its freshness date is updated, too! It's a good idea to date your résumé, anyway, just in case six months after you land a job it lands on your next boss's desk.

Post to Usenet and Newsgroups As a Last Resort

Newsgroups are wonderful communication tools for the online community, but they can be nightmares for job seekers who indiscriminately post a résumé hoping someone finds it. Someone will find it all right, and take your information and sell it to a recruiter, or cross-post in databases without your permission, or call you six months or two years after you've landed a job. After it's out there, it's there forever. You can't remove it, can't modify it, and can't control who sees it, including your boss or a co-worker.

Unless you're currently unemployed, avoid posting to the wide-open spaces of Usenet. It is a good way to broadcast to the world that you're looking for a job, but that's exactly what you don't want if you already have a job. You have absolutely no control over who sees or "borrows" your résumé, and the higher up on the employment food chain you are, the more appetizing you are to identity thieves and recruiters who snag your résumé and sell it to other sleazy recruiters—or just bug you to death.

Techno Talk

What's Usenet?

Usenet stands for "user's network" and it's one of the oldest message board systems on the Internet. Newsgroups operate on the Usenet system. A popular starting point for newsgroup activity is Deja at www.deja.com.

Protecting Your Good Name

With more and more employers doing background checks and prescreening checks on candidates using the Internet, it's more important than ever to know what your online reputation is like. Before you post your résumé online, go to meta search engines such as Google (www.google.com) or Dogpile (www.dogpile.com) and do a keyword search using your name as it appears on your résumé, and see whether you get any matches. Do this, too, at newsgroups to see whether someone with a name like yours (or your actual name) is an active online persona.

Got Any Priors?

Besides employers being able to find out if you have any prior felony convictions, there's another use of the word "prior" in the online job hunt. If your résumé gets picked up and thrown around the online job scene, your résumé might be submitted to the same database several times, marking you as a "prior." If you're "priored" at enough places enough times, you might have trouble getting a response from your legitimate posting. Recruiters say that seeing the same résumé over and over in multiple databases sends the message that the job seeker is desperate as well. Be selective where you post your résumé and try to stick with résumé banks that allow you to remove your résumé after you've landed a job.

"That's a Different John Smith, I Swear!"

Another problem you might encounter if you have a common name, such as John Smith, is that the other John Smiths of the world could be online idiots who post obscene or inappropriate messages in forums, newsgroups, or chat rooms. If an employer or recruiter stumbles across the "dirty" John Smith postings or messages during a prescreening or background check, you might be labeled for life as the "dirty" John Smith, not the John Smith your mother raised you to be. Use your middle initial, or your full name, like John Stephen Smith. It might not offer complete protection, but it's better than not trying at all.

Welcome to the "Team"

Yet another danger involves your résumé being picked up and used by a contract agent to help land a deal. When presenting the contractor's services to a potential client, the contract agent says, "Oh yeah, we've got Joe Smith from Microsoft on our team now. Stanford grad, plenty of C++ experience." There's little danger of the contract agent being found out, as the employer works through the agent and never has direct contact with the "team" members.

Because of these résumé privacy concerns, many of the major job sites and résumé databases are taking steps to increase your online résumé privacy by improving the options you have in allowing access to only registered employers. And through firewalls and other security measures, résumé databases are making efforts to prevent prying eyes and spiders from gaining access to your résumé.

Conceal Your Identity on Your Résumé

A confidential résumé doesn't list your name or contact information, and even goes so far as to exclude any details such as company names (see Figure 8.3). If someone is truly interested in your credentials, they can contact you via a discreet, anonymous email address. Then, you decide whether or not to respond with your full-fledged résumé and cover letter.

Techno Talk

Red Alert! Unauthorized Access Attempt!

A firewall is security software that protects a system or database from invasion by unauthorized users, such as spiders. If you're not sure of a résumé database's security and access-control features, call to find out how your résumé is protected from spiders and unregistered users.

Figure 8.3

This confidential résumé leaves plenty of room for imagination, but no room for identity thieves or crooked contract agents to pick up and go with the person's name or work history.

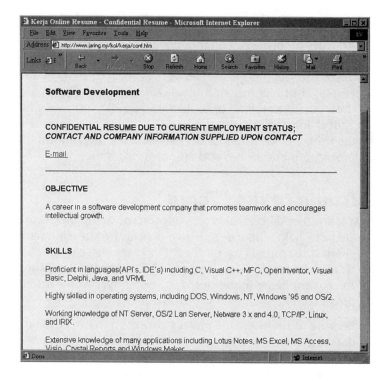

The drawback of the confidential résumé is that some employers and recruiters want to know the names of companies you've worked for, and they also might be put off by having to reply to an anonymous email and then wait for you to respond. If you have stellar credentials or are high up on the food chain (which is all the more reason to protect your name), the confidential résumé is an excellent way to protect your privacy (and confidentiality).

What NOT to Include on Your Résumé

Identity thieves. Résumé hackers. Sleazy recruiters. You name it, there are some real creeps out there bellying along in cyberspace. Don't make it easy for these folks to access and abuse your personal information. Here are some items that you should never, ever, ever, include on your résumé or cover letter:

➤ **Social Security Number**   *NEVER*, I repeat, *NEVER* put your Social Security number on your résumé. It's an open invitation for thieves and hackers to access an enormous amount of personal data that's stored online. With your name and Social Security number in hand, a hacker or identity thief can run a credit report on you and get your credit information, obtain certain medical records, access bank and financial records, and check your marital status. They can perform a complete background check and quite easily adopt your identity.

An identity thief can use your personal information to open a line of credit, apply for a loan, buy a car, and otherwise wreck your credit history. This could come into play during your job search as more and more employers run credit reports as part of the background check, not to mention the nightmare you face in terms of theft and credit card fraud.

You won't be held responsible for having your credit identity stolen, but some reported cases are so horrific that people have had to actually change their Social Security numbers to recover from the mess. And you can imagine the complications this causes.

If you encounter a résumé database that requires your Social Security number to register or make a deposit, run like the wind.

➤ **Licensing Numbers**   Job seekers with certain licensing and certification numbers should not include these numbers on a résumé. It's fine to state that you hold certification or a license in your field, but it is not necessary to provide this information until you have reached the interview stage. An identity thief could take this and use it falsely on his or her own résumé or job application. This is especially true if you have a common name.

➤ **Street Address**   I caution women about putting their home address on electronic résumés. Stick with an email address and your city and state. You never know who's out there lurking in the dark reaches of cyberspace. Better yet, use an initial instead of your first name as well.

If you post your résumé to a database, a phone number (preferably a special job-hunting number or answering service) and email should be sufficient contact information for any employer or recruiter. After you have established the legitimacy of any contacts or requests for a detailed résumé, then it's fine to include your street address. If you feel you need to put postal information on your electronic résumé, go the extra mile and set up a post office box.

➤ **Reference Information**   Don't include references on your résumé for two reasons: First, some wiley recruiters might try to contact your references instead of you with a promising job lead! After all, the folks you list on your résumé are probably in the same field or profession as you, and often in higher levels of experience. Say your résumé comes up in a keyword match, but you just don't have the level of experience required for the job, the recruiter can see your supervisor's name listed on your references and make contact with that person instead of you. You've made it easy for them, in fact, by providing the reference's contact information—phone number and address. Second, a recruiter or employer might contact your references before you have a chance to provide them with the information they need to give you an eloquent and accurate reference. Provide references only when an employer requests them.

127

All this talk sure makes you want to log on and blast your résumé all over the Web, eh? You don't have to be afraid—just don't be foolish. Disasters in online privacy could not only cost you the job you have now, but could cause problems for many years to come if your résumé falls into the wrong hands (or the wrong databases). So, remember to exercise caution and common sense when you venture out to the online job-hunting jungle.

Avoid Reference Redundancy

Besides not including your reference information on your résumé, don't even say "References Available upon Request." Employers assume this, so it's wasted space. Use that extra line for something the employer doesn't already know.

The Least You Need to Know

➤ You can control résumé privacy by limiting postings to password-protected and candidate-controlled résumé databases.

➤ Check résumé-sharing and database access policies before you make a deposit.

➤ Confidential résumés protect your identity but still showcase your skills and qualifications—interested employers will contact you for more details.

➤ Never include your Social Security number or licensing or certification numbers on your career documents.

Part 3

Market Yourself! Tools and Techniques for Gaining the Competitive Edge

Let's face it: You are a product. A mere commodity. If you think of yourself as a hot new product and it's your job to make people (employers) purchase (hire) the product (you), you must make yourself stand out from the competition. This part of the book shows you techniques and strategies to market yourself and be sure you have the competitive advantage when it comes time for the buyer (employer) to make a buying (hiring) decision, plus how to knock 'em dead in the interview.

You also learn how to tap into the "hidden job market" through networking and researching unadvertised opportunities. Although most people don't like to network, it's one of the most effective ways of getting your foot in the door. Plus, it's easy to do online.

After you've got all your ducks in a row and you've targeted the jobs you're going for, learn from the experts about successful interviewing techniques—over the phone, online, and face-to-face.

Chapter 9

Hi-Fi Online Portfolios

In This Chapter

➤ How to wow and woo potential employers with a hi-fi online portfolio

➤ Who *needs* one and who *could use* one to stand out from the competition

➤ How to build a portfolio, even if you're entry-level and don't have any samples (yet)

➤ How to organize your materials before you break ground

➤ What to include, and what to leave out

➤ How to scan images for quick download and optimal resolution

➤ Where to go online for help, which software to use, and how to use online Web-building wizards

For most job seekers, having a hi-fi online portfolio is icing on the cake. Most employers don't expect you to have a career-related Web site, so if you put one together that looks good, downloads quickly, and contains only information that relates to your job qualifications or professional interests, you're going to make a strong impression and really stand out from the competition.

Don't count on your hi-fi Web page alone to get you interviews, though. Rarely will an employer stumble across your site or go to a Web address that's listed in a cold cover letter or even a cover letter sent in response to a job posting, unless your résumé entices the employer to go check it out.

Think of your hi-fi Web site as more of a follow-up tool than a replacement to your plain-text or paper résumé—the fundamental career document that ignites the interest of employers. A hi-fi portfolio simply helps to "close the deal" in most situations.

This chapter covers who should build an online portfolio, and what to include to woo and impress potential employers. I'll cover the basics of good Web page design, how to scan images and printed samples, and where to go online for help, advice on hosting your site, and other things you need to know to build and publish your hi-fi online portfolio.

So You Know...

I'm recommending you use Web page building software (I'll recommend different packages later) or an online Web wizard to build your Web page—I'm not going to attempt to teach HTML code or other stuff you don't need to know to build a Web site yourself. But as you read through the chapter, you'll notice things getting a little technical in terms of scanning images and image file types.

The Extra Mile

Further Reading

The *Complete Idiot's Guide* series includes a number of titles that deal in depth with HTML and Web page building. To learn more about this topic, one of my favorites is *The Complete Idiot's Guide to Creating a Web Page, Fourth Edition*, by Paul McFedries.

The only reason I'm getting into the nitty-gritty of images is because much of what you'll include in your hi-fi portfolio will be scanned samples or other graphic elements, not just text. Unless you're hiring someone to build your online portfolio for you or if your site is entirely text-based, you'll have to deal with images at some point in the Web site-building process, even if you use a wizard or software to build your site.

In addition to what I discuss in the chapter, I'll also point you in the direction of some excellent Web–site-building help sites where you can go to get more information if you need it. So, don't freak out or get in a tizzy over the technical sections of this chapter—but remember, this is hi-fi, baby. Relax.

Who Needs a Hi-Fi Online Portfolio?

Of course, if the job you're looking for has anything to do with visual communications, Web work, or the talent industry, you should think about building or hiring someone to create your online portfolio. If you're involved in new media (Web or multimedia work) and don't have an online portfolio, something is wrong.

Sure, you can include a list of URLs on your résumé and in your cover letter, but most new media employers expect you to have your very own Web site that showcases your work and abilities. Not having one is like being a professional résumé writer and not having a résumé.

Jobs that fall in the categories of written or verbal communications would do well to put together an online portfolio of writing or speaking samples (RealAudio or RealVideo files), and especially links to Web sites where your work or Web content has been published.

Graphic designers, Web designers, Web marketers, copywriters, journalists, illustrators, models, voice personalities—really anyone who otherwise builds and maintains a physical portfolio—can and should think about creating an online version of your best work samples.

What About Entry-Level Job Seekers?

What if you know how to build an online portfolio, but you're an entry-level job seeker and you've got nothing to include except projects you did for class? Course-related samples are a good start. But why not build up your portfolio as well as help out a worthy cause at the same time?

Approach a local nonprofit agency and offer to build their Web site free of charge. Or offer to build your no-tech brother-in-law's online portfolio for him for a reasonable fee, or for free if he's a tightwad. Strike a deal with a local merchant to set up an e-commerce site for "free" in exchange for a percentage of profits for a specified period of time. Heck, start a side business building hi-fi portfolios for all the low-tech people you know, even if they're not looking for a job. Raise your rates as you get more "clients."

Gawow!

Figure 9.1 is a sample from Web designer Amanda K. Erickson's online portfolio (www.gawow.com), which also highlights her writing skills—she's a multitalented gal. Amanda says her online portfolio has been a main topic of discussion in interviews, and that it offers her the opportunity to showcase her many talents in the design and communications arena—it's been instrumental in landing freelance projects, too.

133

The thumbnail images of her Web work (on the right of the screen) are clickable images that take the user to a project overview and a link to the actual Web site. Each sample has a detailed and superbly written case study, describing how she developed the project, what the clients' needs were, and how she went about designing and building the site to meet those needs.

Figure 9.1

Amanda Erickson's hi-fi online portfolio showcases her design and Web technology experience, and includes project overviews and case studies for each sample.

When you start thinking about your online portfolio, remember that you have the opportunity to really demonstrate your understanding of customers' needs and how you think through projects to meet the intended outcome of an assignment, project, or campaign. Don't be shy. The whole point behind building an online portfolio is to blow your competition out of the water, and to impress employers.

Job Seekers Looking for the Competitive Advantage

People who could use a hi-fi Web site as part of the job hunting tool kit include

➤ **Computer programmers** —You include demo versions or scan the packaging and product information of software that you wrote or helped develop. If the server where you're hosting your site allows access to database functionality or scripting, the Web is a perfect place to demonstrate your Java, Perl, C++, or JavaScript prowess. You don't have to be a Web designer to get some credit for making the Web work!

➤ **Teachers**—You can include sample lesson plans, students' art or writing samples, or descriptions and digital photos of science projects. Include excerpts of letters or praise from parents and students, and list any awards (or logos for the award campaign, such as an image of the Golden Apple award logo) you've won with a hyperlink to the Web site that describes why the award is given.

➤ **Salespeople**—You can create or use territory maps, company logos, graphs, and charts that show sales increases, or other visual models of your sales-effectiveness, such as streaming video of a sales presentation.

➤ **Marketers or advertising account executives**—Even if you didn't create the actual artwork or copy for a campaign, you can include samples of the marketing pieces, and a brief overview of your involvement in the campaign or project—creative input, branding or identity development, client services, or other things you did to make the campaign a success.

➤ **Financial planners or stock brokers**—You could create a chart or graph that summarizes portfolio performances over a period of time, or write a narrative description of how your advice and planning led to strong performance on the market. Include excerpts of testimonials from clients or performance review summaries.

➤ **Public relations workers**—Include digital or scanned photos of publicity events, invitations or announcements about special events, press releases, or a line list of your media contacts (no names, just the names of newspapers, radio stations, or other media sources). You could also include case studies or overviews of a media crisis and how you handled the "fallout."

➤ **Media planners**—If you place ads or buy commercial airtime, line-list the publications or stations you work with, and include samples of the actual ads. If you're in Web media planning, include samples of the banner ads and where and why the ads were placed. If there was a measurable increase in sales or traffic due to your ad placement, say so, and back it up with the same data you present to clients to get them to approve your media plan. When necessary, disguise the identity of former clients, especially if you're including budget or spending information.

➤ **Administrators**—Ideas for a health care administrator would be to create a chart (or borrow it from the annual report) of an increase in occupancy and admissions, or a decrease in malpractice suits due to your initiatives to offer more biohazard or other employee training programs. You could also include scans of logos of certifications by governing agencies such as Medicare, JCAHO, or Medicaid.

A school administrator could demonstrate an increase in attendance, retention rates of teachers, fundraising initiatives, or other statistics or programs you might otherwise present to the school board to demonstrate you're doing a good job. If a high number of your teachers win awards, mention this but don't take credit for another person's accomplishments. If parents or students send you letters of approval and appreciation, tactfully include excerpts from letters as testimonials to your leadership skills.

➤ **CEOs or executives**—Productivity-increase charts, organizational restructuring charts, press releases in which you're mentioned or featured, awards, and other accolades are things you might include in your Web portfolio. You could also include copies of annual reports, or other disguised information that you might also use to present to the board of directors or stockholders.

➤ **Architects**—Scan blueprints, diagrams, renderings, or floor plans to showcase your design or building expertise. If you're involved in a high-profile commercial development, try to locate press clippings that mention your name or feature your firm.

➤ **Engineers**—Provide project schematics or design blueprints, or digital or scanned photos of the final design project. If your work impacted the bottom line (say you designed a system to automate mail sorting), use cost-savings projections put together by the sales team. Highlight new or improved designs that you worked on.

➤ **Any Job Seeker**—Anyone with expertise on a topic related to the industry in which you're trying to land a job can develop a Web guide or tutorial that helps people understand or track news and events in your industry. For example, if you're an attorney, you could put together a Web guide or online legal resource site that demonstrates your knowledge of a particular problem or issue in law.

If you've had an accomplishment or achievement mentioned in the local or trade press, scan the newspaper or magazine article or use video or audio clips that showcase your 15 minutes of fame.

Thanks for the Tip

Keep It Professional

Your online portfolio should contain only information and items that are related to your job and profession. Avoid including pictures of yourself or your pets and family or other interests that indicate your religious preference or other personal information.

If you're in a profession that doesn't fit any of the preceding categories, this doesn't mean you can't or shouldn't build a hi-fi Web site to showcase your skills, experience, and background. In fact, anyone who demonstrates Web-building skills is sure to impress an employer, and especially if Web skills aren't required or even common in your line of work. It shows you're a mover and shaker when it comes to learning new techniques and that you're up to speed with current technologies and communication trends.

Back Up the Claims Made in Your Résumé

If nothing else, your career Web site can act as a backup for your plain and simple résumé, offering instant access to your "career story." Say you sent a simplified version of your résumé in response to a job posting at a job site, and you get a call back from the employer. This is an excellent opportunity to mention your Web site (and you did list the Web address on your résumé, didn't you?) and invite the employer to take a closer look at your skills and qualifications before the interview.

Print It Out, Take It to Interviews

Always take a printout of your online portfolio (and your real portfolio if you have one) with you to interviews. Some employers won't have time to log on to your site, and might not even have Web access. But if you have a printed backup of your hi-fi Web portfolio, it's a great way to walk the walk and talk the talk during an interview. Oh yeah, this is a good time to proof the pages for typos, spelling errors, and other blunders—much easier than proofing onscreen.

Thanks for the Tip

The Map Test

Printing out your Web portfolio is also a good way to test the navigation for your site. When you sit down to print it out, ask yourself—from a new visitor's perspective—whether the content areas are easy to find without using your site outline to guide you. Chances are your first portfolio won't be so huge that you'll be challenged to find all the pages, but test it anyway to make sure it's easy to navigate.

You Know You Want One—Where Are You Going to Put It?

Now that you've decided you want to build a Web site, you have to figure out where you're going to "publish," or post your site so others can access it. You have a couple of options. First, check with your Internet service provider (ISP) to find out whether site storage is included as part of your monthly access fee. Most ISPs provide site

137

storage service free of charge and usually provide instructions or support to get you started on building your personal Web site.

If you want to purchase and host your own domain name (www.*yourname*.com rather than www.*yourisp*.com/members/~jcardis.html), you'll probably pay anywhere from $15–$50 a month for site and domain name hosting, plus the registration fees that go along with buying your own domain name.

Get a Domain Name

If you want to *really* market yourself, spend a little cash and purchase your very own Web site domain name (www.*yourname*.com). It costs $70 for two years (if you know where the name will be hosted and have the technical details on hand when you go online to buy the name) or $100 to reserve the name until you figure out the details of where the name and site will be hosted. You can check on the availability of domain names and buy your very own at Network Solutions (www.networksolutions.com). Most ISPs will help you register and purchase your name for a small fee, maybe free.

Again, talk to your ISP and ask your Web-savvy friends. If you don't have any friends, or don't have any Web-savvy friends, go online to look for advice on hosting your site.

If privacy is a big concern, be sure to ask the host site administrator if you can use password-protection to keep prying eyes from accessing your site. Otherwise, unless you go out of your way to make the site findable by search engines, or sign up to be included in your ISP's member directory, no one will probably ever know the site is there.

Second, you can build and post your hi-fi portfolio at a free-hosting site such as Tripod (www.tripod.lycos.com) or HomeStead(www.homestead.com). You might be limited in terms of storage space and having to build your site using the site's Web page wizards, so check out the sites before you start breaking ground with a software wizard. Many site-based wizards are compatible with Microsoft FrontPage, so consider that if you decide to use that as your WYSIWYG Web page builder.

What You See

WYSIWYG means "what you see is what you get." When it comes to building a Web site, using a WYSIWYG software program allows you to type text or add graphics by dragging and dropping the images onto the area of the screen where you want them to appear. No having to learn Web programming code or fret over other technical issues. Most of the free online page hosting sites offer a WYSIWYG interface for building fast, error-free pages.

Go Online for Free Hosting Site Reviews

You have plenty of options when it comes to choosing which free hosting site to store your Web pages. For reviews and guides to free Web-hosting sites, be sure to stop by NetGuide's Free Web-Hosting Services guide which reviews the most popular free hosting sites and links you to each site's main page. To access the guide, from NetGuide's main page (www.netguide.com) conduct a keyword search using "free Web site hosting" and you'll get a link to a quick but comprehensive article on the top free hosting services and what each has to offer.

Or, peruse Yahoo!'s directory to free Web-hosting services—from the home page (www.yahoo.com), click **Business and Economy**. In this subdirectory, click **Companies** and then **Internet Services**. From here, click **Web Services**, and then **Free Web Pages** for a listing of about 50 sites that provide free hosting.

Other Web guide sites such as About.com (www.about.com) and Webmonkey (hotwired.lycos.com/webmonkey/) offer tips and advice on how and where to store your personal Web pages. To access the freebies section at About.com, do a keyword search from the main page (www.about.com) using **Free Web Hosting** to access the information and links on free site storage. For advice and information from Webmonkey, try a similar keyword search or peruse the site contents for information relating to building and storing your site.

Popular Free Web-Hosting Sites

Here are some free Web hosting sites for you to check out. Many of them also have wizards to help you build a Web site, so shop around for the one that meets your needs.

> ➤ **GeoCities/Yahoo!**—This partnership between Yahoo! and GeoCities offers home-page–building wizards and plenty of nifty add-ons such as streaming audio and video. Check it out at geocities.yahoo.com/home/. Figure 9.2 is a sample of the Web-building wizard at GeoCities/Yahoo!

Figure 9.2

An easy-to-use, Web-based page-building wizard can get you up and running in no time.

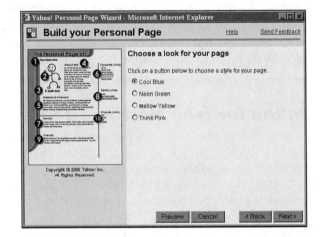

> ➤ **Tripod/Lycos**—With Web-page–building wizards and advanced add-ons, this is another great place to build and host your home page. Visit www.tripod.lycos.com.

> ➤ **The Globe**—Here is yet another freebie site with easy-to-use wizards and lots of bells-and-whistles add-ons. Take a spin around the uPublish section of The Globe at www.theglobe.com/upublish_landing/.

> ➤ **Homestead**—Besides free hosting and site-building wizards, Homestead has a special résumé template that makes building your online résumé a snap. Visit the site at www.homestead.com.

> ➤ **Angelfire**—Another member of the Lycos network provides free Web-site hosting and a variety of templates and wizards to get you started. Visit Angelfire at angelfire.lycos.com.

> ➤ **WebProvider**—This free hosting site (www.webprovider.com) has lots of advanced features and free Web-building software to help you get started on your portfolio.

Ingredients and Planning

In addition to a detailed HTML-formatted and plain-text version of your résumé (for easy download), your hi-fi portfolio can include samples such as those mentioned previously. Be sure to organize and label or have titles for the contents of your site before you start building. This way, you know where everything goes and you can create a plan for users to navigate your site.

Remember, your hi-fi portfolio tells your career story—it speaks on your behalf to interested employers, and lets people learn more about you than they possibly could, even in an interview. Think of it as a sales tool that's used to convince employers that you're qualified to meet their needs. If you approach the portfolio as a sales piece rather than an extension of your ego, you'll do a better job of answering the question on the mind of every employer: What can you do for me?

More Ideas on What to Include

Brainstorm for other ideas on what to include in your portfolio—things that expand on information in your résumé or that otherwise offer more detail about your career interests and expertise. If you're involved with a volunteer organization, include a link to the organization's Web site and a brief description of your activity with the group. This demonstrates your community involvement, and is a highly desired trait for managers and other professional leadership positions. Think about your long-term career plans, not only what you need to do now to get that dream job.

If you're adding "extra" information to your site, break it up in a way so the site visitor doesn't have to scroll through a long page to get to information of interest. Always include a site map and a brief description of what's in each area of your site. Make it easy and enjoyable to get around!

Thanks for the Tip

Build As You Go

Even when you're not looking for a job, you can add to your portfolio. Letters of recommendation, performance reviews, work samples, and other feathers in your cap should be collected throughout your career so that when the time comes to update your portfolio, you don't have to rack your brain trying to think of things to include, or spend time tracking things down. Think of your Web site as a hard-selling extension of your résumé—it's everything the employer needs to know to make the decision to hire you.

What to Leave Out

Don't include things just to add bulk to the site. Ask yourself, "Will this help me get the job, and would I bring this up in an interview?" If the answer is no, or even maybe, chuck it.

And whatever you do, don't include a photo of yourself (unless you're a model, actor, or trying to get a job in the talent industry) or information about your hobbies and personal interests. Save this stuff for your personal Web page, which should be separate from your "professional" Web site, unless your personal interests are a tasteful demonstration of your creativity, personality, and technical aptitude.

Thanks for the Tip

Protect Yourself

Never, never, never put your Social Security number on anything you publish on the Web, on your résumé, or in a cover letter. If an employer needs this information, they'll ask for it after you've been hired, or to conduct a background check. Read Chapter 2, "It's a Jungle Out There: Job Hunters Beware!" and Chapter 8, "Privacy, Distribution, and Access to Your Résumé," for more information on protecting yourself online.

Don't include your Social Security number, salary history, references, or other information that gives away too much about you and gives the employer the upper hand when it comes time to negotiate. And don't include phone numbers or email addresses of your former employers. If the employer you're trying to impress wants to contact them, they'll ask for the information on an application or find the information themselves, if these folks aren't already listed on your personal references sheet.

Make a Site Map

To stay organized and help devise the navigation plan for your site, start with a simple outline of the contents, as if you were getting ready to write a term paper or tackle another large project. Create main headings (home page, writing samples, press releases, radio spots, print ads, white papers, market research, and so on) and then list what falls under each main category. Think about how the contents relate to one another, and note which pages should link together after the site is built.

Collect and organize or create electronic files of the text content of your site so that you can easily copy/paste the content later on. It doesn't matter in which application the word processing files are created or saved. You could even use your WordPad or Notepad to compose and store your Web content for quick and easy cut-and-paste action.

Decide on a Page Layout and Color Scheme

You can tool around with layout and color scheme issues after you get started, but having a basic plan in place will help tremendously when you start designing the site.

Have a short list of fonts that you want to use, and get advice or guidance on basic design principles if you're not accustomed to this sort of thing. A good way to get ideas for design is to visit your favorite Web sites and make note of how the pages are laid out, and how menus and navigation bars are used to help users move through the site.

As far as colors go, I'm not going to tell you what colors you should or should not use. However, I happen to know that if you use blue and green variations, you will subliminally hypnotize your site visitors, and ultimately get so many job offers that you'll have to remove your site from the Web. And, absolutely do not use red. It upsets and angers people, so don't go causing trouble. Ha! Although research does suggest that color has an impact on the viewer's experience and emotional response, don't have a cow if you want to use a splash of red (or other "danger" color) here and there.

A good rule of thumb is to just keep it simple, but tasteful. Visit Web sites of design firms or ad agencies—supposedly, these folks know a thing or two about good design. If you're color blind or otherwise artistically impaired when it comes to matching colors, seek advice from a friend, starving artist, or house painter (who might in fact be your starving artist friend).

Because I'm recommending you use a WYSIWYG ("what you see is what you get") Web page creator instead of trying to teach you HTML code, you won't have to worry about creating page backgrounds or other design elements. These options are usually built in to the wizard menu options. Figure 9.3 shows wizard options that help you choose the design and color scheme for your site.

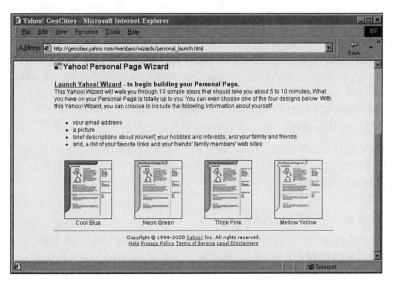

Figure 9.3

Pick and choose page design, site colors, and background colors using wizard menus.

Collect the Images and Artwork

Make a list of the images you'll use, and decide how to go about getting these samples ready for the Web—scanning them yourself or paying to have the images and samples scanned.

As far as artwork goes, I'd say keep non–work-sample artwork to a minimum. A text-based site that's nicely designed makes a fine presentation—you don't need a bunch of cheesy clip art cluttering up your design. But if you do want to experiment with clip art or add a logo-type design element to your site, you can find plenty of free clip art on the Web. Just do a keyword search using "free clip art" and you'll get plenty of matches. Or, go to a site such as Clip Art Review, which is a directory of free clip art sites (www.webplaces.com/html/clipart.htm).

Most Web-building wizards have clip art galleries, too, but don't pick an unattractive piece of clip art just for the sake of adding "graphics" to your site.

A Word on Scanners and Scanning Images for the Web

If you have a scanner and know how to use it, you're in good shape. If you're thinking about buying a scanner for this project and for other scanning needs, you'll be happy to know that scanners are actually pretty affordable add-ons for your home computer. I personally like UMAX and Agfa scanners, but do a product comparison at a site such as ZDNet (www.zdnet.com) before you fork out any cash.

You might even want to consider an all-in-one machine that features scanner, fax, copier, and printer functions—a wider range of features than you'll get with just a flatbed scanner. Again, check prices and get recommendations from expert product reviewers before you make the buy.

If you're ready to buy, you can also do price comparisons online at PriceWatch (www.pricewatch.com) and DealMac for Macintosh products (www.dealmac.com). When making this buying decision, consider the cost of paying someone else to scan your samples for you. At about $25 a pop (the going rate in my area), that adds up fast. Considering good flatbed scanners run in the neighborhood of $100 to $150 these days...well, you can do the math.

You can use your scanner for other things, too, such as to scan photos to email to your friends and family, or to scan documents instead of retyping the whole thing if you don't have the electronic file.

Scanner Settings and Image File Types

If you do decide to scan your own images, spend some time getting to know how your scanner works. Read the software manual and instructions—understanding how to get the best-looking scanned images will be handy later on when you prepare the images for the Web.

After you're ready to scan, place the sample or image on the flatbed, face down. Set the scanner to scan at 72dpi (dots per inch). This is the best resolution for Web images in terms of file size (an ideal file size is no more than 50K, and that's pushing it) and download time. Of course, you can scan the images at a higher resolution and strip them down later. Going from a low resolution to a higher-resolution image doesn't usually work.

File Size

The size of your text and image files will play a major role in how quickly or sluggishly your Web page downloads. To learn more about file size and file compression for the Web—and plenty of other Web-page–building help—visit Webmonkey at `hotwired.lycos.com/webmonkey/99/15/index0a.html?tw=design` and learn some fabulous "fat burning" tips.

Save your scanned images as JPEG files (`.jpg` file extension, such as `.doc` for a Word document) or as GIFs (`.gif` file extension). JPEG files are typically smaller in size than GIFs, but the images are often crisper when saved as GIFs. Most Webmasters use the JPEG format for photographic images, and the GIF format for artwork, especially computer-generated images.

JPEG or GIF?

JPEG stands for Joint Photographic Experts Group—a scheme for compressing images. GIF stands for Graphics Interchange Format. My Web guru buddy, Matthew N. Sharp, offers the following advice on image file types for the Web: "If the images are logo-esque, a `.gif` allows some precise control over color specifics. However, the `.jpg` format allows a wider range of color with a much smaller file size, which counts big-time when people are downloading the files that make up the person's Web page. I won't even bother looking at a site if it's taking too long to download fancy, huge graphics. Use `.gif` or `.jpg`—nothing else. Not `.bmp`, not `.tiff`."

Creating Adobe Acrobat Files

Another option to saving large scanned images (such as a magazine cover or annual report covers or contents) is to create an Adobe Acrobat page. Acrobat documents (PDFs, or portable document files) give you the option to very tightly control the visual layout of a document (from text and image placement, to fonts to kerning to tracking), so that any user on any computer will the see the document as you intend. And, use of PDF files also allows the printout of that document to look the same, regardless of the user's software, printer, or type of computer being used to view and print the document.

However, not all employers will have the Adobe Acrobat Reader software installed on their computers, even though it is indeed a free download from Adobe's Web site (www.adobe.com). But not everyone will want to take the time to do such a thing. You can add a link to the free download page to make the process a little less painless, but don't count on busy employers taking the time to do this just to see your PDF documents.

But even if you can get someone to view your PDF documents using the free Acrobat Reader, you'll have to fork out some cash to buy the Adobe Acrobat software that creates the documents. Unfortunately, this will run you about $250.

Images Ready? Time to Break Ground

After you've got your site map, text files, and images ready for the Web, it's time to start building your site. Here are some popular and affordable WYSIWYG software programs that offer simple point-and-click and drag-and-drop features to construct Web pages.

➤ **Claris Home Page 3.0**—Claris Home Page 3.0 makes it easy as pie to master the basics of Web-site building. Beginning users can quickly and easily build a basic site consisting of several pages, logical navigation, and not-so-cheesy clip art graphics. Home Page's templates actually look good, and come with graphics and a background—all you have to do is type text into the appropriate boxes, and voilà, you have a Web page. If you get lost along the way, help is a mouse click away. Home Page has Assistants that enable users to choose everything from the site's navigation scheme to which logo appears on the site's pages.

➤ **Microsoft FrontPage Express and FrontPage 2000**—The best thing about FrontPage express is that it's free to download and is designed for the beginning user. After you've learned the ropes, you can upgrade to FrontPage 2000, at the tune of about $149. If you use Internet Explorer 4.0 or have Windows 98, you already have Express. Otherwise, you can download it for free from the Internet Explorer site at www.microsoft.com/windows/ie/download/windows.htm

If you're only just starting out, you can use one of several templates or wizards to create a basic page—you're asked a series of questions about how you want your page to appear and a custom page is then generated, which you can edit as

146

you like with easy-to-use editing tools. A cool feature is the "estimated download time" that tells you how many seconds the page will take to download.

➤ **Adobe PageMill**—PageMill is designed for beginning users with little or no HTML experience. A simple toolbar-based, word processor-style editing screen and a pasteboard for storing graphics, text, and links for reuse on multiple pages makes it easy to drag and drop elements to build your pages. Be sure to read through the beginner's guide to get the most from your Web-building efforts.

Don't be intimidated when it comes to learning new technology—the Web makes site building easy for everyone, so just buckle down and get to work! Unless you're trying to change careers to become a professional Web designer, just remember wizards and WYSIWYG editors make page building a breeze. You don't have to become a guru overnight, and just think of the many other ways you can use your Web-building expertise—beyond work-related stuff.

Site for Sore Eyes

Get Help Online

If you need help or have questions about building your hi-fi online portfolio or which software to use, the best place to go for help is the Web. My favorite guides are Webmonkey (`hotwired.lycos.com/webmonkey/`) and WebBuilder 101 (`www.webbuilder101.com`).

Making Your Site Findable

So, you've built a knock-'em-dead online portfolio, but how will employers and recruiters find it? Well, depending on your job search technique, you have several options: You can register your Web site address with the major search engines, you can include it on your electronic and paper résumés that you send to target employers, or you can include it when you upload your résumé to résumé databases and job sites.

A word of caution on registering your site address with the major search engines: After you register, you lose control over who might find your site. If you remember the privacy concerns discussed in Chapters 2 and 8, then you know why it's important to keep your résumé away from prying eyes. Plus, most employers and recruiters will search résumé databases before they do a general search on the Web to find qualified candidates.

Sure, someone might stumble across your portfolio URL and take a peek, but your best bet is to include your Web address on your résumé and to mention it in cover letters, inviting interested employers or recruiters to take a look. Remember, your portfolio isn't a lead generator—it's a qualifier and a great way to convince a target employer that you're the best person for the job. Don't rely on it to bring inquiries your way.

The Web-building guides I've mentioned throughout the chapter contain information on making your site findable if your job-hunting technique calls for wide distribution and access to your information. Otherwise, try the invitation-only approach and let only interested parties access your site.

The Least You Need to Know

➤ Your online portfolio is a great way to woo target employers. Include your Web site address on your résumé and in your cover letter, and always bring a printout of the site to interviews.

➤ You can publish your site for free at free-hosting sites, and use the free site's Web-building wizards to construct your pages.

➤ Building Web sites with wizards and WYSIWYG software is actually pretty easy to do—most programs have a drag-and-drop tool that lets you place text and images on the screen instead of having to learn programming code.

➤ Anyone can build a hi-fi career Web site. Even if you don't have traditional portfolio pieces, such as artwork or writing samples, you can create a Web guide or help site that demonstrates your knowledge of your industry or profession.

➤ It's important to make image files small enough (50K or less) so that they download quickly—you don't want to make a potential employer wait to see your stuff!

➤ Think of your career site as a work in progress. Even after you land your dream job, continue to collect samples and materials that demonstrate your skills and abilities.

Chapter 10

Be in the Know

In This Chapter

➤ How to "romance" your target employer with in-depth company and industry research

➤ How and where to find all your business research sources online, including market and industry information

➤ Get insider company information from third-party reviewers

➤ Spy on your competition at public résumé databases and newsgroups

If looking for a job is anything like dating, applying for a job you don't know anything about is like going on a date with a person you picked up through a blind personal ad. "SWM, 34, likes outdoors, animals, roller-blading. Seeks SWF, 21-31, for weekend fun and quiet dinners by fireside."

Don't you think you need to find out a bit more than that before you decide to actually meet this person for a date? Besides being disappointed yourself, you're not going to impress any of your "dates" when you show up and don't know a single thing about them except maybe their name. They'll probably think, "This jerk doesn't want a date with *me*—s/he just wants a *date*!"

Employers feel the same way, and, in fact, one of the most common complaints from employers is that job hunters don't know anything about their company or industry—they're just looking for a place to spend some time and make some money. Like an insecure date, sweetie, or spouse, they just know that at any moment you're leaving for something better.

Sometimes going on a job interview feels a little like being set up on a blind date. Say a recruiter, headhunter, or networking contact has put you in touch with a hot job lead. They'll fill you in on many of the ups and downs of "dating" Company ABC—someone who knows a little something about both of you has decided it's a good match, so you go with guarded expectations. And just like dating, you usually know right away if it feels right.

But knowing about your "date," the circles he or she runs in, and who the competition is can increase your chances of having a meaningful relationship. We're not talking about marriage, per se, but considering you spend a good chunk of time at work, you had better make sure it's the right fit before you jump into something!

If I haven't yet impressed upon you the importance of doing research, research, research before you begin the job search, this chapter will show you how spending the time up front to investigate the kinds of jobs and companies you want to work for can help you get closer to finding your dream job.

Before the Résumés Go Out...and Before the Calls Come In

Equipping yourself with knowledge about your target employers and their industries can set you apart from the competition during the job hunt and interviewing process—knowing who their competitors are and what those companies are up to is another powerful way to make a strong impression, and can also help you identify ways to customize your résumé and cover letter to get serious attention from your target employers.

Imagine the difference between a cover letter that says, "I'm interested in a position at your company," versus a cover letter that says, "In researching your company and the foodservice manufacturing industry, I see that Hobart has introduced a new incentive program to make inroads toward your Midwest regional distributors. I have some ideas I would like to share with you on how you might challenge those efforts and maintain your status as the top slicer supplier in your strongest and most profitable markets."

But how do you find enough information about your target company to write a compelling statement like that? Go online—it's all out there, just waiting for you to discover it.

Just the Intellifacts, Ma'am

There's so much darned information on the Web these days that simply entering your company research query in traditional search engines often results in thousands of matches—too many! So, to save time and make the most of your online research time, be sure to check out Intellifact's (www.intellifact.com/portal.htm) business

research tutorial (see Figure 10.1). It's a first-and-only starti... seeker, especially those of you who are new to online com... mine of business information and research resources, so b... Bookmarks or Favorites folder.

resea...
research basi...
sources of information.
Why do all the legwork
when these folks have
gathered it for you?

The Intellifact course is grouped into six lessons to help you efficiently perform a variety of business research tasks. Not only will you learn how to quickly locate company, market, and technology information, you'll also learn how to use online resources and tools for finding other important business information.

The subchapters in the Intellifact tutorial include the following topics, as well as links, links, links to resources for each subject.

Online Research Basics

Knowing how and where to locate information can you save you hours of frustration. Intellifact teaches basic and advanced search techniques, and shows you where to tap into the top starting points for your business research needs.

➤ *Use basic search engines.*   A quick overview and tips on using the most popular search engines.

➤ *Use advanced search engines.*   How and when to use Boolean separators (AND, NOT, OR, NEAR), plus links to basic and advanced search instructions for the major search engines, plus an overview of meta-search engines and the latest software (free!) for conducting effective searches.

nd commercial databases. Sometimes you have to pay to play. Commercial databases provide in-depth analysis and market research about companies, trends, and forecasts. Check here for a database directory to sites such as Lexis-Nexis (`www.lexis-nexis.com/lncc/`), Electric Library at `www.electriclibrary.com` (probably the most affordable and effective of them all), and Forrester Research (`www.forrester.com`). You can usually see report snippets, but for the full monty, you'll have to fork out some cash.

➤ *Locate a business.* This section covers using online directories to gather contact information for target companies and competitors. Includes a sublist of business directory links and what information you'll be able to find at each one.

Finding Company Information

Remember, the key to gaining a competitive advantage in your job search is to know your target company inside and out. Intellifact has collected information and links to the richest company information sources on the Web. Those days of old-fashioned hunting for company information are over!

➤ *Get company profiles.* Use Intellifact's company search engine to locate information on more than 350,000 companies. You can also use the Ticker Search tool to find specific company information, plus a list of sites offering company profiles for your target company, if it's publicly traded. In addition, you get links to dozens of services that provide financial information (on specific companies) to complete your company profile puzzle.

Later in this chapter, I also highlight the top sites for company information, so read on.

➤ *Access stock information.* Several sites such as Yahoo! Finance (`finance.yahoo.com`) and CBS Marketwatch (`cbs.marketwatch.com/news/newsroom.htx`) provide free reports and information on publicly traded companies. Intellifact also provides links to dozens of sites covering quotes and charts, analyst information, ownership information, historic data, company background, and stock-screening resources.

Following Business News

The world of business changes at amazing speed, so stay in tune and up-to-date by tracking breaking news, monitoring company news and announcements, and reading online news publications. A handful of sites even let you pick and choose the information you want to follow and deliver it right to your email inbox. How much easier can it get?

➤ *Track breaking news.* For the latest headlines in business, technology, and industry news, Intellifact features headlines from iSyndicate, as well as links to CNN Business (`www.cnn.com/fn`), MSNBC (`www.msnbc.com`), Fortune (`www.pathfinder.com/fortune/fbr/`), The Wall Street Journal (`www.wsj.com`), and Infoseek (www.infoseek.com), which provides access to news sources such as the Associated Press.

➤ *Monitor company news.* There's more than one way to monitor company news, and Intellifact has made it pretty easy for you by providing links to local and regional online newspapers, as well as several sites that offer news-tracking services and monitor news on your target companies. The online newspaper listing isn't complete, though, so to find news in your region, do a keyword search or try a Web directory such as Yahoo!'s News and Media section (www.yahoo.com/r/nm), which lists nearly 6,000 papers, as well as nondaily publications.

To track company news on Excite's NewsTracker (nt.excite.com) pages, click **Company News** for examples and detailed instructions.

The news source formerly known as Newspage is now known as Individual.com NewsPage (www.individual.com). This top-notch site offers a tracking service that includes a personalized news briefing, and access to news from a wide variety of worldwide news publications and sources.

Intellifact also lists Newsedge (www.newsedge.com) as a business research news source, but its product offerings are geared toward businesses and are probably out of budget range for most job seekers. Instead, become a member at its subsidiary, Individual.com (www.individual.com) for FREE information and news feeders, including customized email delivery of the news you want to receive in more than 1,500 distinct topics (and growing!). These topics cover industries and companies spanning high technology, telecommunications, health care, aerospace and defense, automotive, business and finance, travel and hospitality, and energy (among others).

Spanish Town Gives Up Goat Toss

One of the most popular topics at Individual.com is the WeirdNuz section, covering, as you guessed, weird but real news from around the world. With all the hard news and serious business we have to think about every day, why not make WeirdNuz one of your topic choices when you sign up as a member of Individual.com? At least, pay WeirdNuz a visit at www.individual.com and then click through **More Industries** then **General Interest**, and **WeirdNuz**. Who said job hunting had to be all sweat and tears?

➤ *Find online publications.* Even though researching businesses seems like a drag, trust me when I say you don't know how easy you've got it. It used to be that you had to go to the library (yikes!) to gather this information, and even then, you'd be hard-pressed to find free and easy access to as much information as you do online. And so, it follows that most major business publications now have an online version, and Intellifact has made it easy for you to access them by providing links to Web sites of most leading business publications.

Just click on any of the links (such as from `www.intellifact.com/tutorial3c.htm`) for directories of associations, business directories, business news, business technology magazines, computing magazines, electronic journals, finance magazines, government resources (including a link to a bulletin from ourfriends at the IRS), intellectual property, international companies, online newspapers, stock research, and trade shows.

For online publications that aren't listed in these directories, try looking up the publication in a search engine or directory. Meta search engines such as Google (`www.google.com`), Northern Light (`www.northernlight.com`), Dogpile (`www.dogpile.com`), and Metacrawler (`www.metacrawler.com`) scour the major search engines simultaneously to bring query results.

Research Markets and Industries

Employers are impressed with applicants who have deep knowledge of market trends and industry happenings that affect their business. The more information you have about your target company's industry and market, the more power you have to knock-'em dead in your cover letter, and hopefully in the interview.

➤ *Learn about an industry.* Especially for entry-level job seekers and professionals making a career change, you'll need to do a bit of background research to get up to speed on your target company's industry. Again, going online is the quickest and easiest way to do this.

A good starting point is Hoover's Industry Zone (`www.hoovers/industry/resources.html`) for profiles on 25 industry sectors.

For news and information on various industries, try Individual.com (`www.individual.com`) for the latest news articles in a variety of industries. Go to the left column and click on the desired industry to view the latest news articles in that industry. Yahoo! Finance (`www.yahoo.com/r/fi`) also offers comprehensive industry information including searchable news by industry.

The Motley Fool (see Figure 10.2)—no relation to Motley Crue—is a top-notch resource for business information—solid, common-sense business advice and analysis. As an added bonus, the commentary is rather hilarious, which is a characteristic you won't find at many business information sites. For industry information, visit `www.fool.com` and click **Industry and Market Analysis** to research nearly 50 industries. Be sure to check out the Industry Snapshot Reports for a quick and easy overview.

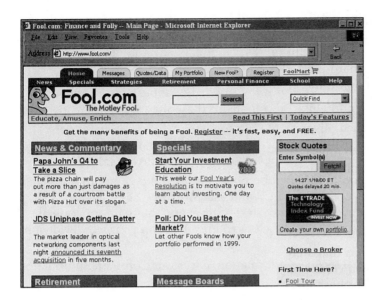

Figure 10.2

The Motley Fool is one of the most down-to-earth business information sites on the Web. Besides a wicked sense of humor and straight talk about business news and happenings, Motley Fool is host to the Ask the Headhunter Message Board—a must-see for any job seeker.

IndustryLink (www.industrylink.com) and IndustryNet (www.industrynet.com) provide you with detailed links to Web sites by industry. To use IndustryLink, click on one of the more than 20 industry buttons. From there, you'll find links to many of the companies in that particular industry.

➤ *Perform market research.* Intellifact recommends Researchinfo.com (www.researchinfo.com) as a comprehensive resource for market research info on a variety of markets and research topics. Read the FAQs or review postings on the message board (Market Research Roundtable) before you post your own question.

Intellifact also links to an article at the Online Women's Business Center (www.onlinewbc.org/docs/market/mk_research_trad.html) that overviews the basics and benefits of market research, so take a gander at that to see how and why you should do this as part of your business research.

To view summaries of market research studies on a broad range of markets and industries, try the following sites:

Forrester Research (www.forrester.com)—Internet and High Tech

Gartner Group (www.gartnergroup.com)—Information Technology

Find/SVP (www.find.com)—All Industries

Freedonia (www.freedoniagroup.com)—Industrial Markets

SRI (www.sri.com)—Technology-based Markets

➤ *Find trade shows.* Intellifact.com offers comprehensive search capabilities to find trade shows by industry, event type, and location, and a list of links to other sites with information on trade shows.

Notable sites include EXPOGUIDE (`www.expoguide.com`), a source for trade show and conference information, and Trade Show Channel (`www.tsnn.com/bclass/tschannel/`), a trade show locator by industry.

➤ *Find international resources.*   If you're searching the world over for that dream job, be sure to tap into the ever-growing international business information resources on the Web. Intellifact recommends these sites as good starting points:

For Intellifact's detailed directory of links to regional information, country-specific information, statistics, trade information, international new publications, and other resources, visit `www.intellifact.com/international.htm`.

For extensive background information on countries and regions around the world, be sure to check the CIA World Factbook (`www.odci.gov/cia/publications/factbook`). There's even travel and safety information at this expansive site, so take a peek before you head out on your worldwide job search.

For more international business information, check out Corporate Information (`www.corporateinformation.com`).

Getting General Technology Information

If you're in the high-tech field or just want to get up to speed on the latest technology offerings that might affect how your target company runs its business, the Web is a never-ending resource for both general and specific information regarding technology.

➤ *Get general information.*   It's no surprise the Web is an expansive resource for technology information. Be sure to check out Intellifact's extensive list of links to sites such as clnet News (`www.cnet.com`), Bloomberg Online (`www.bloomberg.com/bbn/hwy/hwy1.html`), and a host of technology transfer and research sites.

➤ *Research patents.*   Unless you're an engineer or product developer, you probably won't need to research patents or trademarks as part of the job-hunting process, but if you do, Intellifact provides powerful research tools and online resources to help you locate this sort of information.

➤ *Find technology publications.*   For a lengthy list of online technology publications, Intellifact has its own search feature plus a list of the most popular technology publications and sites, including ZDNet (`dailynews.yahoo.com/headlines/technology/zdnet/index.html`) and clnet (`www.news.com`).

Exploring Other Resources

From professional associations to government resources on job markets and employment projections, Intellifact has put together some helpful starting points to round out your business research efforts. Be sure to read the section on using newsgroups to do your homework, as well as researching nonprofits.

➤ *Find government resources.* Link to a long list of government resources and publications, including the Bureau of Labor Statistics (www.bls.gov) and the U.S. Small Business Administration (www.sba.gov).

➤ *Locate associations.* Tap into the ASAE's (American Society of Association Executives) Gateway to professional and trade associations at www.asaenet.org/find/ or the Better Business Bureau at www.bbb.org. Another gold mine is the International Bureau of Chambers of Commerce (www.icc-ibcc.org/), which can lead you in the direction of many local and regional job posting sites, too.

➤ *Use newsgroups.* If you're new to newsgroups, Intellifact offers basic information on where to find them and how to use them. These electronic message boards let you read postings from other participants, and post your own questions and comments. Business research newsgroups can also be found through Deja.com (www.deja.com). To locate newsgroups at this site, just do a keyword search using "business research," or be more specific if you're looking for something like business imports, or special newsgroups for AOL members. Figure 10.3 features some of the job and business-related newsgroups at Deja.com.

Figure 10.3

Deja.com hosts hundreds of newsgroups to help you with your job and business research. To locate a list of topics, do a keyword search for your industry or research interests, or view the menu offerings to find your newsgroup discussion topic.

157

To use newsgroups, you need a newsreader, which is built in to Netscape Navigator and Internet Explorer. Most online services, such as AOL, support this feature, too. Depending on what browser you use, this is how to locate newsreaders:

Internet Explorer—Select **Tools**, **Mail and News**, **Read News**.

Netscape Navigator—Select **Communicator**, **Newsgroups** and then right-click **News**. Select the newsgroups you want to view.

America Online—Select **Internet Connection** on the channels display and then click the **Newsgroups** icon.

Some of the more popular message boards for business research include

`alt.business`

`alt.business.international`

`alt.business.import-export`

`alt.business.marketplace`

`alt.education.business`

`alt.internet.search`

`misc.business.marketing.moderated`

`misc.entrepreneurs`

➤ *Research nonprofits.* GuideStar (`www.guidestar.org`) is a clearinghouse of information on nonprofit organizations for a wide a variety of industries. Another good starting point for nonprofit research is the Internet Non-Profit Information Center (`www.seflin.org/nsfre/npc.mnu.html`) and the National Center for Charitable Statistics (`nccs.urban.org`).

You can also sign up for a free Intellifact.com biweekly e-newsletter that covers new search strategies, business information site reviews, and other tools to help you in the job hunt. I'm serious when I say if you want to learn how to effectively and efficiently research your target companies, its competitors, and the industry, this is a must-see site. Save yourself the headache and the extra effort you'll have to put into your research if you don't know where or how to gather the information you need.

Dig Deeper: More Business Research Resources

The Web truly is a researcher's paradise. Don't settle for one source of information—get second and third opinions to cover your tracks completely. Here are some additional starting points for the full picture of your company, industry, and the job market in general.

Check Out the Riley Guide

Besides wowing your prospective employers with a solid understanding of the company you want to work in, doing industry research before you start on the job hunt might reveal important facts and trends that impact your chances of success. You might just discover that life as a typewriter repair person is a career headed toward extinction, or at least one that you'll have trouble finding work in. The Riley Guide will point you in the direction of just about every information-rich resource for occupational outlooks, industry trends, and other useful resources to help you become a smarter job hunter. Visit "Researching Careers, Employers, and More" at www.dbm.com/jobguide/research.html.

State by State Labor Market Information

Locate labor marketing information and statistics quickly and easily from Yahoo! at dir.yahoo.com/Business_and_Economy/Labor/Statistics/U_S__States_Labor_Market_Information/

Not every state is listed here, so if you're looking for state-specific statistics and can't get to them from Yahoo!, do a keyword search using the terms "labor market information Indiana" or whatever state you're looking for. You'll be taken to the official state Web site to locate industry and labor market facts, projections, and statistics.

JobProfiles.com (www.jobprofiles.com)

JobProfiles gives you an insider's perspective on what a job is really like and what skills and training are necessary for success. Although the profiles tend to be geared toward entry-level and college students, professionals making a career change or folks re-entering the work force can use this free information to get started researching their chosen industry.

Job categories include agriculture, animal services, and natural resources; arts, entertainment, sports and recreation; business support and communications; construction and manufacturing; education and science; government; health and social services; retail and wholesale; and cleaning, real estate, religion, security, and travel.

Profiles are completed by professionals on the basis of membership in associations, unions, and business organizations, as well as site visitors. The first section of profiles covers the respondent's background and what their job is like (accomplishments, time for each kind of task, and so on). The second part covers what stresses and rewards they receive from their job. The third part covers what future challenges and advice they have to give.

If you're at a loss for words when it comes time to do informational interviews or network with an industry expert, this site will give you ideas on what questions to ask. It's also a good way to find out about the "challenges" that you might face in a given profession, so find out before you set out on your job hunt.

What's an Informational Interview?

If you're undecided on what career path to follow or just want to learn more about a specific profession, you can contact an industry expert to ask questions about required skills, the "typical" work day, challenges and rewards, salary ranges, and other on-the-job issues. It's a good way to network, and it might just lead to a real interview! For a list of questions to ask during your informational interview, and tips on sending follow-up notes, visit About.com's Career Guide at jobsearch.about.com/business/jobsearch/library/blquest.htm.

Get an Outsider's Opinion

Getting company and industry information from third-party reviewers is a good idea when doing business research. First, you get an outsider's view of the company, rather than what the employer "wants" you to know. Second, the information in most cases is geared toward job seekers and investors, so you get a broader picture of how a company operates, its corporate culture, financial status, and how it fares in its given industry.

Hoover's Sweeps Together Plenty of Company Information

Hoover's (www.hoovers.com) company profiles cover the largest and most influential public and private companies around the world to give you insight on a company's personality, history and strategy, market position, officers, competition, and financial health.

Many of the reports at Hoover's are free, but for the detailed reports, the monthly membership fee of $14.95 is well worth the cost. Join just for the duration of your job hunt, or sign up for a discounted annual membership to maintain throughout your career to help you stay up to speed with your industry and profession.

For members only, Hoover's advanced search tools let you sift and sort that information to generate customized results that are as broad or narrow as you need on companies, IPOs (initial public offerings), StockScreener, and company news.

Get Your Feet Wet at WetFeet.com

WetFeet.com (see Figure 10.4) has industry profiles and company information to make your business research a breeze. The Company Quicks section has hundreds of company capsules, and Company Q&As is a section where employers deal with "the tough questions for job seekers, and they answer in their own words."

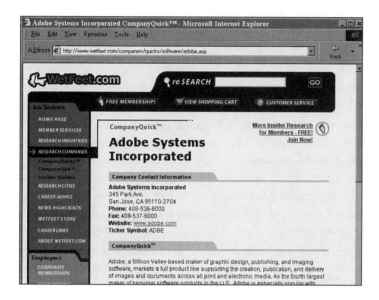

Figure 10.4

WetFeet.com's Company Quicks provides quick capsules of companies—useful especially if you haven't quite narrowed down your list of target companies yet.

The expanded Industry Quicks offers industry profiles and an overview of current trends, the pros and cons of major employers, what's great and not so great about working in each industry, plus general job tips. You'll also enjoy their E-Insider, a monthly newsletter that includes useful career and job search articles.

WetFeet.com is a site you should add to your Bookmarks or Favorites folder, as it is an endless resource for all facets of the job search. I'll talk about it more in-depth in the next chapter, so be sure to read on to find out how this site can answer many of your advanced job-hunting technique questions.

Break into the Vault.com

Vault.com (www.vault.com) is another leading resource for career information—from your first job, to your first career change, and for the tools you need to reach the next level in your current line of work.

At Vault.com, you get research, advice, and career information, plus accurate and timely information from independent research and company insiders. Vault.com interviews and surveys thousands of insiders in 3,000 top companies to bring you the inside scoop on a wide variety of companies and industries.

Even if your target company isn't profiled at Vault.com, you can get a clearer picture of issues and trends affecting companies within a given industry. It's a good starting point, and also has some of the best message boards to ask questions and get answers on many issues facing job seekers at every level of experience.

Get Free and Legal Info from Company Sleuth

Company Sleuth at www.companysleuth.com is another company insider report source. Here, you can get inside financial information, stock and trading updates, and other corporate information—delivered directly to your email inbox. Just select the companies you want to "spy" on and the Sleuth will deliver weekly reports to help you stay current with your target companies. You can also sign up for Job Sleuth services to get job listings based on your preferences and requirements delivered to your email inbox. Visit JobSleuth at www.jobsleuth.com.

Researching *Your* Competition

Although it's pretty much impossible to find out who's interviewing for a position you're trying to get, you can go online before you start on your job hunt to find out what people like you have to offer employers.

Knowing what your competition is up to and what skills they can bring to the table can do two things: It can help you identify your strengths and weaknesses and help you determine whether you need to get additional training; or how to write your résumé and cover letter to set yourself apart from the competition.

For example, if you know that most people looking for jobs as senior copywriters typically have five to 10 years' agency experience, but you only have four years on the job, highlight your experience in new media or Web content—skills or experience those folks might have missed out on. If you know what tools they have in their arsenal, you can decide your plan of action based on that knowledge. It's kind of like getting hold of a game plan before the game, so equip yourself with information to get a leg up on your competition.

Scan Public Résumé Databases

One way to spy on your public résumé databases competition is to visit public résumé databases and just stroll through the postings to see what folks are up to. To locate public databases, just go to a search engine such as Google or Yahoo! and do a keyword search using `"public resume databases"`. Better yet, try to locate industry-specific public databases to home in more closely on the people who want a job in your field.

After you find a public database, just pretend to be an employer or recruiter and search for résumés using keywords specific to the kind of job you're looking for. The more specific you are in your search, the better view of the competition you'll get. Keep in mind that résumé databases seem to attract a certain kind of job hunter, so for all the job-hunter competitors you find in databases, there are many others who forego this technique and instead use more direct job-hunting tactics such as going through recruiters or targeting companies directly.

You might have to register to see résumés, but it's a quick and painless process. It feels a little sneaky, but job hunting is competitive, so arm yourself with the information you need to not only impress employers, but to know what you need to do to beat the competition.

Scan Newsgroups

Newsgroups can reveal a lot of insight about your competition. You won't necessarily know whether the folks you can spy on at newsgroups are the exact same people applying for your dream job, but you can review résumés and see what people are chatting about in terms of industries, the job-hunting process, and other information to find out what the other job hunters of the world are up to.

For easy access to job-related newsgroups, visit Deja.com at `www.deja.com`.

Now that you're equipped with the tools and resources you need to be a business research guru, go online and spend some time "getting to know" your target companies, their industries, and their competitors. The more you know before you go to an interview or send off your résumé, the better positioned you are to make a lasting impression on your target companies.

Be sure to read the next chapter, "It's Who You Know." You'll learn things such as how and when to interview current employees at your target companies, and how to use networking to get job leads and drop names to get an interview. These "deep" research techniques can get you even closer to your dream job, and answer the question, "Is this really the place I want to work?"

The Least You Need to Know

➤ Employers expect you to know about their company, industry, and competitors—go online to gather the information quickly and easily.

➤ You can track your target companies using online news feeders, trade publications, and professional association Web sites.

➤ For a more objective view, third-party reviewers provide in-depth company and industry analysis.

➤ Find out what your competitors are bringing to the table by viewing public résumé databases and scanning newsgroups.

Chapter 11

It's Who You Know

In This Chapter

➤ How and whom to schmooze to become a job-hunting insider

➤ The secret is revealed: where to the find "hidden" jobs

➤ How to expand your community of job-hunting networks

➤ How to conduct an informational interview—in person and online

➤ How and where to network online

Has anyone ever told you, "It's not what you know, but *who* you know"? Didn't it make your blood boil to think that no matter how hard you worked, the good jobs would always go to someone with an inside advantage—the VP's nephew, the account exec's fraternity brother, the delivery guy's next door neighbor. Everyone but you.

Don't get in a tizzy—you might not be one step away from the hiring manager today, but you can get closer by working the same ropes as the "who you know" crowd. It's called networking, and it's one of the most effective ways of ferreting out those "hidden jobs." But remember, people aren't usually just handed good jobs—they still have to submit a résumé and go through the interview process just like anyone else to prove they can do the work.

How do you become part of the "who you know" crowd? You do know people, right? All you have to do is ask for a little help, or at the very least, let people know you're looking for a job and ask that if they know anyone or know of any inroads you can take to get closer to your dream job, you'd sure appreciate their help.

That's what this chapter is all about—building and maintaining a network of friends and business associates to get your foot in the door and uncover those "hidden jobs." This chapter will teach you how to network effectively in person and online, and how to use those contacts to help you get closer—faster—to the job you want.

Who's Hiding All Those Great Jobs?

Given the chance, many employers will do anything to avoid advertising an open position. They'd rather save the time and money and go with someone who has been recommended by a current employee or associate, promote from within, or use a recruiter or headhunter to do the dirty work. Makes sense, doesn't it?

What does this mean to you, oh faithful job hunter? It means you have to consider other job-hunting options outside the online job sites, résumé databases, and sending unsolicited résumés. Networking is one of those options, and if done correctly, it can produce the results you want—job leads.

Nick Corcodilos (also known as "Ask the Headhunter" at www.asktheheadhunter.com) said it best: "The 'hidden job market' is hidden only from people who have their heads stuck in the want ads and Internet job postings." Although Nick takes a fairly aggressive approach to job hunting (see Figure 11.1), he does have some valid points when it comes to the effectiveness of the various ways we look for jobs. His views come from being on the inside of an employer's hiring perspective, and from going out and finding (headhunting) prime candidates to bring back to employers. His livelihood centers around getting jobs filled.

Even if you haven't started looking for a job, the best time to start networking is now. If you have started looking for your dream job and your techniques aren't producing the results you want, it's time to re-examine your approach and ask for help from your networking contacts.

So, to answer the question, "Where are all those jobs hidden?" They're not hidden at all. You just won't find all the jobs openings at online job sites or in the newspapers. You have to go straight to the source to find them.

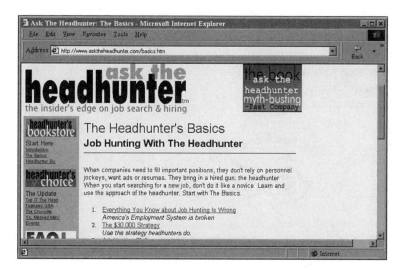

Figure 11.1
Visit Ask the Headhunter for an insider's advice on how to get the job you want. If you're putting all your eggs in the online job site basket, you'll be shocked at the missed opportunities that come from networking!

The Power of Networking

If you don't already realize it, you network every day. When you ask your buddy where he takes his car for brake work, you're networking. If your buddy doesn't know a good brake shop, he gives you the name of someone who does. So, why not do the same thing to learn about careers or job opportunities?

Career networking can do several things to aid you in your job hunt. First, you can gather information and get advice to direct your efforts in a more productive fashion (like not wasting time blasting your résumé all over the Web in hopes that someone, somewhere finds you). You can also ask for advice on ways to best present yourself to potential employers.

Second, networking can lead to introductions to the real decision-makers in companies. That sure beats the pants off going through the black hole of human resource departments or "throwing your hat" into a huge pile of résumés.

Third, networking might get your foot in the door before the job you want ever opens up, which gives you a huge competitive advantage. Why would an employer post a job opening if he's already got a handful of qualified candidates waiting for a call? Sometimes, getting a job is a matter of being in the right place at the right time, and in the hiring cycle, that means being there before the job is advertised to the general public.

Finally, when an insider recommends you or offers a stamp of approval on your ability to do the job, it adds to your credibility and helps the hiring manager make the decision on who's best qualified for the job. Imagine the moment of decision: "Should I hire Joe Blow whose résumé I plucked off the Web and met only one time for a 30-minute interview, or should I hire Jane Doe, who has the same credentials, but comes highly recommended by a colleague I know and trust?"

Get Your Networking Feet Wet

I strongly recommend all job seekers become members (for free!) at WetFeet.com (www.wetfeet.com), a career research portal and a place to get great advice on networking, interviewing—even getting dressed. Articles and insider reports are provided by WetFeet.com career experts and in-the-know folks such as Dick Bolles, author of *What Color Is Your Parachute?* Of particular interest to job hunters is the "WetFeet.com Insider's Guide to Getting Your Ideal Job: Networking, Interviewing, and Landing Your Job Offer." It's a hefty guide to help you land the job you want—your dream job.

How to Expand Your Career Network

A network is more than casual acquaintances and chance encounters. It includes your family and friends, neighbors, vendors, colleagues, classmates, co-workers, clients, and the fellow standing behind the coffee counter. Really, it's anyone you know, online and in person.

In career networking, the goal is to turn your circle of friends and associates into a group of people who can provide you with information, referrals to a larger network, and exposure to job possibilities. These people are the eyes and ears you need to keep you up to speed on what's going on in the industry or job field you're trying to crack.

But networking is not a foolproof technique, and there's always the chance that some of the people you call on for help won't want to talk to you. But don't worry about that just yet. The first thing to do is make a list of your network community including friends and family, as well as professional associates—everyone you know in your industry or profession, including vendors, clients, newsgroup participants you've had direct correspondence with, and co-workers.

Thanks for the Tip

Top 10 Tactics for Online Networking

So, you're in a big hurry and you want to know NOW about networking: what you need to do, how to do it, and when to do it. You're in luck; AltaVista has a Top 10 list of tactics to network your way to a good job, courtesy of WorkLife Solutions. Get the quick skinny at altavistacareers.com/networking.html.

Make a List of Networking Contacts

It helps if you know people in high places, but don't be discouraged if your first stab at compiling a list of networking contacts consists of your Aunt Connie, your next-door neighbor, your parole officer, and the coordinator at the shelter where you volunteer once a week.

Don't forget about people who work in the service industry such as bartenders, waitresses, concierges, hairdressers, and the like. These folks come in contact with a wide variety of people and are generally friendly and well-liked by their customers and clientele. Even if they don't know someone directly who can help you in your job search, they probably know someone who does. If nothing else, they can mention casually as they pour another stiff martini, "Oh, my buddy Dave, who, next to you, is my favorite customer, is about to be downsized from his job in advertising. Know anyone who works in that field?"

So, maybe you should take a martini-induced referral with a grain of salt (or is that the tequila-induced referral?), but the point is, the more people who have their "feelers" out to help you, the better your chances are of getting a good lead.

So, you're off to a good start. Although these contacts might not be able to point you directly to a hot new job, they might be able to review your résumé, offer ideas on how to improve your presentation, recommend how and where to look for a job, refer you to people they know who have friends in high places, or simply encourage you while you look for a job.

Next, make a list of people you want to contact to induct into your networking community—vendors, clients, valued customers, bosses, managers, co-workers, members of professional associations, college professors, and anyone else you can think of. While you're at it, jot down phone numbers and email addresses, activity, and follow-up action items.

Avoid the embarrassment of double-calling or missing an opportunity because you forgot to call or lost a number—it's hard to be organized when you're keeping track of slips of paper or matchbooks with scribbled phone numbers. Figure 11.2 is an example of how to organize and track your networking contact activity.

Figure 11.2

A networking contact and tracking sheet can help you stay focused and organized as you go about making calls, setting up meetings, and to make sure you follow through with thank-you notes and other communications.

network tracking sheet - Microsoft Word

File Edit View Insert Format Tools Table Window Help

Networking Contact and Tracking Sheet

Name	Phone/Address	Email	Contacted Date	Referred By	Response	Follow-Up Action Items
Sis Jones	555-1234	carol@email.com	1/12/00	Carol	Meet for lunch	Sent thank you, confirm lunch date
Skip Townsend	555-1232	skip@marketing.com	1/13/00	Brad the Bartender	Will do info. Interview	Call him 1/20/00
Mary Smith	555-1098	msmith@work.com	1/13	Aunt Connie	Will answer email questions	Send her an email, thank you

Page 1 Sec 1 1/1 At 3.5" Ln 14 Col 1

Making First Contact

So, you've got a list of professional networking contacts, but how do you approach them to ask for help? Don't run up to them and say, "Wanna help me find a job?" Career networking is something that should be approached tactfully and with gratitude every step of the way. Don't be demanding, desperate, or deceitful. You're asking for help, so be gracious, prepared, and direct. Most important, know what you're asking for before you pick up the phone or send off an email.

The Extra Mile

1 KLM.

Make It Easy to Help

After you make a list of networking contacts, decide which ones are in the best positions to help in your job search. Then, send them a copy of your résumé, and a brief summary statement that they can use if they need to make a call or speak on your behalf.

First contact by phone could go something like this:

"Hi, Carol. I'm finally ready to throw in the towel at ABC, just like you told me to do two years ago. I was wondering if I could take you to lunch and pick your brain about ideas on where to look, what to include in my portfolio, and find out what you know about the industry in terms of job outlook and trends in the world of advertising? Don't worry—I'm not asking you to hire me. It's just been so long since I've had to pound the pavement that I was hoping you might know some people or have ideas on who's hiring."

So, you take Carol to lunch and she makes your day by telling you that her brand-new sister-in-law was just promoted at one of the best agencies in town.

Carol then jots down Sis's direct number and email and urges you to call, and to use her name as an icebreaker. "She might not be able to get you a job there, but she does know a lot more about what's going on in agencies around town than I do. She's on the board of the local advertising association."

Don't expect all your networking meetings to go exactly like that, but those kinds of conversations are worth more than a hundred listings at a job site. Trust me. Networking works.

Getting Closer to the Decision Maker

So, you've got Sis's number in your hot little hand. Pick up the phone and give her a call. Your conversation can start off with an introduction like this:

"Hi, Sis. It's Julia Cardis. I worked with Carol at ABC for a number of years and she suggested I contact you about getting a little insider advice. She tells me you were just promoted at your agency and that you're very familiar with the local agency scene through your involvement with the ad association. She says you're the one who knows what's what and who's who.

"I'm ready to move on from ABC, where I've been a copywriter for the last six years. As you're probably aware, ABC is going through some major restructuring right now, and I feel it's time to explore opportunities elsewhere. I'm most interested in agencies that are branching out into new media, so I'm hoping I could set up a brief meeting with you to discuss which agencies are expanding in that area, and whom I should contact. I'd also be thrilled if you could look at some of my portfolio samples and recommend my strongest samples."

At this point, Sis is flattered that you've turned to her for advice, and is willing to help because Carol recommended you to her. She agrees to a lunch meeting the following week.

But what if your networking contacts live in a different city, or come to you via the World Wide Web? No problem. Instead of taking someone to lunch, offer to return the favor—either by sharing your expert knowledge on a related or unrelated topic, or by letting it be known that you understand the concept of "You scratch my back—I'll scratch yours."

In email, your tone and attitude need to convey that you appreciate and respect the person's time and expertise, and that you aren't relying on them completely to help you find your next job. Neediness turns people off more than anything, so being focused and direct about your request, and starting your networking before the need arises increases the effectiveness of your contact with these people. Be sure to read Chapter 7, "The E-Cover Letter," for ideas on how to write networking emails.

Networking with Current Employees

Am I kidding? Do I really think you can call your target company and ask to speak to someone in the department you're trying to get a job in? Absolutely! Getting a feel from the front lines about a target employer will not only answer important questions about company culture and working conditions, but you'll also be better prepared for the interview.

Just how do you go about doing this? It's not as hard as it sounds, but there are some do's and don'ts when it comes to talking directly with insiders at your target company. Know the rules of the game before you go to bat, and you'll come out far, far ahead of your competition.

If you don't want to take this proactive approach to networking, there are companies such as Vault.com (www.vault.com) that conduct interviews such as these with real people at real companies. The only problem is they haven't so far provided profiles for every company in the world, and probably won't ever do so. If your target company is on their list of insider reports, you're in luck, though. If nothing else, read the interviews to get a better idea of how to conduct yourself when you go to do "deep research" on your target companies and network with the troops. You can even get samples of cover letters, emails, and follow-up communications for every step of the way.

How and When to Do It

You can network with current employees before you send in your résumé. Simply scour the company Web site for an employee roster or call the company and ask the receptionist to speak to someone in the marketing department, for example. Start by introducing yourself and explain that you're in the planning stages of job hunting and have learned of an opening in the company. Then, ask the person for a few minutes of time to answer a few quick questions.

Or, if you don't know of a job opening, explain that you're researching the profession and would like a few minutes to get expert advice about trends, opportunities, and strategies for breaking into the field.

Another way to meet employees at your target company is to locate newsgroups or discussion forums that employees of your target company might participate in. Large companies such as Microsoft or AT&T are popular topics in several online communities. (Read on about locating newsgroup networking contacts.)

You'll be surprised how many people are willing to help and are downright enthusiastic about being asked for their opinion on the "state of the nation" at their company. You can even do this via email, although it's advised you communicate through non-work email accounts. If the person has no other email account outside of work, definitely try to talk to them at home or at a remote phone location. Heck, you can even invite them to lunch to do your snooping.

The Extra Mile

Get the Scoop Before You Sign

You can and should ask after a successful first interview for the name of someone in the department to speak with about the details and intimacies of working in that department. Unless the employer has something to hide, they'll gladly give you the name of a manager, peer, or other insider to speak with.

What to Ask

Be prepared with a list of questions. Don't ask outright for negative information, but be prepared to deal with negative feedback. If you happen to connect with a disgruntled employee, take their insight with a grain of salt and try to determine whether the problems are related to the way the company is run, or whether the person just doesn't deal well with authority. And always try to get more than one opinion for a more balanced perspective. You don't have to talk to three people in the same department, but conduct your informational interviews with a variety of people in different levels of authority for the broadest view of life in a given industry.

Here are some sample questions to ask your employee insider:

Can you describe the corporate culture?

How many hours a week do you work?

Do you get along well with managers and owners?

Do you have the support and resources you need to excel in your job?

How are performance reviews and promotions handled?

What's your favorite part of the job?

What's the biggest challenge?

Would you encourage a friend to apply for a job at your company?

How long have you been there?

What is the management structure like?

Is there anything I should know before I send my résumé?

Does the decision-maker have any likes or dislikes I should know about?

What's the average length of tenure?

Other Networking Resources

When you're working on developing your networking contacts, don't forget about your college buddies—alumni associations are excellent places to look for people with insider knowledge in a variety of industries. Hopefully, the folks you went to school with went on to enjoy successful careers, so call on them for networking help. Don't focus your search on people in your graduating class, either. The common thread is your alumni status, so if you peruse an alumni directory and see that Tom Smith, Class of '59, is president or CEO of a company similar to your target company, send him a quick email and ask for an informational interview.

To access alumni associations online, go to a meta search engine such as Google (www.google.com) or Dogpile (www.dogpile.com) and do a search using the keywords *alumni association directory* or the name of your alma mater and *alumni association*. You'll most likely have to register to access the member listing, but that's no big deal when you think about the networking potential of people who think their fellow alums are as smart as they are!

It's amazing how much networking can de done through this channel. I visited the Indiana University Alumni Association (see Figure 11.3) and found a list of pubs and meeting places across the country where IU fans gather to watch football games. All sorts of alumni clubs in larger cities gather to…network, catch up on old times, and oftentimes watch sports events. A great opportunity for meeting people, and some added value for all that money you spent on your college education.

Figure 11.3

The Indiana University Alumni Association Web site includes alumni directories, news and events, and a directory of Hurryin' Hoosier hangouts across the country.

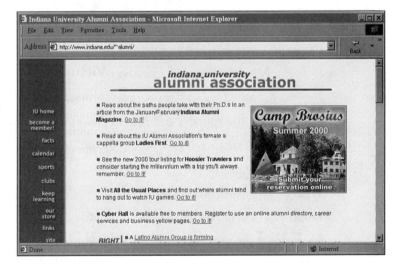

Mastering the Art of Online Networking

You don't need a network of a hundred chat room buddies to have an effective online network. The focus is on the quality of those relationships, and that's something that takes time to cultivate. You also can't expect to "connect" with everyone you meet online, and the chances of meeting a lot of people are good, so focus on a small group of people who interest you, and who bring value to the online community.

To cultivate online relationships, look for discussion forums or newsgroups that you have a personal or professional interest in. You don't have to visit these forums every day, but ongoing participation will help foster relationships and give you a better chance to keep up to speed with what's being discussed, who's contributing, and areas of interest that you can contribute to.

Moral of the story? Start networking now, while you have a job, so that when the time comes to go a-hunting, you'll be much better positioned to ask for help from the people you've identified as having helper-potential. Keep the network alive, too, even after you land a job. You never know what the future holds, and staying in touch allows you to return favors. If you've got a good thing going, don't let it fade away.

Thanks for the Tip

Skip the Meetings: Virtual Associations

No time to attend professional association meetings? No problem. Stay active and in the minds of bigwigs by signing up for emailing lists and discussion forums for your professional association. For a list of online professional associations, do a keyword search using *women in communications listserv* or check Deja.com for newsgroups covering your area of interest.

Watch What You Say!

Keep in mind whenever you post anything online that you're leaving a virtual paper trail everywhere you go of everything you say. If you find yourself in a situation where your contributions or comments are being challenged, resist the urge to fight back. An unsavory online "situation" is nearly impossible to undo, so avoid negative interaction at all costs. If you encounter a difficult situation, it's best to just walk away.

Play by the Rules

To play by the rules of the online networking community, you have to first know what the rules are. Get a refreshing and insightful primer on netiquette from Webmonkey at `hotwired.lycos.com/webmonkey/guides/email/lists.html`.

Where to Network on the World's Largest Network

The Internet is an expansive and expanding domain for all kinds of online communities. Your online networking activity is likely to take place in just a handful of networking forums, which you can participate in anytime of the day or night.

First, you can maintain contact with your business associates through email exchanges. These don't have to be daily events, and you should stick to professional-level information—avoid email chain letters, jokes, and other off-color content. Stick to business. A quick update on your job-hunt progress is appropriate, or sending a Web address of a good online business resource are things you can share through email.

Second, you can participate in newsgroups or other online forums such as chat rooms and message boards. Personally, I've been generally disappointed with unmoderated chat rooms. No matter what the "topic" being discussed, I've always encountered childish babbling taking place. But other chat sites such as Yack! (`www.yack.com`) and Talk City (`www.talkcity.com`) offer generally useful discussions, and plenty of opportunities for meaningful exchange through moderated live chat events with a variety of experts on a number of topics. Figure 11.4 shows chat topics at Talk City.

Message boards, though, are ideal places to track industry trends and "meet" potential networking contacts or locate industry experts. You might even run into people who work at your target companies, so always be on your best behavior. Make sure your postings or comments are professional, to-the-point, and beneficial to the people participating in online communities. And always read the FAQs (frequently asked questions) to make sure you aren't posting questions that have been asked and answered a hundred times before.

Another tip is to "lurk" (look, listen, but don't post) in the online community before you make a post, to get a feel for the group members, their interests, and the style and tone of questions and answers.

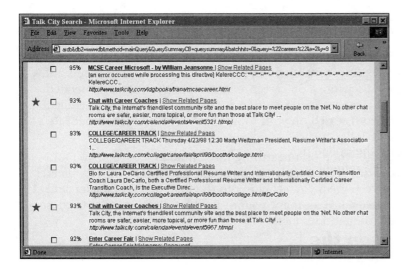

Figure 11.4

Talk City has job-related categories including Business and Professional, as well as live chat sessions with career experts, a special college section, and online career fairs.

Here are some starting points for locating and using newsgroups, chat rooms, or discussion forums.

➤ **Deja.com** (www.deja.com)—Deja.com is host to tens of thousands of newsgroups, so to locate career-related topics quickly, just do a keyword search for topics of interest to you. Some of the more popular job-related forums include biz.jobs.offered, alt.jobs, usjobs.offered, misc.jobs.resumes, and misc.jobs.offered. To locate newsgroups discussing particular companies or employees from particular companies, include the company name in your keyword search.

➤ **Liszt.com** (www.liszt.com)—Liszt.com is a good starting point for locating mailing lists or listservs. These communities function like newsgroups, except that you subscribe to an email list to receive messages in your personal email inbox. You'll find both public and private mailing lists—the public lists are archived online for anyone to see, so watch what you say.

➤ **Reference.com** (www.reference.com)—This powerful search engine will point you in the direction of the many Web forums, newsgroups, chat rooms, and other online communities on the Web. Simply use the pull-down menu on the opening page to look for a specific topic in whatever online community you want to participate. It's one of the best starting points for locating Web forums, which are pretty much the same thing as newsgroups, only less populated.

➤ **Yack!** (www.yack.com)—Yack! guides you in the direction of live Internet events and chats at various places across the Web, such as CNN, Microsoft, Wall Street

Journal, and the Washington Post. Find out what's happening in this ever-expanding world of online events including cybercasts, chats, streaming audio, and streaming video broadcasts.

➤ **Talk City** (www.talkcity.com)—I say skip the unmoderated chat rooms and look for moderated discussions on career-related topics. To locate moderated chat rooms, look in the Live Events section for dates and times of scheduled events, or do a keyword search on your topic of interest. You can also locate discussion forums at Talk City.

So, now that you've got the scoop on unearthing those hidden jobs, and you know how to make friends and influence people, finding your dream job will be a breeze! The Web is a powerful tool to help you get closer to the final decision maker, and at least help you locate people who can point you in the right direction. Get to those hidden jobs before your competition does!

The Least You Need to Know

➤ It's estimated that 80% of jobs are never advertised in newspapers or online job sites.

➤ To get to these jobs, you have to know someone on the inside—networking will help you get your foot in the door.

➤ Expand your career network by putting the word out to nearly everyone you know that you're looking for advice and expert insight on your career of choice.

➤ Conducting an informational interview with a current employee at your target company is an excellent way to get a feel for corporate culture and prepare for the interview.

➤ Newsgroups, mailing lists, discussion forums, and moderated chat rooms can help you locate experts and insiders around the globe.

Part 4

Ready, Set...Hunt! The Online Job Site Landscape

Now that you've done your research, tweaked your résumé, and pinpointed the job or industry you're interested in working in, it's time to put your plan into action. This part of the book covers the various types of job sites and how you can use them to post your résumé, view job openings, find job postings at company Web sites, and get on track for finding your dream job online.

If you're planning on relocating or looking only in your current locale to find the kind of work you're interested in, there are plenty of regional job directories and sites for you. If you do decide to make the move, you'll be glad to know there are lots of tips and tools for relocating, such as calculating your salary requirements based on the cost of living in your new city.

If you want to make a move within your current industry, there are plenty of sites devoted to every type of niche market, such as high tech, new media, finance, marketing, manufacturing, nonprofits, and just about every industry under the sun.

And if it's headhunter or recruiter services you're interested in, you'll gain easy access to these folks through directories and Web sites, and find out when (and if) to use them.

Chapter 12

Starting Points

In This Chapter

➤ Let the Web marketers figure it out—how information and content are shared by Web sites and served to Web users

➤ Using search engine category directories to find career and job sites in a jiffy

➤ Search engines that let you search multiple job site postings simultaneously

➤ The signs of a "good" Web site, and a guide to good Web sites

➤ The crème de la crème of career site guides, and guides to those guides, too

---

Several years ago before the Web became "all the rage," there were estimated to be about 500 career-related sites, including job-posting sites, résumé databases, career expert advice columns, and online newspaper classifieds. Today, there are tens of thousands of Web sites devoted to career development, and unfortunately, not all of them are worth visiting. So, unless you have the time and desire to visit them all, take advantage of directories and gateway sites so you know where to go and what to expect when you get there.

One of my favorite things about the Web is that if you know where to look (or if someone, like me, points you in the right direction), you can tap into directories and gateway sites to save enormous amounts of time when you go online to job hunt. Call it "riding the coattails," call it smart surfing. When someone has gone to the trouble of gathering and reviewing the top job and career sites, why not use these guides to make the most of your online job-hunting and career-development efforts?

This chapter highlights my favorite job-hunting Web site directories and gateways. There are others than what you'll find listed here, but these sites are the best of the best, and should be plenty to get you started using the Web for all your job-hunting needs. Bookmark them all, or bookmark just one—just don't waste time trying to find all this information when the good folks who assembled these directories have already done the legwork for you!

A Brief Lesson on the Ways of the Web

Infoseek, one of my all-time favorite search engines, was acquired by Walt Disney Corporation's Buena Vista Internet Group, and morphed into the GO! Network. Other subsidiaries of BVIG include ABC.com, ABCNEWS.com, Disney.com, DisneyStore.com, toysmart.com, ESPN.com, ESPNStore.com, NFL.com, NBA.com, ABCSports.com, and Family.com, among others. And what does that have to do with search engine directories to help you with your online job hunt? On the surface, it means nothing. When you dig a little deeper, though, some interesting things about Web marketing are revealed.

I'll Support Your Web Site If You Support Mine

First, there's cobranding. This means certain companies align with one another to swap content, information, resources, and market share. What does this have to do with your job search? Well, for example, when you visit the GO! Career center, you see a big, fat link to CareerPath.com, which is one of the most popular job sites on the Web. Yeah, so? When you search for job listings from the GO! Career Center, you're actually searching job listings at another site. Logic would tell you that now you don't need to visit CareerPath.com directly to peruse the job postings.

Affiliate, powered by, featured sponsors, network members, partners—all the telltale signs of a cobranded Web site. Don't waste time spinning your wheels visiting a bunch of different job sites when the content comes from the same source!

I'll Pay to Advertise My Site on Your Site

Another thing about Web marketing you'll need to know is called "push technology." That's when you're presented with quick and easy access to related information or goods and services you "need." It's kind of like the "impulse items" you decide to buy while standing in line at the grocery store. You didn't think you needed a *TV Guide*, but the cover story looked so interesting you decided to toss it on the conveyor belt. Or, you actually needed batteries or a pack of gum, and if these items hadn't been staring you in the face, you would have forgotten to buy them. Thanks, grocery store man, for "pushing" those items our way!

In the world of the Web, this takes shape in the form of all those sidebars (see Figure 12.1) you see after doing a keyword search—say, for example, on something like African killer bees: "Find books on African killer bees at bn.com."

Thanks for the Tip

What Else Is Shared?

When you're dealing with job sites that have alliances and partnerships with other sites, be sure to read the fine print to find out whether all the network members have access to any personal information you supply. For example, if you post your résumé to a database site, do the partners of that site also have access to your résumé? Look for partner logos or a link that describes the network. Find out who belongs to the network and whether your résumé or personal information is shared. After all, knowingly giving your personal information to one site is up to you. When it's shared without your knowledge or consent, your privacy is compromised. If you have to email or call the site administrator to find out about the sharing of information with partners, do so.

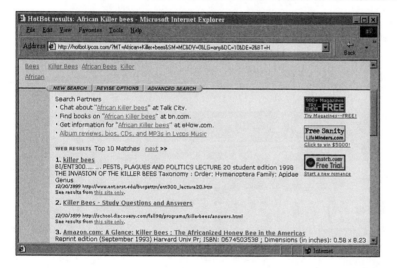

Figure 12.1

After doing a keyword search for beekeeping jobs, the results page had a link to Barnes and Noble's Web site, where I could shop for books about bees, beekeeping, and African killer bees.

The way Barnes and Noble's sees it, it's a good idea to remind Web users that for every topic you research online, including African killer bees, there's probably a book about it. And you can order that book online from the Barnes and Noble Web site. Amazon.com does this, too, as well as countless other commercial Web sites.

My point is that as you go about your online job hunt, be aware of partnerships, alliances, cobranding agreements, cross-marketing, and partnerships. Not only will you save time by not revisiting the "same job site, different name," you can take advantage of this networking by being "led" to related information that the cobranding partners or advertisers think you should know about.

Go the Search Engine Route

Search engines today are much more than tools to find random documents on the Web. The most popular engines also feature Web directories of the most popular topics of interest to Web surfers, such as business, economy, entertainment, news, sports, travel, and careers. To get a feel for what's out there to help you in your job search and career development, check out the directory listings at your favorite search engine. Many of the listings are hand-picked and reviewed by a team of editors, and often feature short descriptions of what you'll find when you visit.

Search Engine Partnerships

After you've spent some timeon the Web, you'll start to notice alliances and partnerships among search engines. This can be very useful if the results from a simple search at Yahoo!, for example, doesn't bring back the results you need. On your results page, there's a link that lets you automatically try your search at a host of other search engines, as shown in Figure 12.2.

For example, I did an advanced search at Yahoo! to find beekeeper jobs. I got one solid result, and a handful of semirelated results. So, I opted to redo the search one by one at AltaVista (www.altavista.com), HotBot (hotbot.lycos.com), and Northern Light (www.northernlight.com). I got the same results. I then did the same search at Lycos (www.lycos.com) and got 104 results.

Figure 12.2

If you don't get the results you want on the first try at Yahoo!, put another search engine to work with the click of a mouse. Yahoo! links you to AltaVista, Direct Hit, GoTo.com, Infoseek, and other popular search engines.

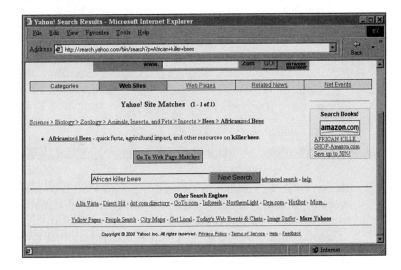

The difference is the Lycos search brought back documents containing either "bee-keeper" or "beekeeper jobs." And that's a good thing, because I found links to bee-keeper associations, news reports on beekeeping, the beekeeping profession, and a link to Bee Culture Magazine. From there, I got a list of who's who in the beekeeping industry and the latest industry "buzz," searchable by location and field of study or associations.

Become a Fast and Savvy Searcher

To learn more about getting the most from your online research and using search engines, be sure to check out Search Engine Watch (www.searchenginewatch.com). The site is used by Webmasters, Web marketers, and others involved with creating and promoting Web sites.

Then, there are search engine users—researchers, librarians, and general Web surfers who want to know how to make the most of their online research. Be sure to read the section on reviews, ratings, and testing of search engines (www.searchenginewatch.com/reports/index.html), which provides a list of comparison reviews, shows which search engines are most popular, and has tests and statistics on how well search engines work.

Even if you're a veteran Web surfer, there's no harm in polishing your Web-searching skills. The technology changes so rapidly that a search technique that worked last year might not bring you the results you want today. Then, there are meta search engines that integrate the results of the most powerful search engines so you can do one-stop searching. Examples of meta search engines include Northern Light (www.northernlight.com) and Dogpile (www.dogpile.com).

Top Search Engine Directories of Career Sites

This is a short list of my favorite search engine directories. This doesn't mean you won't find other directories such as AltaVista, HotBot, or AOL to be just as good. In fact, you might want to spend a little time reviewing each one to compare content and resources. Whichever one is most closely related to your online job-searching needs, use it.

Yahoo! Employment and Work

Yahoo!'s content directories are easy to navigate, intelligently indexed, and constantly expanding. Current offerings in the Employment and Work section include such topics as jobs, career fields, companies, cultures and groups, employment law, organizations, recruiting and placement, salary information, telecommuting, and unemployment resources, among others. Scan the complete listing at (dir.yahoo.com/Business_and_Economy/Employment_and_Work/).

You can also check out Yahoo! Careers (www.careers.yahoo.com), which is a collection of job-hunting advice, career tools, and weekly features from content providers such as WetFeet.com, Ask the Headhunter, and Working Wounded. Daily articles from Wall Street Journal Careers is another value-add of this subsite of Yahoo! Besides being able to search job postings at partner site Career Mosaic, you can upload your résumé, get salary information and negotiation guidance, access relocation resources, and research companies.

GO! Network

Peruse the directory listings at (www.go.com/Center/Careers) to tap into job sites covering résumés (how to write them, where to post them, and where to get professional help), jobs (entry-level all the way to executive, regional job sites, online newspaper classifieds, and occupational information), tips and advice (salary information, job interview tips, cover letters, and self-employment). You can also connect to job postings, get tips and advice, or post your résumé at CareerPath.com.

Lycos (`dir.lycos.com/Business/Jobs/`)

The Lycos Network, which includes HotBot, Webmonkey, Suck, WhoWhere, Tripod, and a host of other top-o'-the-heap Web communities and content providers, is a good starting point for your online job-hunting needs. The Jobs section includes links to sites that have been hand-picked and reviewed by a team of editors, including a Careers section, a job-site section, and niche and regional job sites as well.

I personally don't think it's the friendliest search engine-based directory out there, but after you get familiar with the navigation and content design, you'll find it a useful starting point when you go online to find your dream job.

When You're Hot, You're Hot

Go2Net Network's 100hot (www.100hot.com/directory/business/jobs.html) lists the 100 "Hottest" job and career sites on the Web. How do they determine who's hot and who's not? 100hot collects data on a daily basis from many different sources, representing the Web-surfing patterns of more than 100,000 surfers worldwide, including universities, businesses, and home users. Popularity doesn't always mean quality, but in my review of the 100 hottest job and career sites, I can't argue with the rankings.

A Guide to Career Guides

Come on, already! A guide to guides? Yes, that's exactly what the Argus Clearinghouse provides you with, and it's a good place to learn about what makes any Web site good, not just job sites. Some online directories and gateways are mere compilations and reviews of the most popular sites, and as we all know from having tossed out our own parachute pants and acid-washed jeans, that popularity does not last. There's always a new, faster, better, smarter whippersnapper that comes along and takes over as the hot, new, revolutionary site—"finally, the answer to all your job-hunting prayers."

The Makings of a "Good" Web Site

I strongly recommend you take a look at the Argus Clearinghouse (www. clearinghouse.net) before you spend a lot of time at any Web site. Sometimes when you find a "good" Web site, you can't really pinpoint what makes it good or why you like it. After you read these reports, though, you'll know what to look for when you judge whether to spend your time (or dollars) at a Web site. The lingo and review evaluation criteria are rather fancy-schmancy, but these brief explanations help make sense of the Argus reports and their evaluation criteria.

Guides that have been accepted by the Argus Clearinghouse are rated on the following five criteria, and receive a rating of 1 to 5 checks for each criterion. Then, an overall score is obtained by averaging the guide's score on these five criteria:

➤ **Level of Resource Description**—This can include the site description or "Welcome" copy you read upon entering a site or in the "About" section. It explains what information (content, tools, resources) the site contains, how to use the site, who should use it, and how often the site is updated.

➤ **Level of Resource Evaluation**—The Clearinghouse reviewer looks at the quality of the content, such as whether a message board contains helpful information and meaningful exchange, and an assessment of the credibility of the site author or content provider. For example, a personal home page that had opinions, views, or questionable sources (an interview with a disgruntled employee) about life in the working world wouldn't fare well in this category. In terms of commercial sites, sometimes the content is biased toward a paid sponsor or advertiser. This, too, would affect the rating in resource evaluation. This criterion also takes into account how readable a page is in terms of design and organization.

➤ **Guide Design**—Does the page download quickly? Are the images necessary and attractive? Is there an appropriate use of headlines and subheads for quick scanning? Is it easy to get around, and do you always have a sense of where you are when using the guide?

➤ **Guide Organizational Schemes**—There's more than one way to organize information, and the more ways, the better. Guides can be organized by subject (careers can be broken down into job postings, résumé resources, salary guides, industry profiles, company information), format (Web-site links, mailing list links, discussion board links), audience (job seekers or recruiters), chronology (most recent job postings), geography (regional guides), and by author (career advice columnists).

It's a Keeper

To add a Web site to your Favorites folder (Internet Explorer), click on the **Favorites** pull-down menu and select Add Page to Favorites. In Netscape, click the **Bookmarks** pull-down menu and select **Add to Bookmarks**.

➤ **Guide Meta-Information**—Meta-information is information about other information, kind of like a guide about a guide! In this case, meta-information describes the guide itself, and includes things such as the guide mission (why it was created, what it contains and doesn't contain), how the information was gathered, information about the author or editor (expertise, knowledge of and experience with the subject), how to contact the site and submit feedback, and how often the site is updated.

By all means, don't disregard or disown a Web site if it doesn't meet these standards. Just keep this evaluation tool in mind when you decide what to add to your Bookmarks or Favorites folder. And, admittedly, some of the other directory and gateway sites I list throughout this chapter probably wouldn't fare well in an Argus Clearinghouse review. The point, though, is to help Web users be smarter surfers—to save time and get to the best sources of information without having to kiss a lot of frogs along the way.

The Argus Clearinghouse Guide to Business and Employment Sites

The Argus Clearinghouse also deals with such topics as careers, compensation, employment, jobs, labor, résumés, temporary employment, and workweek reduction. To access the Business and Employment Guide reviews, start at the main page (www.clearinghouse.net) and click through to Business and Employment, and then the Employment subcategory. Here, you have the option to read reviews of guides dealing with an individual's work, the overall state of the nation on getting jobs, and resources for the job seeker. Subsubcategories include careers, compensation, employment (general), jobs, labor, and résumés.

Notable sites reviewed by Argus include myjobsearch.com, Bay Area Jobs (www.bayareajobs.com), Westech Virtual Job Fair (www.incpad.com), Space Careers (www.spacejobs.com), and the Riley Guide (www.rileyguide.com). So, if you're looking for a second opinion, check out what the Argus folks have to say about these sites.

Gateway Sites

Sometimes, no matter how cool and savvy you are with search engines, you just get too darned many results. Why go through the hassle of trying to find what you're looking for when someone else has already figured that out for you? Gateway sites are listings of the most useful career-related sites, and are usually reviewed before being added to the guide listing. Here are some of the best job-hunter gateway sites on the Web.

Job Source Network

From the publishers of *Job Source San Francisco* and *Job Source Los Angeles*, go to www.jobsourcenetwork.com and check out what this impressive one-stop job-search site has to offer. Job sites are broken down by industry, profession, and location; general, popular, and niche job sites; company sites; résumé services; internships; executive job sites; recruiters and job fairs; associations; newspapers; college and university sites, and more.

And through a partnership with Job-Search-Engine (see the following site description) and Job Sleuth, you can search the major job sites with one fell swoop.

Job-Search-Engine.com

Wouldn't it be great if you could search all the job sites without having to visit each one? Well, now you can. Job-Search-Engine (www.jobsearchengine.com) lets you create a search and retrieve a listing of positions from most of the top job-search sites, using a simple search for keywords, job location (U. S. state or Canadian province), and which job sites you want to search—up to 10 at any one time. You'll get plenty of results, as shown in Figure 12.3, but the number of results is approximate, because certain sites indicate only ">25 results," and job sites such as Yahoo! Classifieds feature some overlap with sites like Career Mosaic.

Use the advanced search tool to select the job sites most suited to your job search, and if you have a slow Internet connection, increase the "time out" to 50 seconds. Otherwise, the engine searches for only 15 seconds and won't have time to visit all the sites you select. Or, decrease the number of sites being searched.

Any way you slice it, you can save lots of time by shopping for jobs from this super-search site. The Resource Center also provides links to other career sites, industry- and job-specific sites, and job-related newsgroups, and professional services, such as fee-based résumé-writing services.

Figure 12.3

Job-Search-Engine.com retrieves matches from up to 10 of the most popular job-posting sites and returns them in an easy-to-use table format.

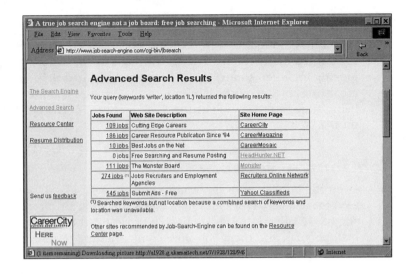

My Job Search

I nearly fell out of my chair the first time I visited this site. I wept tears of joy. I thanked my lucky stars. So, what's so great about it?

My Job Search lists links galore and detailed reviews of the top career sites. Another guide to guides like the Argus Clearinghouse? Well, not exactly. My Job Search is a much, much larger gateway, and the reviews are presented in a one-page table format for easy comparison, as seen in Figure 12.4.

Thanks for the Tip

User Services?

Myjobsearch.com reviewers look for additional user services when evaluating job sites—résumé posting, directly emailed "search agent" results, and job-search advice, as well as registration requirements for use of those services, and how long it takes to register.

Career sites are reviewed by third parties who are not employees of myjobsearch.com and are not affiliated with any career site. Reviews are presented using a four-star rating system, and the Overall Rating is derived from the ratings of three categories: search engine, design/ease of use, and user services. The overall rating also reflects the number and newness of available job postings, along with the likelihood of posted résumés being seen by potential employers. That's what I like to hear!

A big difference between myjobsearch.com and Argus Clearinghouse is the attention to the search features at each job site. For example, at some sites you can search by job title, keyword, or location. At other sites, you can search by salary range, industry, location, and job title. It makes a difference in the quality and quantity of job matches, so pay attention to this part of the review.

I really like this site, and suggest you take a peek at the reviews before you decide which job sites to use or where to post your résumé. In addition to links and site reviews, the job seeker resources and tools are top-notch.

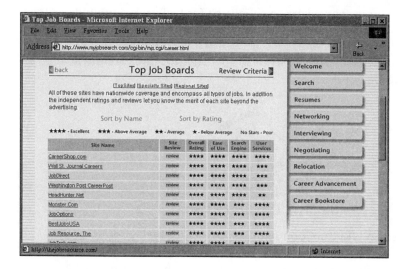

Figure 12.4

Myjobsearch.com reviews are presented in easy-to-read tables for comparisons, with links to detailed reviews of the most popular job sites.

Careerxroads

At the time of this writing, the online version of the most popular print directory and review of the 500 best online career sites was not up and running. I did speak with Mark Mehler, coauthor of the previously mentioned book, and he expects the site to be fully operational in the spring of 2000. The site that's up now (www.careerxroads.com) features reviews, accolades, and ordering information for the book (which, by the way, you should order for yourself), as well as a place for readers to sign up for email notification of updates to the print version. A very nice feature, and something you wish every book publisher would do, especially books dealing with the Web. As we all know, the world of the Web is like life as a dog—for every year in "real time," the Web lives seven.

Look for this soon-to-be-launched gateway site to be a mover and shaker in helping online job seekers get to the good stuff fast!

The Riley Guide

The Riley Guide's A-Z directory (www.dbm.com/jobguide/ or www.rileyguide.com) categorizes and links to every conceivable employment resource on the Net. A real gem for those new to the online job hunt, site creator and maintainer Margaret Dikel is a pioneer in the online job-site world. She takes a common-sense approach to explaining career and Web terminology, and what career services are offered to job seekers. This graphics-free, no-frills collection is an endless resource and includes links to recruiters, regional and international resources, and industry-specific sites, as well as resources for women, minorities, and other underrepresented groups. Every job seeker, entry-level to executive, in every industry, will find something here.

Margaret Dikel personally reviews each site submitted for inclusion, and updates the information on a regular basis. Although you might find the enormous amount of information hard to digest and filter at first, it's worth a few minutes to read through the contents to get a better sense of the scope of this one-stop site. Definitely a bookmark-worthy starting point.

Same Site, Different URL

Have you ever typed an URL (uniform resource locator, or Web address) and a different URL appeared in the location bar on your Web browser? You were redirected to an alternative or primary Web address that contains the same content as the address you typed. Why is this? Well, some savvy Web marketers use different URLs for marketing purposes, and sometimes, the Web address simply changes. It's like forwarding mail when you move, or having your calls forwarded to a new phone number.

Job-Hunt

After a brief hiatus, Job-Hunt (www.job-hunt.org) is back and better than before! Organized categories, a quick-load time, and weekly updates make this site worth coming back for more. Not only are the content areas neatly organized, you get a short list of the best starting points for job seekers who are new to the Web, plus brief but descriptive summaries of each site's content. Considering there are thousands of links listed here, that's no small feat.

Definitely worth bookmarking for future reference.

Okay, comrades. Now that you know where to go to get started on putting your job-hunting plan into action, and have expert advice and reviews to guide you in your choice of job sites, it's time to get down to business! The following chapters describe mega job sites such as Monster.com, plus other noteworthy job-hunter sites such as regional guides, niche sites that list jobs only in specific industries or professions, and where to go to find recruiters.

The Least You Need to Know

➤ Through alliances and partnerships, some job sites provide job-posting search features at search engines or other Web portals—look for alliances so you don't duplicate your efforts.

➤ Search engines feature category directories of career-related Web sites and are good starting points for your online job hunt.

➤ Gateway sites are guides to the best of the best, or the most popular, job-related sites and are often hand-picked and reviewed so you know what to expect at job sites.

➤ There are even guides to job-site guides that provide quick and informative descriptions of site features, intended users, and number of postings.

I SEE A SITE !!

Chapter 13

Mega Sites

In This Chapter

➤ How to pick the mega job site that's right for you

➤ Features, highlights, and tips for making the most out of your time at the most popular job sites

➤ How to make job search engines work for you

➤ Job sites that have personal job agents to bring job matches to your email inbox instead of going out and hunting all the time

One thing can be said about the online job hunt: People are looking for jobs, and jobs are looking for people. The problem, though, is the "needle-in-the-haystack" syndrome; no one knows exactly where the perfect candidates are looking or exactly where the perfect jobs are hidden. It's mayhem, it's confusing, and it's mind-boggling to try to figure out which job site is the best one to use to find that elusive dream job.

Even worse, it's hard to know whether the job posting you find at one site might come up in a search at an entirely different site, or whether it's the same one you find posted at an employer's Web site. It's confusing, darn it! You have to pay attention, and most of us aren't very good at that anymore. We've got speed on the brain— "Must post résumé. Must find job now." Slow down, take your time, and pick the job site that's right for you. And what better place to start than a "mega" site?

How to Find the Job Site That's Right for You

Job hunting is a time-consuming process, although going online is a great way to save time and gain wider access to a larger number of available jobs. If you read Chapter 3, "Getting Ready: Get Organized and Develop a Plan of Action," then you know why it's important to decide on a strategy before you even worry about which job site to use. If you haven't read that chapter, I encourage you to read through it now.

After you've decided on your strategy, though, and if part of your strategy involves using the mega job sites to look for jobs, then you need to know which site to use based on your particular needs. The problem, however, is that I can't tell you which site to use because I don't know a darned thing about you—what kind of job you want, how much experience you have, how important confidentiality is, how soon you need the job, and whether you're willing to relocate.

What I can do is give you an overview of the major job sites and highlight the résumé features, privacy options, job search engine pros and cons, and generally describe each site's virtues and weak points. From there, you can decide which one is most suited to your needs. You might even decide that you need to visit and register as a user at all of them to get the broadest coverage ("Fire Hose Technique") for your job-search efforts.

You might just decide after visiting these mega job sites that the best thing for you is to focus your efforts on regional job sites or industry-specific niche sites, such as those discussed in Chapter 15, "Regional Guides," and Chapter 16, "Finding Industry-Specific Sites." I simply can't recommend any one technique over the other without knowing more about you, the reader.

Keep Track of Your Online Job-Hunting Activities

I can tell you one thing: It's very, very important that you keep close track of all your online job-hunting activities, as you'll discover along the way that employers and recruiters use many different sites to post jobs and find applicants. A job posting you find at Monster.com (www.monster.com) could be the exact same job posting you'll find at another mega site such as Career Builder (ms.careerbuilder.com). Don't spin your wheels, and don't waste time and make a fool of yourself by applying for the same job twice. Read the postings carefully, make printouts of every job you apply for, and pay attention to what you do.

If you skipped the first part of this book, which is all about prehunting preparation and being a smarter job searcher, go back now and read through those chapters. If you know your strategy already and have a solid understanding of how the online job hunt works and you just want to know what to expect at the mega job sites, then go ahead and jump in.

Read the Directions

Either way, be sure to read the "directions" at each job site you visit. Find out how to maximize your job search results using advanced search engine features. Read the privacy and confidentiality policies. Find out how long you can post your résumé, and whether you can remove it after you find a job.

Spending 10 or 15 minutes at each site reading how it works and how to make it work for you isn't going to kill you—it's going to save you time in the long run, and hopefully help you find the best job postings.

My Picks for Top Mega Job Sites (and Why)

The mega job sites reviewed in this chapter and the next were chosen because they meet my very high standards in the areas of design and ease of use; quality, quantity, and variety of job postings; search engine power and ease of use; user services, including job agents, career resources, message boards, and other community-building initiatives; résumé options and privacy policies; and overall quality of the site.

CareerSite (`www.careersite.com`)

Forget the high-dollar advertising campaigns. The site developers at CareerSite have put their money into upgrading and developing a job site that offers both candidates and recruiters a near-perfect solution to the online job hunt.

In terms of résumé-formatting options, confidentiality, and candidate control over the release of information, CareerSite offers users a wide variety of options and control. And the number of job postings and members is growing at a breakneck speed—to the tune of about 15,000 current postings and more than 250,000 registered users. Top this off with one of the smartest job search engines out there, and you've got one heck of a job site.

And taking a look at the featured employer listing, they must be doing something right, or why else would IBM, AT&T, Sun Microsystems, Amazon.com, and Andersen Consulting post jobs here?

Design and Ease of Use

This site is so easy to use, you'd have to be an idiot to get lost! The home page is clean and crisp, and gives users two options: Job seekers go here and employers go here. Cut and dried, eh? After you get inside the site, it's very easy to get around, and the pages download quickly. The site's design is focused on ease of use (no frills or heavy graphics), but this isn't a beauty contest, anyway.

Job Search Engine

CareerSite boasts the smartest search engine around in its Advanced capacity. Entirely keyword-driven, the engine is a thesaurus-based search system that generates synonyms and related keywords that might also come up for the search. Figure 13.1 shows a list of possible keywords and synonyms that employers might use to search for candidates.

Figure 13.1

After completing a keyword summary, the CareerSite keyword generator creates a list of synonyms and keywords that employers commonly use to find candidates—job title, location, and skills criteria.

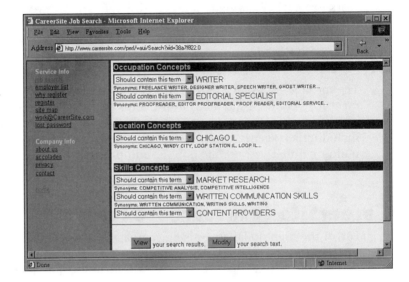

Yeah, what's so special about that? Job titles, skills, and keywords change all the time—what once was called a "customer service representative" is now called a "customer care technician" or "user support specialist." To address this issue in terms of keyword searches, CareerSite employs a keyword guru whose sole purpose in life is to add job-related keywords to the search database.

What this means is that as new buzzwords pop up, if an employer uses a variation of a skills or job title keyword search, you can rest assured that a match will be made even if the new buzzword doesn't appear in your résumé or profile. And if you do a keyword search looking for job postings, the smart search engine delivers matches based on variations of your keyword criteria—not just the words you type into the keyword filter. Pretty smart, eh?

The Quick Job Search function, though, allows you to choose only one location (state or region) and one occupation (from 34 of the most common industries), unlike the Advanced technique that enables you to select more than one criterion at a time for pulling in more results. But, for new users, the Quick Job Search is the recommended technique.

User Services

I love slogans and clichés, and the one that pops into my head every time I visit this site is "Membership has its privileges." When you create a personal profile, you're automatically signed up for emailed search agent results. The brief profile section also works as a temporary "résumé" until you provide a detailed résumé. Have a strong objective statement on hand before you register, and generate a list of keywords and geographic locations you're willing to work in.

Users can also read about registered employers and get links to company Web sites, which saves time in doing company background research, and the Career Resources section offers users links to sites dealing with interviewing, résumés, relocation, career investigation, and everything under the sun that concerns job seekers.

Résumé Options

CareerSite.com's blinded profile and invitation/response system lets you maintain complete control over the release of your identity. After completing your private profile outlining your interests, skills, and preferences, it's added to a database to be searched by employers. If an employer has an opening that matches your profile, the employer contacts CareerSite.com, which in turn confidentially notifies you by email. If you're interested in applying, you can release your identity and résumé with a simple click of the mouse.

Another outstanding feature at CareerSite.com that you won't find at most other job sites is that after you upload your résumé, it's automatically converted to both plain-text format and an Adobe Acrobat file. No other site offers this service, and considering most medium and small employers don't use résumé-tracking software, you might as well take advantage of

Techno Talk

Job Agent 007

A job agent is a "virtual" job scout that notifies you via email when a new job posting matches your pre-determined criteria (job title, geographic region, skills). The concept is based on "push" technology: A Web site pushes information your way based on your preferences and permission to be sent ongoing information, versus your having to revisit a site to see new job postings.

Techno Talk

PDF

Adobe Acrobat is a software application that creates and enables users to read documents that have been saved as PDF files. PDF is a portable document format that can be read by any computer type without losing any formatting or design elements. The software is free, and the employers who subscribe to CareerSite.com will use it to view your résumé if you decide to go with a formatted document. You don't even have to worry about the conversion to PDF—it's done automatically, free of charge.

the opportunity to present a rich-text, formatted document instead of the not-so-sexy, plain-text résumé.

To modify or remove your profile, simply click on the **Members** link and enter your user ID and password. From your personalized **MyCareerSite**, select the appropriate link to edit your profile or submit an updated résumé or make any other changes to your account.

Take Your Pick

When using job-search engines that let you search with multiple criteria, such as location or occupation categories, to select more than one criterion, hold down the **Control** (Windows) or **Command** (Macintosh) key while making selections. Most menus also offer a **Search All Locations** or other general selector that lets you search all locations or all occupations, but you'll get unwieldy results or a message telling you to narrow down your criteria.

Monster.com (www.monster.com)

Everyone knows the Monster. The big, green creature that represents the biggest, most popular, and most populated job site on the Web. With an enormous amount of jobs and an impressive list of employers posting jobs here, this site will probably play some role in your online job hunt. Even if you don't look for jobs here, bookmark this site (www.monster.com) as an ongoing career-development tool. The content is outstanding, and there's something for everyone here. If you're entry-level today, rest assured that as you move into mid-career, the Monster will be there for you.

Maybe you're thinking, "All those jobs...there must be one for me!" Well, you're not the only one thinking that. Lots and lots of job seekers look to Monster.com as a prime source of job leads, so be aware that you're just one of millions of job hunters who come here for the great jobs. If you've read through this book, though, you'll know what it takes to get the attention of employers, so rest assured that if you're looking for a job online, there's a good chance you'll find it at Monster.com.

Users who have been to Monster.com before will rejoice in the newly redesigned and expanded job categories—the site promises "more targeted job searches. Better results." As far as I can tell, they're living up their claim. But be sure to take time to read the job search engine tips and tricks to narrow your results and get matches more suited to your skills, experience, and interests.

Design/Ease of Use

There's nothing scary about Monster.com. A well-designed, logical, and intuitive design makes getting around easy, and quick-loading pages make moving through the site a breeze. And if you do get lost or have questions on how to use the various features in the site, help, tips, and instructions are only a click away.

The only problem I've encountered using the site are error messages that the server is too busy to respond to my job search query. A minor inconvenience, and an indicator of how much traffic the site gets.

Job Search Engine

The job search engine is easy to use, and the newly expanded job category menu offers only 40+ options, and the location filter offers 270 or so U.S. metropolitan areas to help limit your search. You can select up to five in each of the filter categories, and add in keywords to further narrow your results. And if that doesn't work, you can do a subsearch of your results to pinpoint the jobs you're really interested in.

You can also do a search strictly by U.S. city and state, international job postings, or by company, which brings up one of the downsides to Monster.com. A large number of jobs posted here are placed by third-party recruiters such as Management Recruiters International, Manpower, and Hall Kinion. The problem is, you have to go through a middleman, and you don't know what company you're applying to. I find that a little unnerving, but you might not care.

But if a dream job is what you're after, you'd best find out some stuff about the corporate culture and workplace environment before you spend time pursuing opportunities. Of course, a recruiter will argue that all that information will be provided after they see your résumé, but in many ways it's an extra step, and in the job hunt, every move counts. In many cases, though, and at most job sites, recruiters can't be avoided. Just be aware that they're out there, though.

User Services

Hands down, Monster.com has the widest variety of user services, and some of the best original career-related content you'll find at the major job sites—employer information and profiles, newsletters delivered to your email inbox, message boards, career advice, and the Job Search Agent. Monster has your online job-hunt needs covered, but you'll have to register to access some of the tools. Otherwise, much of the content is free to any site visitor. Figure 13.2 shows some of the content areas in the Mid-Career Section of Monster.com.

Improved features include the Letter Management Tool, which stores copies of cover letters you write for the various jobs you apply for online. The improved Résumé Builder allows you to create and store up to five versions of your résumé, and another option allows you to create five different Job Agents.

Figure 13.2

The Mid-Career Section has message boards, chat rooms, expert advice, newsletters, and other career tools for the mid-professional job seeker.

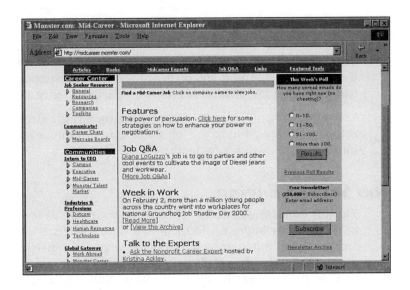

The Job Agent scans new job postings based on your location, occupation category, and keyword criteria, and sends you an email letting you know how many matches have been found. The notice doesn't indicate what the positions are, but a link in the email will take you directly to the results page for quick and easy viewing of job titles, company name, and location. You can choose to have the agent's information emailed to you daily, weekly, biweekly, monthly, or never. If you want to set up an agent and view it from the My Monster site but not receive agent results at your email address, choose "never."

Résumé Options

The Résumé Builder takes you step by step building up to five versions of your online résumé. Although you can create multiple versions, you can choose only one to stay "active" in the database that employers search. You can edit, remove, or add résumés at any time, but posted résumés do expire after one year. Hopefully, your job search won't take that long, but if you're not an active job seeker and are just checking out job sites to see what the possibilities are, this is a nice feature.

As far as résumé privacy goes, your best bet is to not activate your résumé and keep it from the database, as there are no confidential résumé options or any way to block who sees your posting, such as your boss. Use common sense and use only your Monster résumés to apply for jobs instead of posting to the database if privacy is a big concern.

The Extra Mile

1 KLM.

Expert Résumé Advice

Monster.com has an entire section devoted to helping you with your résumé. From résumé makeovers to traditional samples to get you started, this section (`content.monster.com/resume/samples/resumes/`) has something for everyone. If you have a specific question about your résumé, visit the Résumé Expert message board (there's a link from the main résumé page listed previously), and post your question.

CareerBuilder (`http://ms.careerbuilder.com`)

If your goal is to kill as many birds as you can with one site, CareerBuilder.com is the answer to your power-searching prayers—more than 2 million jobs to choose from. This mega site not only has an impressive number of job postings, it also allows you to simultaneously search other job sites using the CareerBuilder job search engine! Another unique feature at this site is the content search engine that helps you find information on CareerBuilder itself. Not many big sites offer you this tool, but if you're stuck, lost, or otherwise having trouble finding information, you're in luck.

Design/Ease of Use

Besides the mildly sluggish download time, this site is incredibly easy to navigate, and as I mentioned before, if you do get lost, the site's search engine will get you back on track in no time. The content areas are clearly labeled with a navigation bar that follows you throughout the site, and overall the mega job search engine is easy to use. You'd think with 2 million jobs to pore through, a power tool like that would be hard to handle. Not the case.

The only complaint I have is that when I entered my job-search criteria, I wanted to add more sites to search. When I pressed my browser's back button to return to the first page, all my information was gone and I had to re-enter my location, occupation categories, and keywords criteria again. Not a big deal, and otherwise I was impressed with how easy the power search engine is to use.

Job Search Engine

When you enter the site from the main page (`www.careerbuilder.com`), a job-search engine prompts you to get started on your search. Skip this engine and go to the Find a Job section. This is where you'll enter your location, occupation, and keyword criteria, as well as select the sites you want to search. Figure 13.3 shows the job-site search selector, which lets you choose from more than 40 other job databases to search.

Figure 13.3

CareerBuilder.com performs a mega job search of more than 40 other job sites. This tool lets you choose which ones to search.

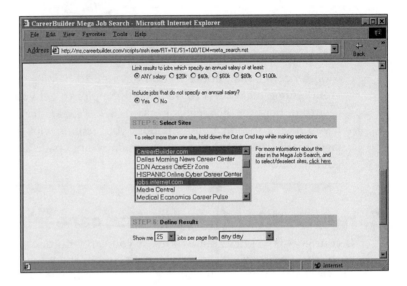

The location filter has more than 200 U.S. cities and major international areas, plus 64 occupation categories. You can also include keywords, minimum salary requirements, and search for postings for full- and part-time, temporary, or contract positions. Postings are supposedly up to four weeks old, and search results usually link you to the employer's profile page and Web site.

User Services

CareerBuilder.com doesn't offer résumé posting, but that's not a bad thing. Where they lack in this feature, they more than make up for it in terms of the quantity and quality of other user services, such as résumé and cover letter tips, career news from *USA Today*, and job-search tools such as salary calculators, relocation tools, and free email. And if you're in the Information Technology field, you can get free certification through the Brainbench online testing and certification system.

There's also an "Ask the Experts" section, where career gurus are "standing by" to field questions and offer advice to job seekers in every field at any level of experience.

The Personal Job Search Agent will also work on your behalf by emailing you job posting matches, along with a job summary and information on how to apply. The job agent only searches jobs posted directly to CareerBuilder.com, but not the 40 other job databases you can search from this site.

Best of all, CareerBuilder.com has a Web guide to the best career-related sites on the Web. Be sure to check out what these folks consider the best-of-the-best and save yourself the trouble of having to go locate these sites on your own.

More One-Stop Shopping

Another job site that searches multiple job sites for postings is CareerShop.com (www.careershop.com). To do a mega search, select which of the 41 job databases (including CareerShop.com, Monster.com, Yahoo!, CareerBuilder, and HotJobs.com) you want to scan and CareerShop will do the legwork for you. Unless you don't care about résumé privacy, I'd forego posting your résumé to this database—after it's posted, you lose all control over where it goes and who can see it.

HotJobs.com (www.hotjobs.com)

If looks could kill, job seekers wouldn't make it out alive from this sleek and sexy job site. Don't worry—HotJobs.com (www.hotjobs.com) has brains, too, and plenty of great job postings to boot. Although the site apparently tries to appeal to the "younger" generation of job seekers, it definitely has plenty of postings for the mid- to upper-level job seeker in all the major job occupations. Who says job sites have to be boring?

Design/Ease of Use

Besides its stunningly good looks, HotJobs.com is easy to navigate and is simplistic in its design. There's a location indicator on every page to let you know where you are, and a standard navigation bar that appears on every page of the site. The only problem I had was locating the non–job-search content, and was temporarily confused on where to go to use the advanced search tools. After a bit of exploration, I discovered that I had to first register as a user before I could get into the "MyHotJobs" section. This is where the good stuff is, so if you really want to get to know this site and take advantage of its tools and resources, you'll have to sign up as a user.

After you've registered, you can create an online résumé, control its searchability, and block certain companies from seeing your résumé. You can also set up automatic job search agents, track your job applications, and view your résumé statistics (how many times employers have viewed your résumé or how many times it's come up in a search). You can also add job postings to a folder so that you can come back at another time and complete the application process.

Job Search Engine

You can search for jobs from the main page, but I recommend you register as a user to tap into the advanced job-hunt features mentioned previously. Either way, the search filters are limited to keywords, job categories, and locations. You can also search specifically by company, international jobs, or by location. The location search technique is rather confusing, as there are no criteria for occupation type.

Thanks for the Tip

Deselect?

When searching by job type, be sure to deselect the "Any Job Type" criteria—just hold down the Control button and click (Windows) or the Command button (Macintosh) and click to deselect. Then, select the specific job types you want to search.

For example, if you want to search for jobs in Indiana, you can either search by keyword or by city, but not both at the same time. After you get a list of all jobs posted in a state, then you can choose a city, and then finally do a keyword search.

An advanced search technique you should try is to select a "channel." All the major occupations have channels, and within each channel are job interest criteria, plus an employer list of companies posting in this job category, and career information about jobs in the specific channel. For example, if you want to search for jobs in Advertising and Public Relations, click the channel. The search feature then lets you select from Job Interests such as account executive, ad sales, art director, copywriter, and media planner among others. Figure 13.4 shows a sample of using the job search engine within a job channel.

Figure 13.4

The channel job search filters let you search for jobs by interest or job title, plus tap into an employer list of companies posting jobs in this job field.

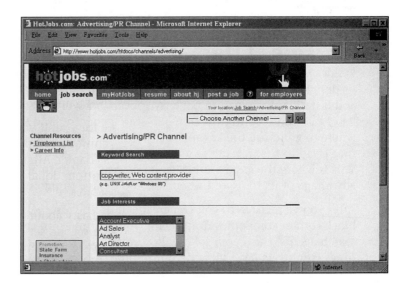

User Services

You'll have to register to tap into the user services section, and then you'll have to dig around for tips, resources, and career information. From the main page of the MyHotJobs section, click **Career Research** to get into the section that contains the *U.S. News and World Report* articles and advice, as well as message boards, industry research, relocation tools, Campus Primer, and Workplace, which deals primarily with diversity issues.

An interesting feature, too, is the Job Exotica section that has features of really cool jobs that probably don't exist anywhere in the HotJobs.com job postings. For example, if your dream job is to write for VH1's Pop-Up Video show, read about someone who really has this job, but don't expect to find an opening for VH1 in the job postings section.

The My Favorite Jobs folder lets you store jobs that you're interested in but don't have time to respond to right away. Jobs remain in the folder for only an hour, unless you ask to save it permanently. But employers don't know who adds jobs to their favorites folder, so don't be surprised if you come back a week later and the job has been filled.

Résumé Options

HotJobs.com offers a variety of résumé posting and privacy options, and lets you set up job agents to send you new job postings that match your search criteria. In terms of privacy, after you build your résumé (or copy/paste your existing résumé into the résumé input field) you can decide whether to add it to the database to be searched by employers, or just store it on the site to use for applying to jobs. You can also select which companies you want to prevent from seeing your résumé by choosing the **Block Companies** filter, and then selecting the member companies you don't want to have seeing your résumé.

If you choose to add your résumé to the searchable database, another unique feature lets you see statistics on how often your résumé has been pulled up in an employer search and how many times the résumé has actually been viewed. And only inhouse recruiters that work for registered member employers are allowed to view résumés, so you don't have to worry about dealing with the middleman.

Any way you slice it, there's a mega job site for you. If you're serious about using the Web in your job hunt, or if it's the only technique you plan on using, spend some time getting to know the sites listed in this chapter. After all, if there are so many job seekers using these sites, you can bet your bottom dollar that employers are going there, too, to post jobs and search for candidates.

Just keep your wits about you, and don't be hasty about posting your résumé indiscriminately. And always, always, always get a second set of eyes to review your résumé before you post or do a quick copy/paste into a résumé builder.

Good luck, and happy hunting!

Darned Good

With the exception of a goofy résumé builder and a high-falutin' claim that your résumé is 100% private, JobOptions.com (`www.joboptions.com`) is a noteworthy and popular site that just didn't make the cut for my top job sites picks. However, you will find standard tools and user services, plenty of job postings, and the unique option to upload a formatted résumé. Most sites take only plain-text résumés, and there's a reason for that—you don't know whether the employer will be able to open your formatted résumé on their end. Either way, check out this site if you want to expand your options.

The Least You Need to Know

➤ Mega job sites contain a mother lode of job postings—learn how to use the job search engine for the best results.

➤ Have your résumé ready and a list of keywords on hand before you apply for any jobs online.

➤ Different sites offer different résumé privacy options, so read the policies before you post, or select options that keep your résumé out of the database.

➤ Most of the mega job sites have job search agents that will deliver job posting matches to your email inbox based on your preferences and search criteria.

➤ CareerBuilder.com not only has its own database of job postings—it will go out and search 40 other job sites for you!

Chapter 14

Other Notable Job Sites

In This Chapter

➤ More top job sites for every level of job hunter

➤ Tips and advice for getting the most from featured job sites including search engine tips and tricks and résumé options

➤ Job site pros and cons and which site to use based on your job-hunting tactic

➤ What to know before you go online to apply for jobs

This chapter highlights some other contenders in the best of the best job-site category. Although every site shares one thing in common (they feature job postings), no two job sites are alike. Some take résumés, others don't. Some have awesome job-hunter resources, others have so-so add-on support. Other sites have top-notch privacy and confidentiality options, whereas others are on par with the average job site.

My point is that every site is different. Not only that, Web sites constantly change. What I've done here, though, is cover the meat and potatoes of each site. But different job hunters at different levels of experience will find some sites to be more useful than others. That's why I'm reviewing them here for you—so you have a better idea of who's who and what's what in the online job-site scene, and can pick and choose which sites to use accordingly.

Disclaimer: If you visit a site and it doesn't look or feel anything like I've described, don't worry. It just means the site has undergone some upgrades or redesigns, which is usually a good thing. In fact, good Web sites are in constant evolution, always striving to improve the site to keep people comin' back, and to attract new users. All they want is to please you job hunters of the online world!

So, here's the skinny on some of the most popular and functional job sites on the Web, including a review of type and number of job postings, ease of use, and user services, including résumé posting options, career information and resources, and job agents—email notification of postings.

Headhunter.net

Headhunter.net is a seasoned veteran in the online job-site scene and a popular starting point for many online job seekers in the sales, marketing, computers, engineering, accounting, and finance industries. With more than 150,000 postings and search options that let you find jobs according to "freshness factor," this site is well worth a visit. Not only can you search for the newest postings, you don't have to worry about stale ads, as jobs are taken off the board after 45 days.

Another unique feature is the upgrade option for job seekers who choose to post a résumé to the Headhunter.net résumé database. For as little as $10 to $30 a month, your résumé will appear ahead of free postings in keyword search results that recruiters use to find qualified applicants. With more than 230,000 résumés in the database, it might be a good idea to pay a little moola and move to the top of the heap. Then again, if your résumé isn't up to snuff, it doesn't matter how much you pay to come up first—employers and recruiters will just think, "Too bad. Should've spent that money on a professional résumé writer."

Design and Ease of Use

Although the site is easy to navigate and there's plenty of help along the way in terms of search tips and links to detailed content areas, the site sections for recruiters and candidates are lumped together, which could make getting around confusing to a new user.

For example, there's a section called "My Stuff." After you've registered as a user, this is where you go to modify your profile or add a new version of your résumé. But it's also where employers and recruiters go to manage job postings and contact information. Kind of confusing at first, but otherwise the site is easy to use.

Even with a high-speed Internet connection, I find the pages are a little slow to download, but speeds can vary depending on many different factors, such as the time of day you go online—Monday mornings are the worst for me. Any way you slice it, though, going online is the fastest way to job hunt, so if you have to wait 45 seconds, just think about the alternative: scouring newspaper classifieds or pounding the pavement.

Job Seeker Profile

Your "profile" is a summary of your work experience, keywords, skills statement (objective), location or salary requirements, and just about anything you want a recruiter or employer to know about you—rather, what they want to know about you before they bother to contact you, also known as a prescreening device. When you complete a job seeker profile, think about the questions from an employer's point of view. And remember to sell yourself!

Job Search Engine

Headhunter.net's job search engine is a shining example of a smart search tool—plenty of options for getting broad or specific results through the use of pull-down menus, basic and advanced keyword search tools, geographic filters that locate jobs within a 30-mile radius of your target city, and input fields for target salary range, your education level, and whether you're looking for full- or part-time or contract work.

Before You Jump In

Haste makes waste. And when you're trying to find a job, the last thing you want to do is waste time or make a silly mistake. As with anything else that's new to you, take the time to read directions on how to use job site search engines and look for a FAQ section. Even though you don't think you have any questions about the site or how to use it, these nuggets of advice, answers, and information are there for a reason—to help you avoid common mistakes and to gain a better understanding of how a site works. Trust me on this one!

Another thing to be aware of is that employers and recruiters have the option to pay for placement at the top of a search result. This doesn't mean you'll get posting matches for jobs that don't meet your search criteria. It simply means some employers take search result rankings seriously and know that many job seekers won't or can't spend the time to read through each one, especially if there are more than 30 matches. Some Web marketers even think coming in past number 10 is like not showing up at all.

User Services

Don't be fooled by the section called "Candidate Resource Center." With the exception of Headhunter.net's CareerBYTES monthly newsletter and a link to a free online personality profile test, the rest of the "resources" are fee-based services from career counselors, executive recruiters, résumé writers, and reference checkers. Although you might very well need these services, show me the free stuff! I like job sites that bring added value for time spent at the site by pooling together content, links, and advice for visitors.

Résumé Options

There are plenty of résumé options, and you can post more than one version of your résumé, so if you're looking for jobs in different fields or different titles, it's easy to customize your profile. After you complete your profile, your résumé goes into the "VIP Résumé Reserve" where it's viewed by recruiters and employers before going to the general access database. You can choose to leave your résumé in the VIP section for added privacy, and can delete contact information and company names for optimal confidentiality. Figure 14.1 shows some of the privacy options you're given when posting your résumé.

Figure 14.1

Privacy options let you post as a public résumé or leave it in the VIP section for review by select recruiters, or you can select to not add it to the database at all and use it to apply to job postings with an online form that goes directly to the employer.

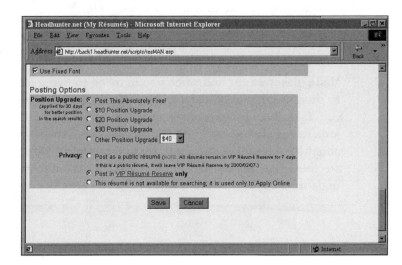

It's easy to remove your résumé, too, which is a nice feature after you land a job. Another cool feature is the statistics that show how many times your résumé or profile has been viewed. If you're a passive job seeker, keep in mind that your résumés are cleared out after 90 days unless you renew them.

6figurejobs.com

If you're lucky enough to fall in the salary range of the business, finance, and IT jobs posted at 6figurejobs.com (www.6figurejobs.com), you might also want to check out Chapter 23, "Just for Executives, High Rollers, and Those in High Demand," for more information and online resources for the executive-level job seeker. Or, if your aspiration is to someday be in this category of job seeker, take a peek at some of the job descriptions at this site to see what employers are looking for and what you have to do to bring home this kind of bacon.

Techno Talk

Filters

A "filter" narrows down search results to those that contain a selected criteria, such as a salary range or job location. If you're casting a wide net to get a wide variety of job possibilities, don't use filters if you have the option not to.

The name of the site holds true to its claim: All 2,500 or so jobs listed here really are in the six-figure pay range. In fact, on the application form, there's a selection filter that asks what your target salary range is. The options start at $100,000 and go up to $250,000. So, if you're looking for a site that exclusively lists high-paying jobs, this is definitely a place to check out.

Design and Ease of Use

There's no getting lost on this site. Three main content areas include Executive Center, where you go to search for jobs, register, and post your résumé; the Career Resources Center, which includes links to company profiles, expert advice, relocation tools, the Executive Library, and a section for products and services; and the Employer/Recruiter section where job postings are managed and résumés are accessed.

Other content areas cover the basics, like FAQs (frequently asked questions), contact information, about the site, and a special feature that lets you "Tell a Colleague" about the site or a particular job posting. A smart move on part of the site developers—make it easy for site visitors to recommend the site to their friends and colleagues.

Job Search Engine

Look for jobs according to industry (30+ fields), skills and function, and state, country (nearly 50 to choose from), or all filters. Postings are date-stamped, and are highly detailed in terms of company information and job description, which is a nice change of pace from the shorter descriptions you'll find at other job sites. Expect to deal with an executive recruiter off the bat.

User Services

Unless you're at this site to shop for pens and organizers, skip the "Marketplace" section. The "Recommended Links" section, though, is worth a stopover, with link categories that include online news sources, career counseling and resources, business travel sites, company research sites, and online investing tools. Another cool feature is the "Ask the Experts" section, which offers thoughtful, detailed advice from career experts.

Résumé Options

This is one of the few job sites that accepts résumés on a review-before-admission basis—if you don't have the skills or experience recruiters and résumé screeners are looking for, you won't be accepted for posting to the database. If you're simply not qualified for the level of jobs posted here, why should you take up database space with your résumé? If you are accepted, though, you'll be pleased with the variety of options you have in terms of who sees your résumé and when, and whether or not you want to reveal your identity—a perfect solution for the discreet job seeker. And you'll be notified via email of jobs that match your profile and requirements, so even if you don't see a job on your first visit, see what lands in your inbox.

After you've completed your registration and profile information, you'll be asked to paste your résumé into the profile form. Then, you can select from three options in providing access to your résumé: If you select Option 1 or 2, you can choose to allow access to your résumé by any member employer or recruiter, or choose to keep hiring companies or executives recruiters from viewing your résumé. Option 3 gives you the option of not making your information available to anyone. It's simply stored at the site for you to include with your online application when you apply for jobs posted at this site.

Thanks for the Tip

E-nailed!

It's a good idea to set up a Web-based email account for your online job search activities to keep sensitive emails from landing in the wrong hands at the office. Several sites offer free email accounts, including Yahoo! (www.yahoo.com), HotMail (www.hotmail.com), and CEOExpress.com (www.ceoexpress.com).

Career Magazine

Jobs, jobs, jobs for everyone at Career Magazine! This doozy of a site (www.careermag.com) excels in the area of user services, content, and job seeker resources, but the search engine is so goofy that it makes job hunting a bit more of a task than it oughta be. Overall, though, I like this site, and if you're willing to spend some time figuring out the search engine ticks and tricks, it's got tens of thousands of jobs to peruse. Postings are date-stamped, and you can find out exactly who's posting jobs here by clicking on the "Employers" link. From this page, you're one click away from researching target employers or viewing all jobs posted by the employer.

Design and Ease of Use

The main page is chock-full of menu bars, feature article lead-ins, and "today's hot topics." Unfortunately, the banner ads and preferred sponsor links make the page cluttered and busy. If you can train your eye to ignore the commercial overkill and focus on the big green navigation menu, you'll be fine. After you get inside the site, though, the pages are much cleaner and easy to negotiate.

Job Search Engine

You might have to spend some time figuring out which search feature produces the best results for you—a standard keyword search, advanced search, and a proximity search (choose a city to get job matches within a 30-mile radius). If location isn't your first priority, try the standard search.

If you're looking for a very specific kind of position, the advanced search allows the use of Boolean operators (marketing NOT sales, programming AND C++, writer OR technical writer). If you have no idea what a Boolean operator is, or don't have much experience using search engines, educate yourself. Spending a half hour learning how these things work will save you enormous amounts of time in the long run and produce better job search results.

Understanding Search Engines

To learn more about how search engines work and which one is best based on what kind of information you're trying to find, be sure to visit the Nueva School Search Engine Guide at www.nuevaschool.org/~debbie/library/research/adviceengine.html.

User Services

Hands down, Career Magazine does a darned good job in the user services category. Articles, expert advice, company research, job fair announcements, employer and recruiter directories, message boards, relocation resources, entry-level tips and resources, and help for getting started on the entrepreneurial path. Figure 14.2 shows some of the topics covered in the articles section, which also features a search tool to help you locate articles of interest to you or to locate a certain columnist.

Figure 14.2

Career Magazine's articles cover a range of topics and usually include links to sites and resources for more information, or a link to a discussion board covering the topic at hand.

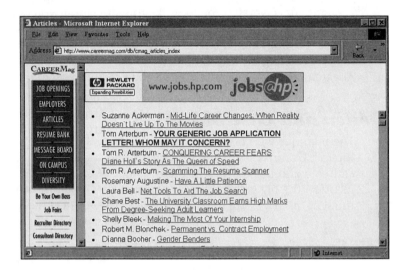

Résumé Options

After you've registered, you'll complete a profile that asks for a keyword summary, objective statement, education, and fields of interest. You'll also input (copy/paste) your résumé into the profile form, so have these items ready before you log on to register.

You have options on whether your résumé can be viewed by recruiters and employers, or to use it only to apply directly for jobs. A word of caution: If you abandon your résumé, after 120 days it goes to a public-access area where anyone can view it. But you can go in at any time and delete your résumé and profile, so be sure to stay organized and keep track of where and when you post your résumé during your online job hunt.

Another notable feature at CareerMag.com is the JobMatch, which allows you to sign up for email notification of new job postings that match your criteria—a real convenience rather than having to revisit the site until you find a job posting that matches your criteria.

Vault.com

Across the board, Vault.com delivers in all areas of "what makes a job site good." Extensive (200,000+) job posting pool, a whiz-bang search engine, intelligent information, and moderated forums make this a site worth visiting. What sets Vault.com apart from other job sites is its extensive company information, including insider reports and discussion forums by and for people who really work at the companies. Although you should take the discussion commentary with a grain of salt, it's an excellent way to find out whether you fit with the corporate climate and to establish networking contacts. Overall, I give this site a "two thumbs way up!"

Design and Ease of Use

What used to be a slow-loading site is now a fast and smart job seeker's paradise. Plenty of menu options in this superbly designed magazine-style format make the site easy to use and quickly locate content areas. Figure 14.3 shows the home page, which is clean and sharp, and provides plenty of content areas to choose from.

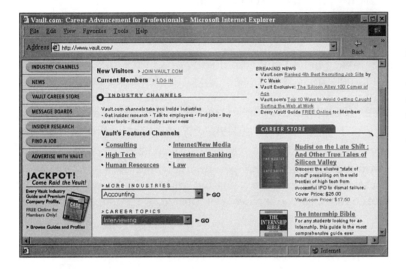

Figure 14.3

Vault.com is a magazine-style format with navigation menus, pull-down search features, and plenty of content categories to help you locate top-notch information quickly and easily.

Job Search Engine

The Vault Report's search engine is a dandy, offering search options in 25 pull-down job categories and another 28 subcategories. For example, you can search broad-based job categories such as communications, or dig deeper into art and graphic design, public relations, or general writing such as journalism and editorial positions.

The location filter lets you choose multiple options from 145 U.S. and Canadian metropolitan areas, and additional filters include a keyword search, experience level, posting date (jobs are on the site for up to three months), and the option to exclude postings placed by recruiters or headhunters. You can also choose to view search results by date or category.

User Services

One bit of advice to job seekers: Become a member of Vault.com, although you don't have to join to access most of the content areas. But you'll want to check out the site's company profiles, insider reports, industry channels, message boards, and newsletters—the site covers every area of your job search needs. Learn how to schmooze, how to write a killer résumé, how to network—all the advice and information is timely, engaging, and takes a "new economy" approach to life in today's working world. Plus, members get deep discounts on reports, career- and business-related books, and other goodies in the Vault Career Shop.

Be sure to check out the Electronic Water Cooler message boards. Use the message boards to contact other company or career insiders, network with other professionals, and get the inside scoop on the latest workplace news and gossip. You can search for discussions by company name, industry, and career topic.

Résumé Options

No worries about résumé privacy here! Vault.com doesn't accept résumés. No big deal, though. Instead, you apply directly to the employer or recruiter's site. Members can also (and should) sign up for the VaultMatch service, which allows you to complete a profile (takes about 10 minutes to complete) so the Vault job search engine can keep an eye out for new postings that meet your criteria and send you an email when matches are found.

Remember, take a tour through each site before you decide which ones to use. Read the FAQs. Learn how to use the site's job search engine. And always keep track of your online job-hunting activity, especially where you post your résumé.

The Least You Need to Know

➤ When you complete a job seeker profile, do so from the employer's point of view—profiles are prescreening devices that could make or break your chances of getting a response.

➤ Some job sites have the option to pay an added fee to get your résumé to the top of the heap when an employer conducts a résumé search.

➤ Before you register at a job site, have a proofed and ready résumé, a keyword summary, and a short but powerful objective statement on hand.

➤ Keep track of where you post and how long your résumé stays in the database, and remember to go back and remove your résumé after you land a job.

Regional Guides

Regional job sites come in handy for two types of job seekers: those who are firmly planted and those who are not. Maybe you know exactly where you want to live, and finding a job there is your second consideration. Maybe you're tired of your sleepy little town or can't find a job in your area of specialty. Maybe there's no way, nohow, you'd consider moving.

Whether you're staying put or hitting the road, going online is often easiest way to job hunt, and by far the easiest way to find geography-specific information, such as apartment and housing information, weather statistics and climate conditions, cultural events, and local news, if you do decide to make a move.

Although many of the mega job sites such as Monster.com and Career Mosaic (www.careermosaic.com) will allow you to search for positions by geography, these sites simply don't list every job posting that you might otherwise find in a local or regional job site. So, you need to get out your spy cap and find other ways to job hunt—namely using regional job sites and other sources for the geography-oriented job hunt.

Who Should Use Regional Job Sites?

First, let's make a distinction about regional job sites: There are *general* regional job sites, and then there are *industry-specific* regional job sites. Different types of job hunters will have better luck using one or the other.

For high-level executives and those lucky job seekers in high demand positions such as programmers and authors (ha!), stick with industry-specific sites—regional or otherwise. You folks are worth flying in for interviews and picking up relocation expenses, right? So, use any darned job site you want. There are thousands of regional job sites in California (Silicon Valley) and the East Coast (Silicon Alley), so take a peek at what's out there. Heck, you might not even have to go looking—the headhunters are already hot on your trail!

Thanks for the Tip

Locate Recruiters in Regional Directories

If you're counting on contacting recruiters as part of your job search technique, there are some that deal with placement in specific regions of the country. That's where their clients are, so look for regional recruiters in regional directories such as Get Local Yahoo! You can also do a keyword search using "recruiters New Mexico high tech jobs" or some variation of that.

For entry-level and mid-career job seekers, if you don't have a target company and are looking to newspaper classifieds and online regional job sites (which are essentially online versions of newspaper classifieds), you're in luck. The Web is chock-full of geography-specific Help Wanted job sites to help you locate your next job in just about any town across the globe. I don't recommend this as your only stopping point on your online job search. You might get a job, but aren't you supposed to be looking for your dream job?

For out-of-the-region job seekers, however, keep in mind that one reason employers use regional job guides is because they're not interested in drawing on a national candidate pool. Why? It's expensive to fly in 10 candidates, put them up in a hotel, and pay their expenses when the employer has plenty of able-bodied job seekers to choose from right in his own back yard.

Another disadvantage you might face is the lack of a local network. Sure, you might know people online who live in different parts of the country, or even in your target destination, but living in a community is a definite networking advantage, so be prepared to do a little extra legwork in this department if your heart is set on high-tailin' it out of town.

Getting Started at Search Engines

A quick and easy way to get started on a job search by location is to use your favorite search engine or gateway site. Yahoo! (www.yahoo.com), HotBot (hotbot.lycos.com), Dogpile (www.dogpile.com), Google (www.google.com), and most other popular starting points feature job information according to region, and often list Chamber of Commerce and state department of labor information and links, as well as local media sources to check out online classifieds.

Either click through the directory headings until you find the category or location you're looking for, or use keywords such as "jobs AND Lafayette AND Indiana" to find job listings in your location of choice.

Other Regional Job Site Starting Points

Remember, there are thousands of regional job sites, and even industry-specific regional sites. Again, I urge you to use your search engine prowess to locate regional job sites that fit your skills and area of experience, unless you're relying on general regional job sites for relocation purposes, or are trying anything you can think of to just get a job!

But before you go scouring the Web for regional job sites or employment directories, stop by Duke University's Career Center. The Job Resources by U.S. Region at cdc.stuaff.duke.edu/stualum/employment/jobresources/jregion.html (see Figure 15.1) is a smart guide that breaks down job sites by region and also helps you locate industry-specific job sites in a particular state, as well as state employment agencies. A real winner!

Another awesome starting point is Yahoo! Besides the awesome Yahoo! Metros— mini-Yahoo!s for select U.S. cities, including links to local job boards and other job-seeker resources—the Get Local Yahoo! directories are growing at a feverish pace. If you're moving to a hot-shot city such as Austin, Dallas, Chicago, Boston, Minneapolis, Miami, Washington, D.C., New York City, Los Angeles, Seattle, or San Francisco, pay a visit to the Yahoo! Metro at metro.yahoo.com for your city of choice. To get to the job listings, the directory features are the same as the big Yahoo!, so under **Business and Economy**, click the **Jobs** link and you'll be on your way to scanning the local classifieds in the top U.S. cities. Otherwise, be sure to check Get Local at local.yahoo.com.

Figure 15.1

Duke's Career Center Regional job guide lists job sites as well as industry-specific sites by geographic region. An excellent resource for relocating job seekers.

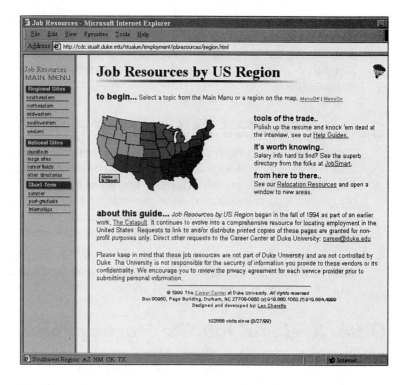

Digital City

America Online's Digital City (www.digitalcity.com) is the nation's largest online network with a local focus, delivering locally relevant news, community resources, entertainment, job listings, and commerce for more than 60 U.S. cities.

A popular site, yes, but I didn't have much luck finding job listings in the cities I want to move to. But that doesn't mean you won't have better luck. The content is good, and the nonjob information is timely, engaging, and up-to-date. Even if you don't use the jobs feature, you'll find something of interest at Digital City.

Online Help Wanted Classifieds

Another way to locate job postings in specific cities is to access the local newspaper classifieds. Although you're in competition with local folks who read the daily paper, it's at least a good way to get a sense of available jobs, and maybe catch up on local news and events. Here are a few of the more popular online classified sites:

➤ **CareerPath** (www.careerpath.com)—CareerPath.com provides one-stop shopping for the Web's largest number of the most current jobs listings. The listings come from two sources: They're pulled from the Help Wanted ads of more than a hundred of the nation's leading newspapers, and from the Web sites of leading employers. Job listings stay posted for two weeks, and are updated every morning, bright and early at 6 a.m. The newspaper jobs database is searchable by geography, newspaper, job type, and keyword. The employers' listing database is searchable by geography, employer, job type, and keyword.

➤ **Excite Classifieds (**`classifieds.excite.com`**)**—The Web site formerly known as Classifieds2000 has hundreds of thousands of postings pulled from newspapers across the country. I like the Start-Up Central feature, which lists jobs at cutting-edge startups, plus the Job Search Agent that sends listings to your email inbox. You'll also find career research tools and advice, as well as a résumé bank. It's more of a one-stop job-hunting site, but it does specialize in newspaper classifieds, so I listed it here.

➤ **Classified Warehouse** (`www.classifiedwarehouse.com`)—Scan more than 100,000 daily job ads from more than 800 U.S. newspapers, including community newspapers and buyers' guides. You can also check out Metro and Regional guides for select cities, or use the search feature to see all postings by state or regions within states. Unfortunately, if you don't know exactly where in the state your city is located, you might have a heckuva time finding city-specific listings.

Leave No Stone Unturned!

You are hunting for a job, right? A good hunter often knows where to expect the prey, but always keeps an eye out for unexpected discoveries. There are many ways to skin the gotta-get-a-job cat, so try these sources of local jobs, too.

Local Business Publications

Another good place to hunt for jobs in specific geographic areas is to track down local online business publications, which often include classified ads. One place to start is the Association of Area Business Publications at `www.bizpubs.org/directory/members.asp`. It is a membership organization, so not every local business magazine will be listed here. To find more, use your trusted search engine and do a keyword search with `"Indianapolis business magazines"` or whatever city you're looking in.

Thanks for the Tip

Research Local Companies Online

Reading local business publications is also a good way to do research on target companies to customize your résumé and cover letter, and to prepare for the interview, and possibly establish networking contacts.

University Employment Sites

If your main objective is to get a job in a certain city or region, don't leave any stone unturned. Turn to higher education as a source of employment—in many "college towns," universities are the largest employers. For a directory of colleges and universities, again get started at your search engine and look for a link to job openings. Don't get off track clicking through to the Placement Office or Career Center—those services are for outplacement, not bringing in new blood to keep the school running.

The Pros and Cons of Relocation

Ahh...to relocate or to not relocate. These days, that is the question for many job seekers. With quick and easy access to national job sites and online relocation tools and resources, making the big move for a new job is really not a big deal anymore. Plus, there's a ready willingness for many job seekers to move to the Silicon Valleys and the Silicon Alleys of the work world in search of those high-tech "hot" jobs. But simply put, you're either willing to relocate or you're not in order to find that elusive dream job.

My mom stopped entering my address in her little black book many years ago and claims that if she writes down address information at all, it's in pencil. In fact, she claims to have used two whole pages in the "C" pages just for me!

The Extra Mile

Long Distance Networking

Although personal contact is probably the most effective way to work your circle of network friends and associates, it's not always an option when you're looking at a company that's halfway across the country. Instead, work the Web using email and newsgroups. Or locate national professional associations online and ask for member directories in your city of destination. Alumni associations are good resources for getting connected in a new city, too.

But I absolutely hate moving. Sometimes, though, you have to bite the bullet and make the move. Before you make the decision to hit the road to make a career change, be sure to do your research and weigh the pros and cons before high-tailing it across the country (or the globe).

Relocating for whatever reason can be an expensive, stressful, and time-consuming endeavor. Add in the stress of starting a new job and relocating suddenly seems like a big decision to make. Yes, it's exciting to get a start on a brand-new life in a brand-new town with a brand-new suit in a brand-new firm, but when you stop to think about all the stinkin' legwork that has to be done just to get there, it's not as exciting as it seems.

But lucky for us movers and shakers of the world, there's help online to make the transition to our "new life" smooth sailing. From relocation assistance to online apartment previewing, you can accomplish a lot of the to-dos before you turn in your resignation.

Get the Scoop on Your Destination City

Another site to check out is Relocation Central at www.relocationcentral.com. A comprehensive relocation resource with everything from where to live to how to get there, who's hiring to what's cooking, with products and services from apartments to zoos. Includes international relocation information, too.

Before You Take the Plunge

Spend some time investigating the "hidden costs" of relocation before you sign on the dotted line. An excellent source of information and tools to help you make your decision is Home Buyer's Fair at www.homefair.com.

The More You Make, the More You Spend

Don't forget to do a salary comparison before you make your final decision on that great job offer! Even though you could be making five grand more a year in your new dream job, you might find yourself paying more for transportation, housing, food, work attire, entertainment, and taxes. Be sure to calculate your salary requirements based on the cost of living in your new locale before you make the move.

Even if you're an apartment dweller or are planning on temporary housing upon arrival, you'll find all kinds of cool calculators and comparisons between your city of departure and your city of destination. Or, if you can't decide on a destination city, there are tools to help narrow down the options.

Highlights at homefair.com include city and school reports, home or apartment finders, job and loan finders, community information, temporary housing options, self-storage options, and utility information.

Homefair.com also features tools and calculators to help you add up the dollars and cents of making a move, as well as lifestyle and housing considerations. Figure 15.2 shows the Salary Calculator which helps determine whether a salary offer is good based on the cost of living in a particular city.

Other cool tools to check out include the Relocation Crime Lab, which provides crime statistics for more than 6,000 U.S. and international cities, a Lifestyle Optimizer, and tips on organizing your move.

Figure 15.2

The Salary Calculator at homefair.com calculates your current salary and location's cost of living against a salary offer and cost of living in a new location to help you determine whether it's a smart move.

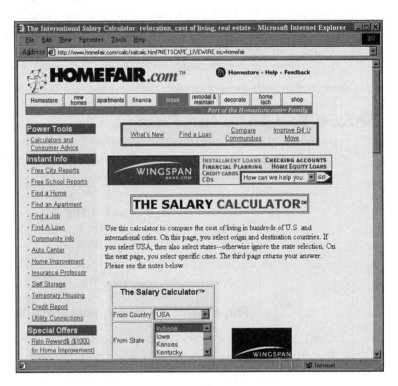

Best Places to Live...and Work

Maybe one of the factors of deciding where to live is how a place ranks on the annual lists put out by Money and Fortune magazines: Best Places to Live and Best Places for Business, respectively. Economy and the job market impact the ratings on Best Places to Live, as well as cost of living, weather, culture, schools, and other lifestyle features. And it would make sense that a city listed on the Best Cities for Business would also be a hot place to look for a job. Check out these lists for 1999 results.

➤ Read Fortune's Best Cities for Business at www.pathfinder.com/fortune/bestcities/index.html

➤ Get the scoop on Money's Best Places to Live at www.pathfinder.com/money/bestplaces/

BestPlaces.net

The folks at Best Places designed the research methods for Money's "Best Places to Live" poll, so be sure to check out BestPlaces.net (www.bestplaces.net) for 1,000 City Profiles in 30 categories, including housing, cost of living, crime, education, economy, health, and climate. You can even choose any two cities and see them displayed in a side-by-side comparison. The "Find Your Best Place to Live" tool lets you describe your ideal place to live, and then compares your preferences with BestPlaces' database of hundreds of cities, and ranks best places to live for your personal preferences.

Dealing with Long-Distance Interviewing Issues

So, you found the perfect job, but the employer isn't quite ready to drop a fortune flying you in for an interview. Instead, you'll probably have to do a phone interview, but prepare for it the same way you would a face-to-face meeting. But besides convincing the employer you're a worthy candidate, you'll have to really knock 'em dead in the phone interview to be invited for round 2, so be prepared.

One way to knock the socks off any long-distance interviewer is to ask that they call from a phone that's near a Web-connected computer so you can take the person for an online virtual tour of your Web-based portfolio. You don't have one? Build one yourself! Chapter 9, "Hi-Fi Online Portfolios," shows you the ropes on assembling a knock-out presentation that's sure to impress any interviewer.

International Jobs

If you're looking at international job options, you'd best be prepared to spend a lot of time doing research, completing paperwork, and gathering information. It might seem like a cinch to just head over to "gay Paris," but it's a real can of worms after you start investigating your options and opportunities.

Hitting the road for an international job is a much more complicated matter than I can possibly cover in one chapter. But lucky for you, there are tons of resources online to help you make the transition as smooth as possible.

For your one-stop researching needs, be sure to check out The Riley Guide, the venerable Margaret Dikel's lengthy list of relocation employment links (see Figure 15.3) at www.dbm.com/jobguide/internat.html#info. Information gathered here covers job listings by region and country, cross-cultural communications, country guides, taxes, finances and Social Security, and other international relocation concerns and considerations.

Searching regional job sites is one way to locate a job based on location. However, using these sources can often unearth postings that you won't find at your general national job sites such as Monster.com or CareerMosaic.com, so give it a try.

Figure 15.3

The A–Z directory at The Riley Guide includes everything you'd ever want to know about career-related Web sites, including international job sites, relocation information and resources, and expatriation and repatriation issues.

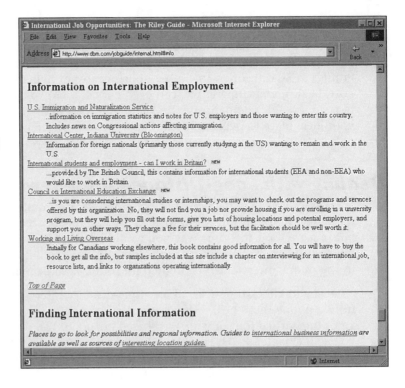

Of course, in these days of high technology and global communication systems, you don't even have to move to find your dream job. With the increase in telecommuting, contract work, and work-from-home job opportunities, you might just find that staying put and getting a home office set up is all you need to do to find that dream job. But more on that in Chapter 24, "Just for Entrepreneurs and Free Agents."

The Least You Need to Know

➤ Regional job sites often post jobs not available at national job sites.

Online classifieds are most effective for the "I need a job, and I need it ⌐l" types, although there's additional competition from local newspaper too.

᠈s its ups and downs, but going where the jobs are has never ᠈ks to online relocation tools.

᠈ind regional job sites, including industry-specific ᠈ start at a search engine.

᠈earching is simplified online, but relocating abroad is ᠈ut there's help online for that, too.

227

Chapter 16

Finding Industry-Specific Sites

In This Chapter

➤ From agriculture to zoology, there's a job site for nearly every industry

➤ Use search engine directories and Web guides to quickly locate niche and industry-specific job posting sites

➤ Mining industry-specific sites for additional job search resources, such as company profiles, news, forums, and local resources

---

If you're not finding the kinds of jobs you're qualified for or interested in at general job sites, or you're just getting too many matches, a good move is to scour industry-specific, or niche, job sites. These sites feature jobs in a general category such as accounting, manufacturing, or health-care. Broad fields such as computers are often broken down even further into niche sites such as information technology or programming.

Even if you're entry-level, you should check out sites specific to your major or area of study and interest. These industry-specific sites aren't just for established professionals—we all have to start somewhere.

Starting at a Web directory or search engine reveals hundreds of career field categories from accounting to zoology and everything in between. In this chapter, you'll get links and descriptions of directories and gateway sites that can help you locate sites specializing in positions just in your area of expertise. I also highlight some of the more popular niche sites as examples of what to look for when choosing industry-specific sites you'll use.

Search Engine Directories

The great thing about search engine directories are the cross-reference features. If you go to a search engine to locate industry-specific job posting sites, for example, you'll often also get links to publications, news, company information, and Web site links, and other career-related information. Most search engine directories are set up in this fashion, so get started at your favorite site. Here are some examples of what you'll find at some of the most popular search engine directories.

Yahoo!

Yahoo!'s Business and Economy section breaks down job-related sites into several subcategories, one being Career Fields (dir.yahoo.com/Business_and_Economy/ Employment_and_Work/Career_Fields/). Featuring nearly 300 categories, you'll find niche job sites, plus industry-specific resources, publications, recruiters, and newsgroups (see Figure 16.1). This is definitely a fast and smart way to home in on your field of interest.

Figure 16.1

Yahoo!'s Career Fields cover general industries that you can tap into to find niche job sites and other resources specific to your area of expertise.

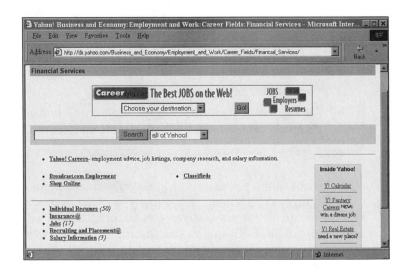

page (www.looksmart.com), click **Industries** under the **Work** 's will take you to a list of industry subcategories, including 'eting, computers, and other major industry categories. 'e link. This will take you to a sub-subcategory listing ....s. Many of the categories have links to online recruit- .d **Directories** links will point you in the direction of . profession. From there, you can easily locate job posting , where you can post your résumé.

Industry-Specific Job Site Directories and Gateways

Don't waste time searching the vast reaches of the Web for sites and information when others have already done the legwork for you. Here is a handful of starting points in locating industry-specific sites if your search engine directories come up short, or you want to get your leads from people in the know, such as the folks who assemble these Web guides to industry-specific sites.

My Job Search

Hundreds and hundreds of specialty sites are alphabetized for searching by name, or select from the menu of specialty areas (see Figure 16.2) such as automotive, cruises, food and beverage, and an impressive collection of computer job sites. An extensive listing, and a great general career site to boot! Visit www.myjobsearch.com/specialty/name01.html to get started sorting through this endless guide to niche job sites.

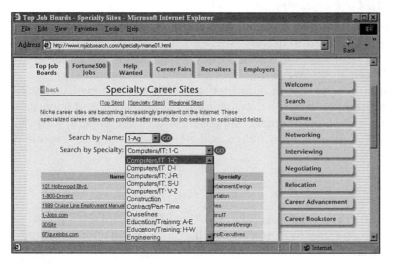

Figure 16.2

My Job Search features one of the most comprehensive guides to specialty niche job sites—more than 500 in every job field you can imagine!

The Riley Guide

Margaret Dikel's "Riley Guide" is a good starting point for any aspect of your on-line job hunt. The "Resources for Specific Industries and Occupations" section (www.dbm.com/jobguide/jobs.html#spec) lists Web sites and brief descriptions in fields including agriculture, arts and humanities, business, public service, high-tech, manufacturing—every major occupational field. The site is updated regularly, and Margaret visits every site for a personal review. A good starting point, but be sure to check other general directories, too, in case she hasn't gotten the chance to review the site, or if it hasn't been submitted for review.

Get a Second Opinion

Although Web guides and gateway sites are good starting points, keep in mind that the guides are usually assembled by an individual or a team of editors who collect links, or review links submitted by site owners. Unlike a search engine, it can be easy to miss a new site, or update links and site descriptions, so always use more than one gateway site to be sure you're getting the full story on online resources.

Skillbot Community Finder

Although it's not exactly a niche site directory, Skillbot is a software package used by recruiters to locate résumés posted to industry-specific sites. Skillbot has collected a lengthy list of links to specialty sites in a wide variety of industries and specializations. Check out this great starting point at www.skillbot.com/community/ community.htm for finding niche sites in industries including arts and media, computers and information technology, construction, education, engineering and science, executive sites, finance, industrial, international, leisure and entertainment, medical, and professional, which includes administrative, real estate, insurance, management, business, and nonprofits.

Career Resource Center

Be sure to scroll down the page at www.careers.org/topic/01_023.html to get to the thorough listing of niche sites in agriculture, archaeology, architecture and landscaping, arts, construction, contractor's labor pool, horticulture, legal, health-care, sports, physicians, industrial plastics, science, training and development, trucking, and hospitality.

Although many of the sites listed here are specifically job-posting sites, some are links to associations or general communities, so you might have to do some digging to get to the jobs section. Most sites, however, provide links on the home page to the jobs section.

Stale Job Leads

With small industry sites, be sure to check job-posting dates, and when in doubt, try to locate the employer's Web site to see whether the job is posted anywhere on the company site. Sometimes it's up to the employer to remove a job posting after the position has been filled, so if you don't get a response in a reasonable amount of time, email or call the employer directly to find out whether the position is still available.

Featured Niche Job Sites

The sites listed here are only the tip of the iceberg when it comes to niche job sites. The ones featured are some of my favorite specialty, and generally offer more services and resources than just job listings. Things to look for in choosing which job site to use include ease of navigation, job-posting expiration dates (who wants a stale job possibility?), and user services such as the option to post, edit, and remove your résumé, job agents, and clearly stated résumé privacy and access options.

Also keep in mind that many of the sites in this chapter are national niche sites, but usually include a location filter so you can focus on jobs in certain areas. If you want to narrow your search by geographic region, you can locate regional niche sites by doing a keyword search such as "information technology jobs San Francisco".

incpad by Westech

Westech Career Expo joined forces with High Technology Careers Magazine, a recruitment publication for technical professionals. Today, incpad is the Web's largest technical career site, with 36,000 positions at more than 1,200 companies and millions of visitors per month.

Witness the evolution of one of the earliest niche job sites at incpad (the site formerly known as Westech Virtual Job Fair) at www.incpad.com. This technology information and career portal offers the best of the Web, including high-tech information, news, company profiles, white papers, career-management tools and resources, and one of the most comprehensive job databases for computer professionals.

Besides its online recruiting tools, Westech is the nation's biggest high-tech job fair producer, with the country's best-attended technical career fairs—up to 90 each year in more than 25 major U.S. markets.

Aspiring Faces

Forget the office job. You really want to be a movie star, don't you? Talent, talent, talent—that's what the scouts are after, and they'll go half way around the world to find it. Make it a little easier for them to find you, Oh Talented One, by making use of high-traffic entertainment recruiting sites such as Aspiring Faces (www.aspiringfaces.com). Be sure to have a scanned 5×10 glossy of yourself—this site will store your headshot and vital statistics for you. Other site features include tips and advice on how to get started, audition, find an agent, break into commercials, put a résumé together, select a photographer, get your child into the business, get a movie part, and convey what casting directors are looking for.

Truck Net

All you need are 18 wheels and a crowbar, or at least access to trucker jobs in a central location. Truck Net has put together an impressive online trucker recruiting site at www.truckingjobs.com, where drivers can access trucking company Web sites or apply for jobs through Truck Net. Figure 16.3 shows the online application form, which quickly and instantly sends the driver's application information to any of the selected trucking companies. The form includes fields for the driver to indicate preferences, driving certifications, driver license and safety record, and other driver information.

Figure 16.3

The online application form at truckingjobs.com allows drivers to submit application information to multiple trucking companies.

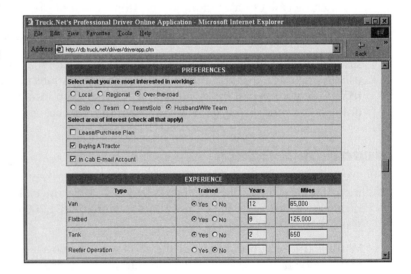

ArtJobs

Even starving artists need jobs, so go online to find national opportunities and links to arts organizations and support services. This site lists plenty of jobs in the arts field, including full-time, part-time, and internship positions, plus links to academic artist opportunities, arts organizations, commercial sector, libraries, museums, presenting organizations, publications, public sector grants, commissions, fellowships and more. Check out ArtJobs at `www.artjobs.org` for a continually updated listing of jobs in arts.

United States Secret Service

The Secret Service has two responsibilities: protection of our nation's leaders and criminal investigations. The Secret Service was established in 1865, solely to suppress the counterfeiting of U.S currency. Over the years, it's expanded to include investigations of crimes such as counterfeiting of currency and securities, forgery and altering of government checks and bonds, thefts and fraud relating to electronic funds transfer, identity fraud, computer fraud, and telemarketing fraud.

For employment opportunities as a special agent or uniformed officer, or technical, administrative, or clerical, and physical security specialist positions, check out `www.treas.gov/usss/opportunities.htm`. While you're at it, check out the Most Wanted section to see whether you or anyone you know made the list.

Remember, there's always more than one way to do something. If your job searches at general sites such as Monster.com or CareerPath don't turn up the leads you're looking for, industry-specific sites are always a good bet. Employers use these sites to home in on qualified groups of candidates, so find one that fits your skills and interests.

The Least You Need to Know

➤ If your online job search at general sites turns up too many duds, try industry-specific job sites for positions in your area of expertise.

➤ Search engine directories and Web guides are good starting points to locate industry-specific job posting sites and recruiters.

➤ Niche sites are good starting points for general research, too, including links to newsgroups, online publications, and current news and trends.

Chapter 17

Headhunters and Third-Party Recruiters

In This Chapter

➤ Who's who and what's what: inhouse recruiters, private recruiting (third-party) agencies, government placement services, and headhunters

➤ How to locate and choose recruiters, and what to know about online recruiters who find you

➤ How to know when you're being hunted, and when you're being recruited

➤ Directories of online recruiters, and how to find agencies that place job seekers in your industry of choice

---

Employers use a variety of techniques to fill job openings, including the services of outside agencies, commonly referred to as recruiters and headhunters. Then, there are public employment services, such as state employment agencies, that match candidates with jobs in a variety of what I might call "non–dream-job" industries and professions.

Chances are, if you've posted your résumé online, it's been picked up by recruiters who scour résumé databases to find candidates to match with job openings at their client companies. If you're a highly sought-after executive or specialist, you might have dealt with a headhunter at some point in your career, even if you weren't actively looking for a new job.

This chapter explains how these outside agencies work, and what they can and cannot do to help you find your dream job. You'll learn how to locate recruiters, how to tell the good, the bad, and the ugly, and what you can do to make your skills and qualifications more attractive to these "middlemen."

Making Sense of the Recruiting Business

There are thousands of recruiters placing job seekers in every industry in every corner of the world. And now with the ever-growing popularity of online recruiting, it seems that more and more recruiters are popping up all over the place. So, how do you know how to work with these folks to move through the job-hunting process? First, you need to understand who's who and what's what.

Inhouse and Third-Party Recruiters

An inhouse recruiter is a personnel jockey that works full-time to fill positions for one company. They do things such as represent the company at job fairs and campus visits, and handle all the legwork that goes into attracting, screening, and placing candidates. A third-party recruiter, on the other hand, works for an agency that is hired by many companies to do all the dirty work of filling positions. Fees are usually paid after a successful match has been made, so to get the attention of a recruiter you have to present yourself to them the same way you would to the actual employer.

Thanks for the Tip

THANKS!!

Read the Fine Print

When you register with a recruiting agency or placement service, be sure to read the application materials closely. Usually, the employer is responsible for paying any fees associated with your placement, but you could be held responsible if the employer doesn't belly-up with the dough. You could also be penalized if you take a job offered through another recruiting agency, so be sure you know the rules before you play the game.

Why would a recruiter want to mess around with a job hunter who doesn't have a clear objective statement, or who doesn't stand a good chance of getting placed? They wouldn't. And they won't, so don't start contacting recruiters until your résumé is in good shape and you've at least targeted the industry you want to work in.

First-Come, First-Served

Sometimes employers post job openings at their company Web site or at online job sites at the same time they're using a recruiter to fill the same position. Keep records of all your online job-hunting activity, including when you send a résumé to an employer, when you post it to résumé databases, and when you're contacted by recruiters. If you get contacted by both the employer and a recruiter for the same position, ethically you should go through whichever one got there first.

Keep in mind that the employer has to pay a finder's fee to the recruiter, which could knock you out of competition if you're one of a small group of qualified candidates vying for the same position. Sometimes if the employer has to pay to play, that could be the decision-making factor in who gets hired.

U.S. Employment Services (USES)

Do you know anyone who's found a dream job using a government employment service? If so, I'd like to meet them. While you can gather information and get practice interviewing or get help with your résumé at government job services, federal and state employment services are known for listing nonprofessional and low-paying jobs. In fact, you'll be hard-pressed to find a dream job through USES—jobs are usually listed here only after employers have done everything else to try to fill the position.

The placement rates vary from about 15% to 30%, but almost half the people who find jobs through this avenue have quit or are "let go" within a month of being hired. Either most of the job listings are for temporary work, or there's just a really high turnover rate for jobs that are supposed to be permanent.

My advice? If you're looking for a dream job, you probably won't find it here.

Headhunters, Body Snatchers, and Things That Go Bump in the Night

Oh, to be so good at what you do that you've got people trying to steal you away from your current job. That's exactly what a headhunter does—they're hired by an employer to find a very specific candidate, and sometimes the specifics include your name and where you work. How would a person know so much about you?

Usually, hunted heads are CEOs and other high-level executives and professionals who are in such high demand that recruiters and employers just don't find scouring résumé databases or out pounding the pavement. These hunted heads are active in professional associations and often serve on boards of directors, or are written about in press releases and feature articles in trade publications. Quite simply, they are considered experts throughout their industry. And employers will pay any price to get you on their team. This is where the headhunter comes in.

So, why the bad rap for headhunters? Well, if I were an employer and my top-notch employees were lured over to my fiercest competitor by a headhunter, I wouldn't like them, either. Then, there's the confusion over people who aren't headhunters at all calling themselves "executive recruiters" and "talent scouts" and "headhunters." A headhunter will scout you out for only one specific job. No more, no less.

The fees charged by headhunters might be another reason why they have a bad rap— compared to recruiters' fees (which can also be steep), headhunters' fees usually account for upwards of 30% of the candidate's annual salary. When you think about the salary ranges of the high-level heads being hunted, that adds up. But, if employers are willing to pay to get the best of the best, headhunters deserve every penny. After all, it's not the easiest job in the world.

I Asked the Headhunter, and He Answered...

Nick Corcodilos is an executive recruiting consultant, famed author, and the man behind the curtain at Ask the Headhunter (www.asktheheadhunter.com), a formidable career resource site that every online job seeker should sneak a peek at. Not only will Nick's insider view on how headhunters work open your eyes to the highly competitive world of talent scouting, he offers tips and advice on acting as your own headhunter if you're not quite at the level where hunters are hot on your trail.

Thanks for the Tip

Don't Let the Name Fool Ya!

Headhunter.net isn't a directory of headhunters at all—just a place to post your résumé for recruiters to see, and a place for you to peruse job openings placed by employers and recruiters. Just don't get confused thinking you're dealing with a headhunter if you get responses to posting your résumé here—that's all.

"Headhunters hunt the people their clients want. You will not be hunted unless a company has a great need for your abilities. Headhunters find you because your professional community thinks a lot of you," explains Nick. "That doesn't mean you're famous. It means you are known to, and respected by, people who frequently talk to headhunters. To get 'known,' circulate among your professional community's associations and publications."

Nick also warns job hunters to know whom and what they're dealing with when it comes to being "hunted" to fill a position. "Understand the most important thing about headhunters: Most people claiming to be headhunters are not. They are employment agencies. Headhunters work on specific assignments for their client companies, and they will consider you *for one specific job only*. They will not 'market' you to lots of companies. That's what an agency does," says Nick. "Having your name and résumé spread around your professional community can hurt you. Be careful who you're working with."

Recruiter Do's and Don'ts

If you don't already know it, finding new employees is as stressful for employers as it is for job hunters. That's why employers hire recruiters to do the dirty work!

Recruiting agencies perform a variety of functions in the job search, from writing and posting ads, scouring résumé databases, screening applicants, and sometimes even conducting interviews. The first thing you need to realize is that they don't work for you—they work for the employer. In fact, consider recruiters extensions of or a replacement for an employer's own human resource department.

The good news is you usually won't have to pay a fee to use a recruiter's services, but the bad news is they're not necessarily concerned with your interests—finding your dream job. Their job is to fill the position, and when you're just one of a thousand job seekers using their service, you're just another number.

Don't expect career counseling or help from a recruiter in terms of your job search objectives. Their job is to match the best candidate and fill as many positions as quickly as possible. The business runs on volume, so don't be surprised or disappointed if your recruiter doesn't do a lot of hand-holding. In fact, if you're a career changer or have little experience in the field you're trying to be placed into, many agencies won't even deal with you.

So, just like other techniques used in your job hunt, you need to do some research and figure out which recruiters to target, and which ones to deal with when you're contacted about a résumé you posted in a résumé database.

Thanks for the Tip

Success Rates Vary

On the average, only about 5% of job seekers that go through recruiters or placement agencies actually get jobs using this technique. To increase your odds, try working with multiple agencies, and work with recruiters that have high placement rates in your industry or field. And by all means don't rely on your recruiter as the only tool in your job-hunting bag of tricks. Consider them part of your career networking community, and you won't be disappointed.

What to Look for in a Recruiting Agency

A good way to choose a private recruiting agency is to ask around. Remember all those networking contacts you've been talking to? Ask them whether they've ever worked with recruiters, what their experience was like, and start with those agencies. You can also get recommendations from recruiters themselves. For example, you find a recruiter (or a recruiter finds you), but the agency doesn't place employees in your field of expertise. Ask the person which agency they'd recommend. A good recruiter should be able to rattle off a handful of names of local, noncompeting agencies.

Also, ask how long the firm has been in business and what percentage of employees are placed. They might not be willing to share this kind of information, but you can ask. You can also ask to speak to candidates they placed, and sometimes the employers they work for. One question to ask is whether or not the employees placed through recruiters are aptly suited for the position, or whether there's a high turnover rate with recruits.

Some recruiting agencies get paid by the number of applicants they provide an employer—not actual placements. Don't send your résumé until you've been given the name of the employer and a job title. And also beware of recruiters who try to talk you into interviewing or accepting job offers you're not totally gung-ho about.

And just like any other professional service, such as a doctor or accountant, follow your instincts. The first time you meet your recruiter, ask a few tough questions such as, "What do you think about cold-calling an employer about job openings?" or "Can you recommend any networking strategies that might accelerate my job-search efforts?" Compare the answers you get with what you've learned about job-hunting techniques, and see whether the person is up to snuff or in agreement with the knowledge you've gained (by reading this book, and by gathering advice online from career experts).

Prescreen Your Recruiter

After you've determined the agency is legit and you want to test the waters in terms of how the recruiter does the actual job of matching candidates with open positions, ask questions such as:

> "What can you tell me about the company you represent?"
>
> "What kind of person is the individual I would be working for?"
>
> "What are the particular things that the interviewer looks for in a candidate?"
>
> "What makes you think my skills are right for this particular job?"
>
> "What types of jobs with which kinds of companies would be suitable for someone with my particular experience?"
>
> "What training will be provided with this job?"

Good recruiters will always ensure you go only to interviews that are relevant to your qualifications and aspirations. The biggest complaint from employers and candidates about the recruitment industry is that it is responsible for wasting vast amounts of time by setting up interviews that are pointless.

Last, contact your local Chamber of Commerce or Better Business Bureau or see whether your state regulates employment agencies. Find out whether any complaints have been filed against the agency, and find out what credentials are required for approval and review by a regulatory entity, or whether the agency belongs to any professional associations, such as the National Association of Personnel Services. Although it's not the same stamp of approval you'd get from a regulatory body, it does at least demonstrate a willingness on part of the agency to participate in ongoing certification and education on human resources and other employment issues.

National Association of Personnel Services

The National Association of Personnel Services (www.napsweb.org) certifies recruiting and staffing professionals as Certified Personnel Consultants (CPC) or Certified Temporary-Staffing Specialists (CTS). Certification is a seal of excellence, and a way for you to screen agencies in terms of credibility and general ability.

NAPS certification was initially established as a self-regulation vehicle for the staffing industry as an opportunity to expand the professional knowledge base in employment law, changing regulations, best business practices, and the highest standards of ethics.

Work with a Specialist in Your Field

There are literally thousands (tens of thousands, in fact) of recruitment agencies to choose from, so spend time locating recruiters that specialize in placements in your specific field. If your experience is too general or varied to be categorized in just one field, by all means experiment with a number of agencies.

One of the problems job seekers face sometimes in dealing with recruiters is that they get pigeonholed into too specific or too general of a category. This means you might get overlooked for jobs that you're nearly 100% qualified for, or too many leads for jobs you'd never consider interviewing for.

And, ideally, a specialized recruitment agency typically provides a much broader knowledge than you have about what's happening in your field as far as jobs are concerned. Don't expect or rely on them to know everything that's going on, but they should have thorough knowledge of the main players, what it's like to work for them, and who pays what. They know who's recruiting at the moment and who isn't, as well as those companies who are always on the lookout for new blood.

The Extra Mile

Getting Extra Mileage from Your Recruiter

A really good recruiter will provide you with feedback after your job interviews to help identify your strengths and weaknesses. They might also be able to give you a copy of the job description and company information such as an annual report or an overview of products and services. If they don't, it's a good idea to obtain it yourself, which you can do online.

Quick Tips for Working with a Recruiter

The recruiter's job is to fill a client's open position, not act as your personal career coach. Use your recruiter as a member of your personal job-search network, and use these services to augment other job-hunting activities. Here are some quick tips for deciding which recruiters to add to your job-hunting bag of tricks.

Choose a recruiter who

➤ Works in your field of specialty

➤ Deals with the level and type of position you want

➤ Has a good reputation within your industry

➤ Passes a reference check or is recommended by a reliable source

Maintain a relationship with your recruiter by

➤ Having periodic contacts to give updates on your achievements and accomplishments and other job-hunting activities

➤ Expecting a give-and-take relationship

➤ Making a strong impression so the recruiter represents you in the best light to potential employers

Avoid recruiters who

➤ Show unethical behavior

➤ Contact you with "blind ads" just to get hold of your résumé

➤ Charge a fee for their service, unless you are aware of and accept the terms of the agreement

➤ Release your résumé without permission

➤ Have a personal chemistry that doesn't click with yours

➤ Call themselves headhunters when, in fact, they represent a number of clients seeking similar types of job candidates

What's a Blind Ad?

A blind (or vaporous) ad is a job posting for a bogus job. Recruiters sometimes post blind ads to attract the attention of unknowing job hunters and to get people to send résumés for the recruiter to add to a database or sell to another recruiter. Avoid getting scammed by blind ads by always asking any recruiter who sees your résumé online what company he represents, and the exact job title. If the recruiter can't or won't provide this, politely end the conversation and ask to not be contacted again.

Locating Online Recruiters

To be most successful working with recruiters, you have to shop around for the agency that's best suited to your needs and skill level. Another good idea is to use more than one recruiter. If you have multiple skill sets or an interest in more than one facet of, say, advertising, it's a good idea to use recruiters who specialize in general industries, as well as agencies that have more narrowly defined areas of placement.

Some recruiters do placement only in specified geographic regions, too, so be sure you're working with a national-reach agency if you're open to relocation. Either way, be sure to specify whether you're willing to relocate when you get started with a recruiter.

Remember when you're looking for online recruiters that you need to deal with a human being at some point. At the very least, look for "virtual recruiting" sites that allow you the most flexibility and the most options in terms of how much information you provide and how you can limit your job requirements.

When in Rome, act like the Romans, right? When trying to find recruiters, act like a recruiter trying to find job seekers. These days, the easiest way is to go online.

Start with a Search Engine Directory

The obvious way to locate recruiting agencies is through search engine directories. Browse categories, as seen in Figure 17.1, or do a search using keywords like "industrial engineering recruiter" or "entry-level marketing recruiter". Most recruiter sites also list positions they're trying to fill, so before you make contact, read through the job descriptions, and also be prepared to fill out online miniapplication forms or have an electronic version of your résumé on hand. But don't send it to anyone until you've learned of a specific opening.

Figure 17.1

Yahoo!'s Career Fields categories feature recruiters in nearly 300 industries, from accounting to zoology. View this list at dir.yahoo.com/ Business_and_Economy/ Employment_and_Work/ Career_Fields/.

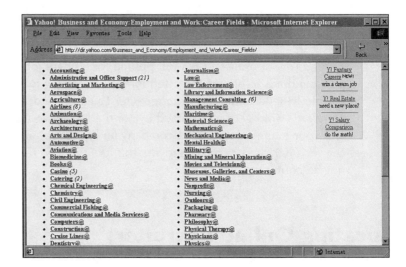

Oya's Recruiter Directory

Oya's Recruiter Directory (www.i-recruit.com) lists recruiters by location and specialty in the following categories: broadcasting, new media, publishing, computers and information technology, data warehousing, hardware, networking security, executive finance, accounting, banking, international and bilingual, entertainment, food, travel, advertising, insurance, legal, management, marketing, engineering and science, research and development, aerospace, environmental, and telecommunications. It's a nice, no-nonsense site that's easy to navigate and search for recruiters in your industry.

BrilliantPeople.com

Management Recruiters International is one of the largest private employment agencies in the world. This functional site (www.brilliantpeople.com) with a name that makes you feel real good about yourself has all the bells and whistles of a mega job site (see Figure 17.2), and more advanced features to not just help you locate recruiters, but to help MRI's team of 4,500 recruiters locate you. Take a few minutes to complete a profile and a job requirements description, scan the job listings, and register as a job hunter to see what comes your way.

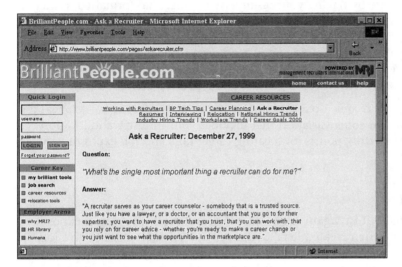

Figure 17.2

Let MRI decide whether you've got the brilliance it takes to be placed by their agency in one of thousands of MRI client companies. With more than 4,500 recruiters in locations around the world and job postings from a wide variety of industries and geographic locations, it's worth a shot.

Recruiter's Online Network

One of the most comprehensive listings of recruiters, staffing agencies, and headhunters on the Web. Search more than 8,000 listings by industry, location, or keyword or take a peek at the thousands of job postings. Visit www.recruitersonline.com for one of the most highly referenced recruiter directories on the Web.

College Recruiters CareerSearch

Many colleges and universities subscribe to CareerSearch, a directory of recruitment agencies that specialize in every imaginable industry for every level of job seeker. Many college Web sites have career sections where you can access CareerSearch with a password supplied by your school's placement office, so cruise the directory from the comforts of home, whether you're a recent grad or budding alumnus.

Reaching Recruiters Through Virtual Job Fairs and Career Expos

If your goal is to kill as many birds as possible with a single stone, a job fair is a good way to go about such a task. Virtual and in-the-flesh job fairs put you face-to-face with recruiters (both inhouse and agencies) in a job hunter's smorgasbord where you can visit as many company booth exhibits as you want.

If you attend a job fair, remember time is not on your side. Although some recruiters will seem interested in getting to know you, expect less than 10 minutes of time at each booth, and prepare by having your résumé (remember that formatted, print version I told you about in Chapter 6, "Get Help with Your Résumé Writing"?) on hand and a hard-selling "speech" that summarizes your greatest accomplishments and skills. You're essentially going around conducting mini-interviews with numerous companies, so be prepared for any kind of question. Grab a plastic bag, too, to tote around all the company literature and goodies you'll pick up along the way.

To locate job fairs in your area, do a keyword search for "`career fairs information technology midwest`" or some variation that includes your industry and location. Here are some other starting points for locating career fairs and job expos in your area, and online.

WorkSeek.com

This company started out in organizing retail, sales, and marketing career expos across the nation, and then created RetailSeek.com and SalesSeek.com to give job seekers and hiring managers a great tool for connecting with one another online. WorkSeek.com combines all these tools and recruiting features in one central location at www.workseek.com. Find out where and when career expos are taking place, or register as an online member for recruiters to check you out. You can also conduct company and industry research on participating WorkSeek.com client companies. One-stop shopping!

JobsAmerica

Westech, one of the most well-known and respected high-tech recruiting services in the country, has branched out into a diverse area of job categories to help employers and job seekers meet, both online and at a host of career expos across the country. Find a new job quickly and easily by choosing the company you want with the benefits and wages you need in the professional, comfortable setting of a JobsAmerica Career Fair. Whether it's full-time, part-time, entry-level or a temporary position you're looking for, even advanced training to update your skills, JobsAmerica is a great place to start. Visit it at www.jobsamerica.com.

Industries include accounting and finance, administration, banking/lending, clerical/secretarial, customer service/tech support, data processing/misc, marketing, insurance, management/operations, hospitality/restaurant management, retail management, manufacturing/production/technicians, sales, medical (select markets), and trainee and temp positions.

So, now that you know who's who and what's what in the world of employee recruiting, you can add this trick to your bag of job-hunting tactics. Remember, don't rely on a recruiter to help you find your dream job—use these services to augment your job hunt, and if nothing else, take the opportunity to practice your interviewing skills and gather important information about your industry.

The Least You Need to Know

➤ Recruiting agency services are used by employers to locate qualified candidates and perform prescreening and other preliminary steps in the hiring process.

➤ Don't send your résumé to a recruiter unless you've been given the name of the company and a specific job title.

➤ Beware of recruiters in headhunters' clothing—a headhunter tries to place you in only one specific company, whereas recruiters try to market your skills to a host of their client companies.

➤ Use more than one recruiter, and focus on agencies that offer placement in your industry and area of specialty.

➤ Remember that recruiters are working for the employer, so make a good impression and remember that their job is to match you with available positions, not provide career counseling.

➤ You can kill many birds with one stone by attending career expos and job fairs—go online to get schedule and event information.

Chapter 18

Go Straight to the Source

> ## In This Chapter
>
> ➤ Finding company Web sites to locate job postings
>
> ➤ How to use Web business directories to locate your target company's Web site
>
> ➤ How high-tech, Web-based, and large companies use their Web sites as recruitment vehicles
>
> ➤ How to get your foot in the door even if you don't find job postings at the company Web site

Going online to do research on your target companies is a critical step in preparing your résumé and cover letter, as well as making a good impression during the interview. Employers want to know that you're interested in more than just getting a job.

Another plus of visiting a company Web site is to locate job openings. Many large companies rely heavily on their own job posting sections for recruiting. They can analyze their site visitor statistics and see just how many people visit their Web site each day. Why not advertise available positions on their own home page, instead of hoping someone comes across their postings at a mega job site?

Remember, though, if you visit a company Web site and don't find a job posting section, or don't see a listing for the position you're interested in, don't give up. Employers often post job openings only when there's a very immediate need to fill the position. Otherwise, receiving a "cold" letter of inquiry from an interested and informed candidate might make them want to rethink their staffing needs!

Getting Started at Search Engines

Employers that use the Web for recruitment are trying to reach a wider candidate pool at a lower cost in the quickest way possible. They want you to find their Web site and job postings, so don't expect a great deal of difficulty when you go online to find your target company.

But not every company is Web-savvy enough to know that they have to register their Web site address at some search engines to be picked up and added to the database or directory. So, depending on the company, you might have to do a little more digging. I'll tell you later how to use other Web directories to locate hard-to-find companies.

If you don't find the company Web address using a search engine, try using a meta search engine such as Dogpile (www.dogpile.com) or Google (www.google.com). These power search tools perform simultaneous searches through many of the major search engines and bring back the results in one location (see Figure 18.1). Call it one-stop searching.

To get started at a search engine, simply type in the company name in the search box, and add the name of the city for good measure. If you're looking at large companies with multiple locations, you might have to start at the main corporate Web site, and dig for job leads there if each local office has its own personal Web site.

Figure 18.1

Google (www.google.com) is a meta search engine that performs simultaneous searches at major search engines based on your keyword query.

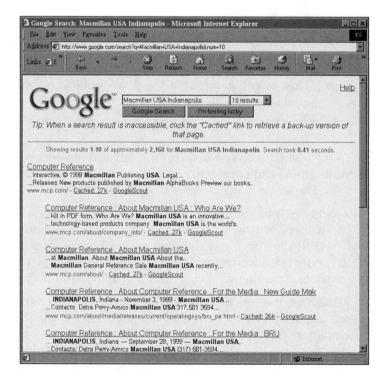

Another trick to making sure you get fast results is to capitalize the company name or put it in quotation marks, as in `"First Chicago Bank"`. Be sure to read the instructions for whatever search engine you use, as they each have their own little quirks when it comes to getting proper name matches and other types of keyword search results.

Thanks for the Tip

Zero In on Search Engine Queries

If you find you're getting too many results from your search engine queries, try using a plus sign (+) between keywords or AND or NOT to narrow your results. For example, you're looking for First Bank of Chicago's corporate Web site, and you're getting matches of documents with the word "first," the word "bank," and the word "Chicago," but not the three words together. Try this simple technique, but read the directions at whatever search engine you use to make the most of your online research time.

Using Search Engine Business Directories

Search engines aren't just search engines anymore. Most have developed detailed hierarchical directories on topics such as business and economy, entertainment, travel, computers, education—the most popular subjects that people search for to help you locate information quickly.

In your job search, this is good news if you have a target industry, but haven't quite narrowed your job search down to a handful of target companies. For example, you know you want to get a job at an advertising agency, but you don't know which agencies are in your town, or which ones specialize in consumer advertising. Clicking through search engine directories such as AltaVista's Business and Finance section (see Figure 18.2) is a smart and quick way to find out what companies suit your interests, and from there, you can locate the ones you want to home in on. Access AltaVista's Business and Finance Directory at `dir.altavista.com/Business.shtml`.

Figure 18.2

Popular search engines such as AltaVista also contain Web directories of the most popular topics and Web site categories.

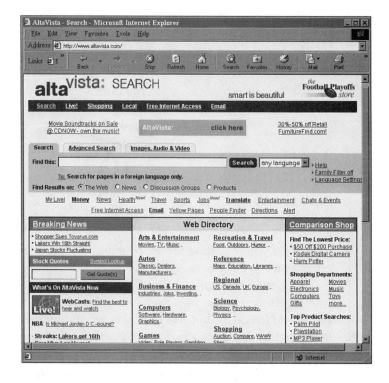

Find Other Goodies Using Search Engines

So, you found the company Web site, but you also got a bonus search result that links to a feature article in an area newspaper about the company's recent layoffs and how they have affected the local economy. Or, you stumbled across the company name in a search result that takes you to an industry publication that has a profile of the company's philanthropy program. See, you're just uncovering all kinds of goodies at search engines, aren't you?

Be sure to read Chapter 10, "Be in the Know," too. It goes into detail on how to do deep research on your target company, including snooping in newsgroups or participating in forums to get the inside scoop on the corporate culture or earnings record.

No Luck at Search Engines? Try a Web Business Directory

There's so much darned information online, some very useful Web directories have been developed to help you find information quickly. A directory like BigYellow (www.bigyellow.com), which is the online equivalent of the Yellow Pages, can yield results in a snap. You can search by company name and city to get results for companies listed in these directories.

The basic listing provides address and phone number information, maps, and directions, but not all listings link you to the company's Web site. Having more detailed location information can help you narrow your search results using the search engine technique.

Another feature of BigYellow is that the directory listing indicates what categories the company is listed under. If you know you want to work for a company similar to ABC Corporation, but don't know exactly how they classify their product or service, this is an excellent way to find out more about the industry and market, as well as who the competition is. This is good information to have during the interview, or just to find similar companies you want to research.

Another directory of businesses with an online presence is the QuikPages Business Directory at www.qpg.com/directory.shtml. This directory includes company name, address, URL, and email contact information, as well as an interactive map with directions to the company headquarters. You can search for companies by geography, business category, or keyword. Hundreds of thousands of listings make this a site worth checking out. Again, Chapter 10 has plenty of power search and snooping tips to help you uncover important and valuable information about your target companies.

How Large Corporations, Web-Based, and High-Tech Companies Recruit

Many employers realize that their site visitors are also their target talent pool. And many also know that they don't have to do a lot of advertising to attract interested candidates, and so they set up their very own mini-Monster-like job sites within their company Web sites.

A great example of how a high-tech company uses its own job site to recruit is Electronic Arts at jobs.ea.com. The company is growing so fast, in addition to having offices across the globe, that the centralized recruiting system is best run through their own job site, versus posting and tracking all those jobs on all those mega job sites.

Techno Talk

Bookmark Your Findings!

Remember to Bookmark (Netscape) or add Web pages to your Favorites (Internet Explorer) folder when you come across a company Web site or other information during your online job research. It's also a good idea to open your bookmark folder and organize your findings by dragging bookmarks or Favorites links to appropriately named folders.

Not only can you view current openings, you can deposit your résumé, and fill out a skills and criteria registration form (see Figure 18.3) to be contacted via email when a job opens up that meets your requirements. You can even preview a recruiting video, read the annual report, or research the company's investors.

Figure 18.3

Electronic Arts knows many of its interested applicants go to its corporate Web site looking for jobs, and have developed a standalone recruiting feature to help candidates view job postings and send in résumés.

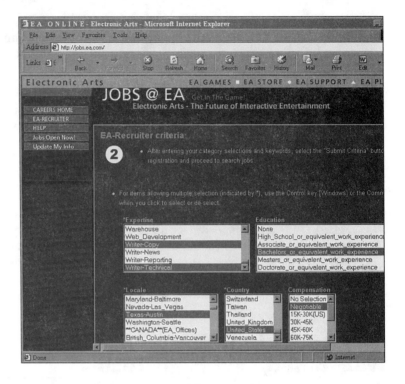

At other popular Web sites such as eBay.com, Amazon.com, Electronic Arts, HotBot, or Yahoo!, you'll find a jobs section. In fact, there's usually a link on the front page. If your target companies fall into Web-based and technology-oriented categories, go straight to the source when looking for a job. More than other industries, these types of companies rely heavily on their own mini-job sites to attract and recruit new employees, so don't spend all your time looking in mega-job sites. Go straight to the source!

Job Safari

Job Safari (www.jobsafari.com) is a fee-based directory of companies that have employment sections in their Web sites. You can search by company name or by geography, including U.S. states and limited areas in Canada and Europe. The links take you directly to the employment section, or click on the **Home** link to start at the company's home page.

Microsoft has a hard-selling recruiting section in their corporate site (www.microsoft. com/jobs/) that not only lists job openings, but has interviews with managers and employers, plus links to life in the Northwest, a campus map, and special job sections for college grads and MBAs.

Tips for Responding to Company Web Site Job Postings

So, you tracked down your target company's Web site, found your dream job, and you're ready to fire off your résumé. Before you press **Send**, invest some time visiting the entire Web site (if possible) and look for news, press releases, product information, contact names, and other tidbits you can draw on to customize your résumé and cover letter.

Also, try to locate a posting date for the position you're applying to. Although some companies rely heavily on the Web for recruiting, others aren't as good at keeping postings up-to-date. If you're not sure of the posting date, look for a number, call the company, and ask whether the positions listed on the jobs page are current. If not, ask whether you can obtain a list of current openings.

Can't Find the Jobs Section?

If you land at a company Web site and don't find a link to the jobs section, look for a search feature or site map to point you in the direction of the job postings. If you can't find job postings at all, look for a department or personnel directory, and see what the titles or positions are. Then, find an email address or make a phone call to find out whom to email your résumé to.

The most important thing to remember is to follow directions! If the employer wants you to fax your résumé, fax it. If you're told not to send your résumé as an email attachment, include it in the body of your email message. Remember, attachments sometimes carry viruses, so most employers will prefer that you copy/paste your plain-text résumé in the body of your email message. Be sure to read Chapter 5, "Understanding the Electronic Résumé," before you hit **Send**.

Another reason to not send your résumé as a rich-text–formatted document is that you don't know whether the company has the software or the same version needed to read the file. Not every office in the world uses Microsoft Word, so play it safe and follow directions.

Not following directions on how to send your résumé is sure to raise a red flag, if not automatically land your résumé in the trash. Take the time to read application instructions and make a good first impression.

You Found the Site, but No Job Listings

So, you tracked down your dream company's Web site, searched and searched for a job postings section, and came up empty-handed. Does that mean they're not hiring? Maybe, maybe not. Don't let this stop you from finding out. Sometimes a company posts openings only when all other channels have been exhausted and the need to fill the position is immediate.

The Nutshell Version of How Employers Fill Openings

The way things work when a company determines there is a need to bring in a new person doesn't always start with advertising the position at a job site or newspaper. Usually, the company will post the opening internally to see whether any existing employees are interested in a transfer or promotion. If that doesn't produce results, the company will ask employees for referrals—someone they can vouch for in terms of skills and corporate fit. If that doesn't work, the employer might turn to a recruiter or headhunter for help locating the right candidates.

But recruiters and headhunters charge hefty finders' fees, and employers would rather hold on to that money if possible. This is where you come into the picture.

Warm Things Up with a Cold-Inquiry Email or Letter

Say you visited the company Web site a month prior to the employer deciding to fill a position. Although the company wasn't hiring at the time of your visit, they are now. If your letter of interest happens to be on file or somewhere in the employer's email inbox as the result of your "cold" inquiry, you might be in luck.

Notice I said your "letter" of interest is on file, and notice I said "luck." Employers sometimes treat unsolicited résumés like junk mail—they throw them away, or at least forget about them. So, unless you happen to be in the right place at the right time (the day the employer decides to fill a position), your résumé will probably not strike much interest from the employer. Or worse, it could end up in a dusty filing cabinet in human resources, never to be seen again.

That's why a "cold" letter or email (see Figure 18.4) inquiring about possible openings is a better bet—but it is a gamble. First, try to find out the name of the decision-maker. Avoid sending your unsolicited résumé or letter of inquiry to human resources. If you can't find the decision-maker's name by scouring the company Web site, call the company and explain that you're researching career opportunities and would like to talk to an expert in the field. Explain you're not applying for a job.

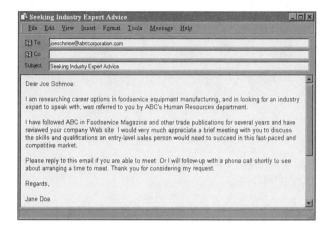

Figure 18.4

The "cold" inquiry letter states your interest in the company, and briefly explains why you're qualified for a position with the company.

You'll probably be given the name of a department manager or the ultimate decision maker/"expert" in the field. Ask for the email address, too, and then pick up the phone and request a brief informational meeting with the expert, stating that "you were recommended as someone who could answer some questions about the industry," or ask whether you could email a few specific questions about your research efforts. Follow that up with your "warmer" email (see Figure 18.5), thanking the person for agreeing to meet with you or answer your questions.

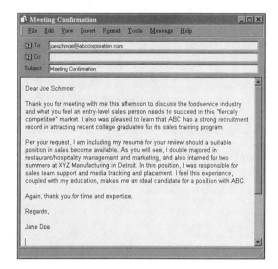

Figure 18.5

The "warmer" email helps open doors and can lead to a request for your résumé, or at least being remembered when you do send it in!

259

Now your foot is in the door. Because this is not perceived as anything other than "helping out a person who sees me as an expert in my field," you have a better chance than you did before. If you do your homework and research, and come prepared with insightful and interesting questions for your "expert," you'll definitely be remembered when you do send your résumé.

So, don't give up hope if you don't find the position you're looking for when you visit a company Web site. Be persistent, but not pesky, and be brief, but make the letter work hard—it has to pack a punch in place of the résumé.

And if you do find your dream job posted at a company Web site, make sure your cover letter and résumé are customized for the position. Put all your research efforts to work to let the employer know that you're interested in more than just a job.

The Least You Need to Know

➤ Company Web addresses can usually be found by conducting a simple keyword search at a search engine.

➤ Meta search engines send your search query to multiple search engines for maximum results.

➤ High-tech, Web-based, and large corporations often have "mini-Monster"-type job sites within the company site.

➤ If you don't find a job listing in your area of expertise, carefully compose and send a "cold" email inquiring about possible openings.

Part 5

Resources for Every Type of Job Hunter

It would be impossible to write a book about career development and online resources without making a distinction among the various levels and types of job hunters: passive or active; unemployed; entry-level; high-level executive; entertainer; free agents; laborers; and anyone who's a member of the working class. No matter what category you fall into, there's something online for every type of job seeker.

As things move to a global market, the issue of diversity in the workplace is a hot topic on the minds of minorities as well as employers. Find out which companies embrace diversity in the workplace, and where to find job sites specific to women, people of color, and people with disabilities.

Or, if you're curious about going free agent or telecommuting, be sure to read Chapter 24, which deals in-depth with the job and career opportunities in startups, contract and project work, franchises, temp work, and Web-based work.

Chapter 19

Just for Entry-Level Hunters

In This Chapter

➤ Getting the most from your college career services offices, now and after graduation

➤ Career advice sites just for entry-level job hunters

➤ Prime job-hunting sites for young professionals

➤ Looking for an internship? Where to find them and how they can help you get closer to finding your dream job

Well, well, well. Seems the time has come to face the music and dance—you're about to enter the working world! No more summer vacations. No more extended holiday breaks. No more all-night cramming sessions (hopefully). Aren't you glad those college days are behind you so you can go out to the real world, get a good job, and start paying back those student loans?

As much as I hear college students express angst, frustration, uncertainty, and anxiety over taking the first steps in the job hunt, I have to tell you one thing: You've got it easy. I don't mean landing a job is easy. I mean people entering the workforce today are better equipped than any other generation of job seekers to use the Internet to its full potential to aid in your job search.

Employers know this. That's why they use the Web to find you, as much as they expect you'll use the Web as a major tool in your job search. From posting your résumé online to visiting entry-level-friendly job sites or locating a killer internship, it's all online, ready for you to log on and get started on your career path!

A word to the wise, though. I can't get over how many college grads and midlevel professionals I run into who rely 100% on the Web for job-hunting. Although this technique might work for some people, I advise you to read through Part 3 of this book, "Market Yourself! Tools and Techniques for Gaining the Competitive Edge," which discusses more old-fashioned ways to find your dream job. After all, the Web is a wonderful tool in your job-hunting arsenal, but it's not the best way to uncover those hidden jobs.

Get Your Feet Wet: Online Career Resources

I'm assuming you've spent some time thinking about what you're going to do with your life after the glory days of college end. Otherwise, what have you been doing for the last four or more years? In case you missed the boat on taking advantage of your college career placement services, or you just didn't find the help you needed, I've located some online resources to help you get started, or restarted on your career-planning strategy.

And if you're still in school and are taking a more proactive approach to your post-college plans, this information will only enhance your efforts. It's always a good idea to get second opinion, so even if you're a regular at the college placement office, log on to the Web to do additional research and job-hunting preparation.

Getting the Most from Your College Career Placement Office

Make the most of your on-campus career counselor services by preparing a list of questions to ask before you make an appointment. Although these good folks are fully equipped to answer your questions, the more prepared you are to ask for help, the better they can assist you in your career planning. Whether you're new to campus or getting ready to enter the job market, here are some tips on making the most of the information and advice available from the career services staff. And don't forget, even after you graduate most career centers offer access to resources and information to alumni.

➤ *Get a head start.* It's never too early to start thinking about your career. If you're a freshman, a career services counselor can help you figure out what occupations fit your personality and interests, help you find occupational information, offer advice on selecting a major that's related to your career interests, provide internship information, and help you locate alumni in your career areas of interest to get started building your networking community.

➤ *Your senior year.* Have you always wondered where the career center is located? If you're starting or finishing your senior year without ever having located your campus' career services office, you still have time. Very little, but there is hope. Make an appointment today to get expert advice on writing résumés, cover letters, and follow-up letters. Sign up for on-campus interviews and learn how to research target companies. These services are free to you—your tuition dollars help pay for them. Plus, this might be your last opportunity to receive free, professional career counseling.

➤ *Develop a strategy.*   When should you declare a major? How and when do you apply for internships or co-op programs? What's an informational interview and whom do you interview? Having never held a job before, what the heck are you supposed to put on your résumé? Even if you're running behind with your career-planning activities, the counselors can help you catch up.

➤ *Keep up with career services special activities.*   Pop over to the career services office or visit its Web site to find out what's going on: career fairs, on-campus interviews, special workshops or presentations, mock interview sessions, and other special events and offerings.

➤ *Fine-tune your online job-hunting skills.*   Most career centers put together impressive collections of online resources to help students use the Web in their job hunt. One advantage to using your school's directory is that they might go the extra mile and pull together information about employers that recruit heavily at your school, or offer resources and advice for career services in your area, such as professional résumé writers. Most college career services Web sites include links to résumé databases, internship openings, links to online recruiting sites, and tips and information on writing and designing an electronic résumé.

If you find your school's career services Web site isn't quite up to snuff, use another school's site. To locate a college career resources directory, either access the school's main Web site and locate the career services section, or do a keyword search at any search engine using "college career services" or "university placement office".

➤ *Go to on-campus interviews.*   With the exception of career fairs, this might be the last time in your career that employers or recruiters come to you to do interviews. It's a good idea to practice selling yourself to potential employers, and a good reason to get dressed up.

➤ *Speaking of getting dressed up...*   Many career services offices offer lessons on interview etiquette, even how to handle a lunch or dinner interview, such as what to order, what not to order, when to take a bite, and when to break to speak. Some schools also offer workshops on how to dress for interviews and how to "behave" after you start your new job.

➤ *Going to grad school?*   Maybe your career ambition right now is to be a professional student as long as possible. Lucky for you, most career services offices provide schedules, study guides, and general information for grad school entrance exams such as the GRE, GMAT, LSAT, and MCAT. Many career services offices provide input on what program is best-suited to your needs and review of your grad school applications.

It's About Your Future

About.com has tons and tons of resources for entry-level and college grad job hunters, including links, networking center, articles, and advice from About.com's career experts. Take a look at `http://collegegradjobs.about.com/business/collegegradjobs/`.

Experience Network

Experience Network (`www.experienceonline.com` and `www.experiencenetwork.com`) is a national online member organization for young professionals just getting started launching their careers. It's free to join, and features include Career Explorer, a tool to help you figure out the right career path, and to jump-start your career with a close look at 25 of today's most popular industries. You can also read company profiles that feature interviews with hundreds of insiders at more than 350 top companies in 25 industries.

Members can also connect with other young professionals to get advice and share war stories. And be sure to read *Experience* magazine, a guidebook to help you achieve success in the new world of work, with a focus on the ever-changing lives of twenty-somethings in the workplace.

JobWeb

JobWeb is sponsored by the National Association of Colleges and Employers—two groups that would really like to see you get a job. To help you do just that, JobWeb (`www.jobweb.org`) has put together links to colleges and universities, including medical, law, and business schools; employment centers that feature job listings, internships, and post-grad options; job search and industry information in business, government, not-for-profits; professional associations; and relocation resources.

Another cool feature is Job Choices magazine. Content areas include quick tip articles on topics such as "E-Mail Tips for the College Grad Job Hunter," "Managing Student Loan Repayment," and "Top Secrets for Achieving Your Dream Career."

You'll find a range of features to help you search for your first "post-graduation" job. Check out the "Preferred Employers of College Graduates" list, or find out about organizations through the Employer Profiles section. You also get direct links to company Web sites to review current openings, and learn how to build a résumé that gets attention. Need help acing your interviews? No problem. "Ask the Experts" and read career stories from people who've been there, done that.

Be sure to check out JobWeb's affiliate site, Career Planit at `www.careerplanit.com`. A little hipper with the just-as-smart content and solid career-planning advice. Just for fun, be sure to play a round of the Career Interest Game to determine your suitable fields of employment.

Many college career resource sites have career interest and planning tools, too, such as the University of Missouri's Career Interests Game at `web.missouri.edu/~cppcwww/holland/e.shtml`.

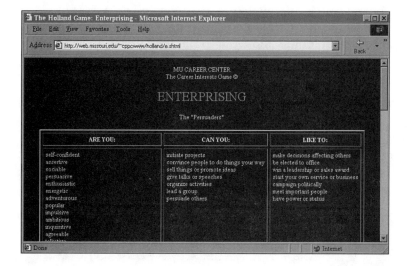

Figure 19.1

Are you an enterprising and persuasive individual? Try the University of Missouri's Career Interest Game to find out the right career fit for you!

Prime Spots to Hunt for Jobs Online

Every spring, I go morel mushroom hunting. I have a group of friends who also like to hunt for morels, but we never, ever tell one another where we're going or where we find a prime hunting spot. Why would we be so selfish? Because morels are tasty vittles, and they're hard to find. If I tell everyone I know where I hunt, they're going to beat me to the punch. I'll have no morels.

There's no moral to the story (pun intended), but to make up for my selfishness in keeping the prime mushroom-hunting spots to myself, I'm going to point you in the direction of some prime job-hunting sites that are geared toward entry-level and intern positions. It's up to you to decide whether to tell your buddies or not.

Thanks for the Tip

Custom Made

Of course, you can and should check out other job sites such as Monster.com and CareerSite (www.careersite.com). You're sure to find entry-level positions, but the sites listed in this chapter are designed just for you! Plus, you get content designed for your information needs.

JobTrak

If your college or university subscribes to this veteran online college-grad job search site, all you have to do is get the secret password and log on to find job listings, post your résumé, do research, and gather information to get started on your career-hunting adventure. If your school doesn't subscribe, you won't be able to access job listings, but you can participate in forums and tap into the site's timely and engaging resources.

College Recruiter

This is one of the most heavily trafficked sites by job seekers and employers looking for interns and both entry-level and midlevel professionals, so be sure to pay a visit. Besides email notification of job openings, at College Recruiter (www.college-recruiter.com) you can tap into the Learning Center for tips, advice, and plenty of job-related reading material, as seen in Figure 19.2.

Figure 19.2

In the Ask the Experts section of the Learning Center, you can read or post questions for employment experts. Post your question at www. college-recruiter.com/ pages/asktheexperts.htm.

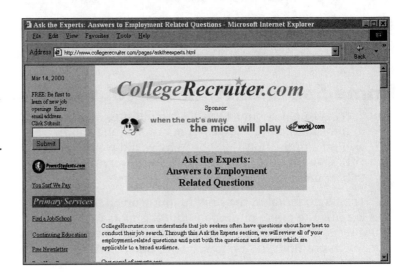

JobDirect

The first step at JobDirect (www.jobdirect.com) is entering your résumé, step by step, in the database, so be prepared to spend a little time getting into the meat and potatoes of this site. The job listings are updated often and are sent directly to your email inbox as new postings become available, and the career resource center is worth a look. Even though I think it's a pain to have go through a lengthy registration process, it's worth the time. One user of JobDirect said, "JobDirect brought me some great opportunities with quality companies. You have to be an idiot to not utilize this site. Thanks!" Enough said.

CollegeCentral.com

Like JobTrak, your school has to be a member at College Central (www. collegecentral.com) for you to gain access to the job postings at this site. There's a Top Employer Profiles section with job openings, but many of the postings I saw were quite old. If you're not sure how old the posting is, click over to the employer's Web site and see whether the job is posted there. Hopefully, the employer's site is up-to-date, so if you don't see the listing there, it might not be open.

College Grad Job Hunter

This top-notch site at www.collegegrad.com is ideal for first-time job seekers and recent college grads. Sign up for email notification of job openings that fit your skills and interests, read up on employers, and tap into the career resources section. Again, the postings at this site were not dated, so take a quick peek at the employer's Web site to see whether the job is still open, and to check out other opportunities.

Internship Opportunities from Career Planit

Career Planit has pulled together some of the best internship Web sites to make it as easy as pie to locate both summer and co-op opportunities. Besides the wonderful learning experience and on-the-job training benefits of an internship, you'll be glad you did something during college to put on your résumé. Besides that, it's a great way to network and a source of references and letters of recommendation.

➤ *The Carter Center Intern Program* (www.emory.edu/CARTER_CENTER/intern.htm). The Carter Center offers opportunities for undergraduate juniors and seniors interested in today's international and domestic issues.

➤ *Idealist* (www.idealist.org). This directory, maintained by Action Without Borders, lists nonprofit and volunteering resources on the Web and has information provided by 15,000 organizations in 130 countries.

➤ *INROADS* (www.inroadsinc.org). Inroads develops and places minority youth in business and industry and helps them prepare for corporate and community leadership. Preference goes to African-American, Hispanic, and Native American high school and college students with 3.0 or better grade averages.

➤ *Internships in Youth Development Agencies* (www.nassembly.org/html/search.html). This database lists more than 2,000 paid and unpaid internships in more than 500 national nonprofit human service organizations. It's maintained by the National Assembly of National Voluntary Health and Social Welfare Organizations.

➤ *Intern-Net* (www.vicon.net/~internnet). This database provides up-to-date internship listings and resources to students interested in recreation and parks, hospitality, sports and health-related professions.

➤ *National Institutes of Health (www.training.nih.gov/student/index.asp).*
This site provides summer internship opportunities in Biomedical Research.

➤ *Smithsonian Internship Opportunities (www.si.edu/youandsi/studies/infell.htm).* The Smithsonian's museums and many of its research institutes and offices offer internships. Its centralized internship application referral service (see Figure 19.3) makes it easy to locate the variety of opportunities at one of America's leading learning institutions.

Figure 19.3

The Smithsonian Internship Opportunities describes the projects you can participate in, the skills that are necessary, and how you can apply. You can also get a unique perspective on the many opportunities by reading actual quotations from current and former Smithsonian interns.

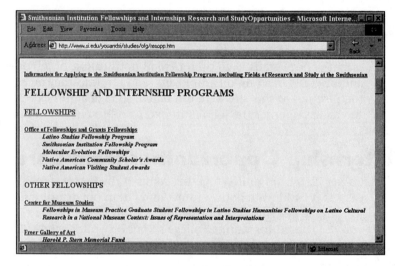

➤ *TV Jobs: Broadcast Employment Services (www.tvjobs.com/intern.htm).*
For opportunities in the broadcast field, this is the place to shop around.

➤ *The Washington Center (www.twc.edu).* The Washington Center for Internships and Academic Seminars provides internship opportunities in Washington, D.C.

➤ *Washington Intern Foundation (www.interns.org).* The Washington Intern Foundation is a nonprofit organization that provides information on internships on Capitol Hill and in the Washington, D.C. area.

With all these job-hunting resources at your disposal, job-hunting seems easy, doesn't it? Don't worry. It might seem like the first job is the hardest one to get, but there are plenty of employers who specifically target entry-level students and go directly to the Web to find you.

The Least You Need to Know

➤ It's never to early to start planning your career—get a head start or get up to speed at your college career services office.

➤ Attending on-campus interviews is a great way to practice your "sales pitch" and take advantage of the luxury of employers coming to you with job openings.

➤ Employers know that most college students will use the Web in the job search, so many, many sites are devoted just to jobs for entry-level professionals and students looking for internships.

➤ Interships are excellent opportunities for gaining real on-the-job experience and for forming networking alliances.

BEFORE
AD EXEC

AFTER
CHEF

Chapter 20

Just for Professionals Making a Career Change

In This Chapter

➤ Good reasons for throwing in the towel on your current career

➤ Online resources to help you find the "right" career based on skills, interests, and goals

➤ How to land a job in your new career field and what to expect when making a radical career change

➤ Online resources and tips to help you revamp your résumé for job hunting in a territory you've got no "real" experience in

Chances are if you're reading this chapter, something has happened to cause you to sit back and evaluate your current career situation. Maybe you're bored with your day-to-day routine, or you've discovered that your job has come to a dead end. Maybe you spent time with an old friend or relative who has a dream job that they absolutely love and you wonder why you don't have similar feelings about your chosen profession.

It could be a change in your personal life, too, that's caused you to re-examine your chosen career path. Maybe you just got married or divorced, had a baby, suffered through an illness, or simply came to the realization that your work life is out of balance with your personal life.

A major career change can be a big leap to make, so calm those prejump jitters and read on—this chapter points you in the direction of some very valuable (and free!) online tools, such as assessment quizzes and value surveys, to help you make such a decision. You'll also learn about the most common mistakes career changers make and how to avoid these pitfalls and blunders. And if freelance, contract, telecommuting, or other nontraditional work arrangements are options you're thinking about, be sure to read Chapter 24, "Just for Entrepreneurs and Free Agents."

You Gotta Know When to Walk Away...

Know when to run? Whoa, horsey! Before you make any rash decisions about changing careers, make sure you have a good reason for making a move, and that you have an understanding of what it will take to succeed in your new career, assuming you've figured that out already. Even if you don't know what you're going to do just yet, here are some darned good reasons for making a career change.

➤ You're sick and tired of your job, or worse, plain bored. You dread going to bed on Sundays because you know when you wake up, you have to face the monster that is "Monday Morning." Maybe the thought of doing your job for the "rest of your life" makes you sick to your stomach.

➤ You're not getting paid what you're worth, or you've reached the limits of salary ranges in your chosen profession.

➤ You're not challenged by your responsibilities, or you want to take more chances and reap the rewards that go along with risk-taking.

➤ Technology advancements, market fluctuations, or industry trends have changed the nature of your work so much that you can't stand your job anymore, or your job is headed for extinction. Or, perhaps your company is moving to a new location, or your management team has turned over and the new leaders want to bring in their own team.

➤ You're STRESSED out to the point of not enjoying *anything* about your life—at work or outside of work. Job unhappiness or dissatisfaction can take a major toll on your health and your spirit—it's time to re-evaluate your priorities, such as staying alive.

➤ Your job is too demanding, and you don't have time for the important things in life, such as living, seeing your children grow up, or taking time for the simple pleasures in life.

➤ Your personal interests have changed over time, and your line of work is totally meaningless now. You've been reading up on new technology or a newfangled business model and want to add these skills and experiences to your bag of tricks.

Avoid Making the Wrong Move for the Wrong Reasons

All sorts offactors and events can affect the way we think and feel about our work life. Before you make the leap to a new career path, spend some time asking yourself the hard questions to make sure you come up with the right answers. That way, when your family questions you on why you decided to quit your very promising career on Wall Street for a new life in the nonprofit sector, you can say, "Because I know myself and I know what makes me happy."

Regardless of your career change strategy, avoid these common mistakes, and take advantage of the tools, resources, and advice on the Web to help you work through the career-change decision-making process.

Leaping Before You Look

Monster.com's "Career Changers" (content.monster.com/careerchangers/) resource center and Web guide is an excellent starting point, and walks you through a three-step process to help you decide the best career-change strategy based on your specific needs and interests.

Step One: Do Your Homework

There's no point spending time looking for a job in a new career field if you haven't done some homework first. Monster.com's Career Changers channel has wonderful cross-referenced tips and resources for getting started on the research before you start the job search, including how to revamp your résumé for a new career field and how to assess your transferable skills and interests. Here are some highlights of the current topics covered in "Step One" to help you get started on your homework.

➤ **"The Ten Worst Mistakes Career Changers Make"**—A notable feature in this article by career change expert Barbara Reinhold includes links to sites that have tools and tests to help you determine your skills and interests, Career Key (www2.ncsu.edu/unity/lockers/users/l/lkj), and the "Self-Directed Search," a widely used career-interest inventory tool (www.sdstest2.com).

➤ **"Assessing and Re-Assessing Yourself: Be Sure to Start Here!"**—This section covers personality tests and other assessment tools, such as the University of Waterloo Career Development Manual (www.adm.uwaterloo.ca/infocecs/CRC/manual-home.html), which is a series of printable forms to help you determine and organize your interests, values, and skills. Another site worth checking out is "The Best Tests For Career Hunters" (www.queendom.com/test_frm.html) that has online, real-time testing and scoring in career-related areas such as success likelihood, leadership, sales personality, assertiveness, and burnout. Try not to get sidetracked on the other psychology tests at this site, such as the relationship satisfaction evaluator. You might end up dumping your sweetie instead of focusing on the issue at hand—finding a job in a new career field!

➤ **"Is Self-Employment for You? The Quiz for People Who Want to Work for Themselves"**—Before you quit your job, take Pat Boer's quick quiz and ask yourself a few key questions to determine whether you have what it takes to succeed in starting and running your own business. Even if you're not ready to set out on your own, you might be in a position to create a more flexible work situation or increase your current responsibilities. This article shows you how to know whether you're ready to go solo or what you can do to improve or locate a more "independent" work-for-hire situation.

➤ **"Retooling Your Résumé to Change Fields"**—This quick article highlights the most important things about revamping your résumé, from highlighting transferable skills to focusing on networking contacts over your résumé to get you job leads. Also recommended is devising a functional or skills résumé instead of a chronological career history, but be sure to include a brief work history somewhere on the skills résumé so you're not red-flagged as a job hopper.

The Pros and Cons of Skills Résumés

Although a skills or functional résumé might be an effective way to demonstrate your general, transferable skills when breaking into a new career, most employers interpret a skills résumé as a cover-up for an inconsistent work history or lack of direction and focus. Many résumé experts discourage this résumé format, but it might be your only choice. Always include a timeline of employers and job titles, and include a brief lead-in to each skills category that demonstrates your understanding of the new career requirements and how your transferable skills can get the job done.

Step Two: Talk to Others

Monster.com's message boards let you ask career experts questions and exchange thoughts and ideas with other job seekers. If you've never used a message board before, be sure to click on the **Help** link at the bottom of the page. The Monster.com forums work just like any other online forum, but if you're new to this method of online communication, take a few minutes to learn how the system works. And as with any chat room, discussion board, or newsgroup, always read the FAQs (frequently asked questions) and guidelines before you post a question or reply to another member's posting.

➤ *Career Guru hosted by Pat Boer.*   This Monster.com board focuses on Mid-Career issues such as changing careers, relocating, re-entering the workforce, working from home, job hunting, advancing your career, leadership training, and returning to school.

➤ *Career Coach hosted by Barbara Reinhold.*   The Career Coach answers questions and offers advice to executives, career changers, and professionals considering becoming free agents or wanting to become more successful at working solo.

➤ *Transition from Military to Civilian Work hosted by Gale Kennedy.*   Whether you're about to retire or are separating from the military, making the transition to work in the civilian world can be a big change in your life. Veterans, retirees, spouses, and family members of transitioning service people can post questions or comments. Be sure to check out the Military to Civilian Toolkit (look for the Toolkits Menu on the right side of the Monster.com Career Changers main page).

➤ *Résumé Tips hosted by Kim Isaacs.*   Definitely pay a visit to this online forum if you're making a career change. Kim Isaacs ("The Résumé Expert") takes questions from job seekers at all levels and occupational fields, and will provide a brief review of your résumé to offer general starting points for improvement. If you're considering using a skills (functional) résumé, Kim can offer advice on how to make this style of résumé work for you, or can offer tips on how to transform your chronological résumé into a hard-selling career document for breaking into a new field.

Step Three: Keep Informed

It's always a good idea to get more than one opinion when considering making a career change—and I don't mean from your mother-in-law, neighbor, and workout buddy. If these people have expert knowledge on the subject, that's one thing, but with all the free career change information on the Web, why not take advantage of this advice and find out from the real experts how to succeed in making the switch? After all, this is your livelihood we're talking about here. Monster.com has graciously pulled together some great starting points and online resources, as well as some books you might want to check out.

➤ **Links**—Career Changer Web guides include links to the Career Doctor section of Monster.com, as well as sites such as WetFeet.com and other sources for research information on different industries and fields, as well as insider guides and company profiles. Don't forget to check out Vault.com (as seen in Figure 20.1), Hoovers.com, and CompanySleuth.com, too, for this valuable insider information.

For a fee, you can also access online quizzes to help you identify what's wrong in your work life—as if you don't already know! But, even if you know what's wrong, maybe you need to do further introspection and evaluation to find a career that fits with your personality, work style, and skills.

➤ **Books**—Monster.com has a recommended reading list for career changers, and you can even read reviews and editorial summaries of each recommended title. Another recommended book not on the Monster.com list is *Working for a Life, Working for a Living* by Dr. Mark Albion. Be sure to check out his Web site at www.makingalife.com for the full story on how this Harvard professor walked away from a promising career in academia and consulting to pursue other dreams and ambitions.

Figure 20.1

Vault.com provides industry insider reports and profiles for career changers and job hunters at every level of experience in the top "hot" industries.

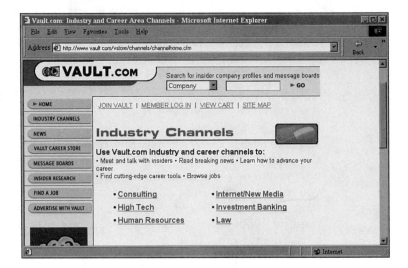

Jumping into a Hot or "Interesting" Field

In many ways, the "hot jobs" of tomorrow haven't even been invented yet, and what's hot today might be only lukewarm by the time you're ready to enter that career field. There are certain industries that have staying power, such as technology, communications, and service-oriented professions. Banking probably won't go away, and neither will legal professions. But these are wide-open categories of job industries, and knowing you want to go into computers doesn't even begin to narrow it down.

Either way, changing careers to enter a hot field without determining whether it's the right fit for you is like jumping on a fast train to Burnoutville. Even though flexibility and an eagerness to learn new skills are important in today's job market, it's best to begin building on what you already have. Starting from scratch in a new, uncharted field just because of media buzz or hearing rave reviews from people who work in these hot jobs might be the worst move you could make. What's good for the goose isn't always good for the gander, right?

To learn more about industries and professions, visit sites such as WetFeet.com (as seen in Figure 20.2) and Vault.com, or hunt down industry trade publications using a Web directory such as Yahoo! Web site:Business and Economy Category listing of trade publications (`dir.yahoo.com/Business_and_Economy/Magazines/Trade_Magazines/`).

Figure 20.2

WetFeet.com is an outstanding resource for career and industry information. Members get discounts on reports, and other free tools and information to make a smooth career transition.

Basing Decisions on Prestige and Income

If money or status are the only things you care about, go ahead and look for a new career that promises fast money and fast cars. But as you go about breaking into your hot, new promising career, remember something Lily Tomlin said: "The trouble with the rat race is that even if you win, you're still a rat."

Believe it or not, there's more to life than a fat paycheck and external material objects. Being fulfilled and challenged in your daily work life is as important to your well-being as financial security, and given the demands of many high-salary positions, you might just find yourself so consumed by your job that you have no time or interest in a life outside of work. That can only last so long.

I'm not suggesting you throw out your plans to get an MBA and get started on a new, fast-track career. I'm reminding you only that there's more to life than money. So, when it comes time to change careers, don't forget the other factors that go into the decision-making process such as working conditions, travel requirements, demands on your personal time, work-related stress, and cutthroat competition. Think very carefully before you chuck your core values to pursue a prestigious, high-paying position.

Going It Alone

Making a major career decision isn't something you should do on your own. Talk to friends, family, and business associates (confidentially, of course) to get advice and guidance, and even begin building a career network with people in the know about career fields you're interested in.

Locate industry experts and request a short meeting to conduct an informational interview. Monster.com's Career Changer channel has links and resources to show you the ropes on how to locate and approach experts, and what kinds of questions to ask.

It's also a good idea to ask people who know you well or who understand your work style and attributes what profession they think you're suited for. Someone might surprise you with an idea that you never thought of before, further expanding your possibilities and re-energizing your quest to find a more appropriate or meaningful career.

Relying on Others to Make the Decision for You

If you find yourself looking to career counselors or a career transitions agency to help you make the decision to switch career fields, maybe that's a sign that you're not sure about your career goals or why you think you need to make a change. Maybe you need to go back to step one—self-introspection—before you start looking for someone to push you in for the "Nestea Plunge."

And certainly don't look to recruiters, headhunters, or placement agencies to help you make the switch. If you're not prepared to demonstrate to these folks that you're ready and qualified to land a job in a totally new field, do you think you're going to be able to convince an employer, either? Do your homework and be confident in your decision before you even think about sending out a résumé or contacting a recruiter. And don't be surprised if they don't want to deal with you at all—they tend to focus on moving people along the continuum of the same career field simply because it's easier to do.

Expecting Too Much, Too Fast

If changing careers is anything such as moving from an apartment to home ownership, it's not something you decide to do one day, and the next week you're packing your boxes and signing mortgage documents. It takes time, and it takes planning. It often requires training or additional education, so the earlier you start preparing, the better off you are.

But before you enroll in school or spend a dime on training, consider alternatives such as internships, volunteering, or taking on a moonlighting contract assignment to test the waters. It's a smart way to make your investment dollars pay off in the long haul. The only thing it will cost you is your time.

America's Career InfoNet

America's Career InfoNet (www.acinet.org) is an excellent starting point for job seekers looking for a new career. This nonprofit network, which includes America's Job Bank (www.ajb.org), is broken down into two levels—general and specific information relating to industries, trends, occupations, salaries, and a lengthy list of resources for any level of job seeker. Don't skip the Career Resource Library, either, which links you to Web sites and books with information on occupational information, job search aids, job and résumé banks, and relocation information.

Level One

To get started on general research about your career fields of interest, start with Level One to get a feel for general trends, required levels of experience or education, and what the job outlook is like according to geography.

➤ **General Outlook**—This provides the general trends of the current job market, either overall or for different levels of education and training.

➤ **Wages and Trends**—This section links to second-level pages that display information about the occupation and state that you select. Be aware that some of the salary information is dated, so get a second opinion at sites such as WageWeb (www.wageweb.com).

➤ **State Profile Search**—This section provides each state's demographics, economic data, educational institutions, cultural resources, and recreation sites.

➤ **Resources**—The Career Resource Library helps you locate other sites related to your career interests, plus skills assessment tools and information. Read more about the Career Resource Library later in this chapter.

After conducting an occupation search, you can select from Level Two resources for more information specific to the occupation you're researching. Figure 20.3 shows a Knowledge, Skills, and Abilities overview for the financial-planning industry.

Figure 20.3

America's Career InfoNet provides information on what skills and knowledge are required and desired in a variety of professions and career fields.

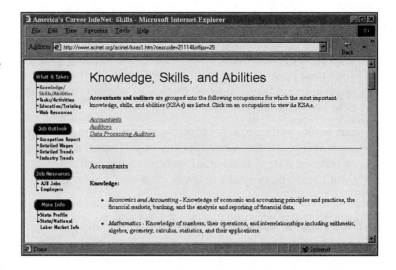

Level Two

This level of information at Career InfoNet digs a little deeper than general occupational research. Here's what you'll find in the detailed information section.

➤ *What it takes to work in a specific occupation.*   "Skills" lists the knowledge, skills, and abilities required in the occupation. "Tasks/Activities" gives you an idea of the typical work day in specific occupations. If you think you might need a different or updated skills set, the "Education/Training" profile lists the typical education level and training areas for people in specific fields and occupations. For more information, there is a "Web Resources" section that lists Web sites that have information related to the occupation.

➤ *Job outlook for a specific occupation.*   "Detailed Wages" displays the national, state, and local wages for the occupation, and "Detailed Trends" displays the national and state occupation projections. To learn about "Industry Trends," read the national data on your industry of choice.

➤ *Locate a job in a specific occupation and geographic region.*   Link to America's Job Bank jobs—nearly a million to choose from in all industries and experience levels. You can also post your résumé here. The "Employers" section has contact information and brief profiles for companies with job postings in the job bank.

➤ *More Info on a specific occupation.*   "State Profiles" contain general information about the 50 states if you're considering relocation, and the "State/National Labor Market Info" links to a page in the Career Resource Library that provides access to local, state, and national labor market information sites on the Web.

Career Resource Library

The good folks at Career InfoNet have put your tax dollars to use and assembled a Web guide to some very informative and useful sites and resources to flesh out your online career planning efforts.

➤ **Occupational Information**—This section contains links to sites covering career information, education, training, and financial information; guidance and counseling associations and services; local, state, and national career and labor market information sites; and other industry-specific sites.

➤ **Job Search Aids**—Visit the sites listed here for tips and information on job searching, resources for diverse groups, professional and trade associations and labor unions, employment law and publications, or to research employers.

➤ **Job and Résumé Banks**—This section lists job banks, meta guides and job clearinghouses, job resources by occupation, state and local resources, miscellaneous opportunities, tips for posting your résumé online, and directories of recruiting and staffing services.

➤ **Relocation Information**—Making a move? Visit the relocation section for city and state guides, realtors, moving guides, reference materials and directories, and tips on conducting online relocation research.

The Least You Need to Know

➤ Besides the realization that you went down the wrong career path, there are valid reasons for leaving your profession, such as technology advancements or inevitable extinction of jobs requiring your skill set.

➤ Making the decision to change careers takes careful thought and planning, and often takes about six months to a year to put into effect.

➤ Online sites such as Monster.com and About.com provide outstanding starting points for researching your career interests, options, and change strategies.

➤ Before you pick a new career, find out what the occupational outlook and salary trends are so you know you won't find yourself in the same boat two years from now.

➤ One of the most common mistakes career changers make is leaping before looking—with online experts and industry information at your fingertips, it's an easy mistake to avoid.

Chapter 21

Just for the Currently Unemployed

In This Chapter

➤ What to do before you start looking for another job

➤ Examining why you were let go, and taking steps to make corrections or redirect your career goals

➤ Negotiating a separation package or applying for unemployment benefits

➤ Exploring temporary or "contract" work options

➤ What to tell potential employers

Losing a job to downsizing, layoffs, outright firing, or unexpectedly quitting puts you in a stressful and anxiety-ridden situation. No one responds well to finding themselves without a job. In fact, it feels pretty lousy. Even if you quit on your own accord, it might have felt good at the time, but after you come down from the initial charge, you're probably going to be faced with bad feelings and a sense of urgency.

But being without a job doesn't mean there's not work to do. Some experts advise that you go get temporary work right away, even if it means you have to "reduce" yourself to menial work that's completely below your skills and interests. Others will tell you to spend at least 40 hours a week looking for a job. "Mass mail your résumé to thousands of employers, knock on every door of every company you can find," they tell you.

So, what are you supposed to do? How can you look for a job when you're flippin' burgers? The key to dealing with job loss is balance—balancing your bank account, balancing your mind and emotions, and balancing your time between working and looking for work if your length of unemployment goes beyond a certain amount of time.

This chapter explores your options and strategies on dealing with job loss, including how to answer the dreaded questions that will inevitably come up in forthcoming interviews: "What have you been doing for the last two months? Why were you let go? Why did you leave without having another job lined up?"

Sad part is, you're going to get these same questions from yourself. The shame, guilt, and frustration you might feel when dealing with the loss of your "work identity" is enough to send even the most resilient person into deep depression. Try to exercise, eat regular healthy meals, and try to maintain structure in your life. And when you need it, lean on your family and friends for love and support.

You won't find all the answers to your unemployment problems online, but there are lots of resources for advice and support, as well as options in terms of finding temporary or consulting work. And, of course, you can use the Web as a tool in your job search. I warn you, though—don't think the Internet is a magic bag of beans that lets you just post your résumé or apply to online job-site postings and leave it at that. You have to do a lot of legwork and self-examination, and set standards for your next job.

The "F" Word

Okay, so you messed up and got FIRED. Now what? How will you ever recover from such a blow? Here are some tips for dealing with job loss due to termination.

➤ *Reflect on why you were fired.* You probably know why you were fired, and your employer might or might not give you an exact reason why. Examine things you did that led to your termination, and take steps to correct those things so you don't face a similar situation in the future. Learning about your shortcomings and devising a plan of correction can help build your self-esteem. It's better than just resolving yourself to believing you can't do a job because you're not capable of improving yourself. You might also discover that you're not in the right line of work.

➤ *Decide what you need to succeed.* Developing a plan of correction can help you decide whether your personality fits better with a different kind of company. You might also discover that your reasons for being let go were purely political, and that you did nothing wrong. Perhaps then you need to hone your office politics skills so that you're better equipped to deal with similar situations in the future. If you determine that the reason you were fired is because you don't have the skills to meet the standards for job performance, get training or explore other career paths that are more suited to your skills and interests.

➤ *Develop a marketing strategy.* After you've determined your skills and interests, determine how to present those selling points to prospective employers. Do company research, talk to an industry expert, and do a thorough investigation of your chosen field. Know what you're getting into and what you need to succeed in selling your skills and contributions you can make. A marketing strategy is more than just a spiffy résumé. If you need ideas on how to market yourself, be sure to read Part Three, "Market Yourself! Tools and Techniques for Gaining the Competitive Edge." This part of the book is all about the tools and techniques you can use to position yourself ahead of the competition.

➤ *Decide how you'll answer the dreaded question: "Why were you fired?"* Be honest if asked, but don't volunteer the information. If (when) you are asked, a perfectly good answer might be something like: "I was experiencing personal difficulties at the time that interfered with my getting to work on time. I have since resolved those problems, but at the time of my termination, my supervisor was under orders to reduce the workforce anyway. To be quite honest, my tardiness gave him the reason he needed to let me go. We are on good terms, and he will verify that up to the time I experienced personal problems, I was never late, and even stayed beyond my scheduled time to get projects complete." Try to focus on what you learned from the experience, and that you recognize the value in your supervisor upholding standards. Throw in a comment such as, "I learned the hard way that commitment and responsibility are not to be compromised."

If you really were unjustly fired, resist the urge to blame others. Hopefully, you can gather facts and evidence that you were not the only person fired, and that "in fact, I was one of 15 people let go in less than four weeks." And always focus on what you learned from the experience.

Hold Off on Sending Out Your Résumé

Resist the urge to start sending out your résumé the day you get home from your last day at work. First, devise your next career move and plan of action. Make sure you've defined your goals and objectives and researched a target list of potential new employers. Next, update your résumé to focus on quantifiable accomplishments and transferable skills, and rehearse your answer to the questions about why you're out of work.

Dealing with a Layoff

Layoffs and downsizing are completely out of your control. Keep this in mind as you go about finding your next job, and use it to your advantage. First, if you're laid off you might be eligible for unemployment benefits or severance pay. Your company might also offer outplacement service, which is usually part of a severance package. For sound advice on dealing with a layoff, Monster.com's Career Center has articles that cover various issues related to this topic, as seen in Figure 21.1.

Figure 21.1

Monster.com's Career Center has articles on dealing with downsizing, and how to respond to unemployment questions in the interview. Read this article at `midcareer.monster.com/articles/recoverdownsizing.html`.

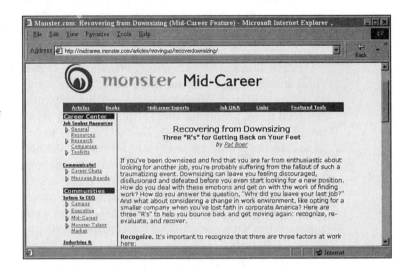

Unemployment Benefits Eligibility

The U.S. Department of Labor Employment and Training Administration has a quick overview of unemployment insurance eligibility at `www.doleta.gov/programs/claims.htm`. The overview will tell you how to apply, how much to expect, and how long you're eligible to receive these benefits.

Unemployment laws are governed on a state level, so to file a claim or get more information, visit the unemployment agency state directory at `www.doleta.gov/region.htm`. Filing by phone, mail, fax, or the Internet is now routine in many states, and in states which require initial filing in person, follow-up reporting can be done by phone or mail.

Negotiating Your Severance Package

A general rule of thumb when negotiating your severance package is to expect a month's salary for every $10,000 in annual pay. Here are some standard packages:

➤ **Senior executives**—Twelve months' salary or more

➤ **Midlevel executives**—Six to 12 months' salary

➤ **Junior executives**—As little as three to six months' salary

➤ **Midlevel managers**—Six months' salary and not less than a week's pay for each year of service

➤ **Exempt professionals**—Three months' salary or a week's pay for each year of service (the greater of the two)

➤ **Nonexempt, hourly, and blue-collar**—These workers usually receive a week's pay for each year of service, but sometimes much less. Two weeks' pay is the norm for many small employers.

Outplacement Services

Designed to help downsized or laid-off employees find new jobs, outplacement services range from one-day seminars to ongoing programs that provide counseling, the use of an office, job-opening monitoring, and other ways to provide you with job leads. Some larger companies automatically offer this service to displaced employees, and some even have full-time outplacement counselors on staff to help during layoffs.

Even if your employer isn't picking up the tab to cover the cost of outplacement, it might be something worth investigating. To locate outplacement services in your area, do a keyword search using *outplacement services* to locate agencies in your area. Often, recruiters and human resource agencies provide this type of service.

Web Sites for the Unemployed

Maybe this is the first time in your life you've been without a job. If that's the case, you probably have no idea where to begin, what to do, what to feel, or how to turn things around in the shortest amount of time. Believe me, many people for many different reasons find themselves in the unemployment boat at one time or another, so learn from others and from career experts how to deal with your situation.

Here are some very useful Web sites you can visit to help organize your plan of action, get some support, and learn from others how to start putting your work life back together.

Wall Street Journal Careers

Many experts offer sound advice at the Wall Street Journal's Career Center (public.wsj.com/careers/resources/documents/cwc-afterjobloss.htm). Here are article titles you can read online. Many include links to other resources, so spend some time reading these wonderful nuggets of advice.

"How to Reduce Stress When You Lose a Job," by Barbara Mende

"Overcoming the Stigma of Losing Your Job," by David R. Caruso and Alan S. Harris

"Turn Your Job Loss into a New Beginning," by Taunee Besson

"Don't Allow Shame to Hinder Your Job Search," by Amy Eldridge and Virginia K. Gordon

"Why Job Security Is an Oxymoron," by Freda Turner

"How to Negotiate a Fair Severance Package," by Paul H. Tobias and Susan Sauter

"While Between Jobs, Consult Part-Time," by John M. Hartigan

"Keeping the Family Calm After a Job Loss," by Jeri S. Miller

Amby's Work Site: The Unemployment Blues

This personal home page offers a long list of links and other online resources for the unemployed, including how to develop and survive on a budget, how to help family members deal with job loss, next steps after a job loss, and other articles and advice to help you get back on track. Visit Amby's at amby.com/worksite/unemployment_blues.html.

Tips for Quitters

If you walked off the job out of disgust, anger, to avoid getting fired, or in response to horrible working conditions, you're going to have some explaining to do to potential employers. No matter what your reasons for leaving before securing a new job, it seems to reflect poor or no planning on your part. Your best bet is to frame this in interviews as, "I wanted to study and broaden my skill set," "I wanted to spend time exploring all my career options and investigate new opportunities." Another good one is, "I worked very hard for a very long time, and wanted to spend time with my family before I jumped back into a career."

During this time off from work, too, you might want to spend some time reading Chapter 2, "It's a Jungle Out There: Job Hunters Beware!" which covers issues such as finding out what your former bosses say before you apply for jobs. You can hire a professional reference checker to call your boss and find out what he might say to real potential employers. If you left on bad terms, this is highly recommended.

Locating Temporary Work Online

If your length of unemployment is longer than you expected and more than 10 or 12 weeks, consider doing part-time temporary work. Be sure to leave time for your job-search efforts and try to get assignments that offer flexibility for taking time off for interviews and making calls during the day.

To locate temporary agencies in your area, or to locate contract work online, do a keyword search using *temporary placement* or *temporary staffing*. Include the name of your city or use a regional directory such as Yahoo! Local or just general regional directories for your area. The yellow pages list temp agencies, too. Aquent is a national talent service (see Figure 21.2) that hails contract work as the wave of the future. Maybe you just stumbled into a new career path?

Keep your eyes and ears open to networking opportunities while temping. You may not have any interest in the line of work you're temping in, but if you fall into good graces with your manager or other co-workers, they might just know someone, or know someone who knows someone who can help you get your job search in motion.

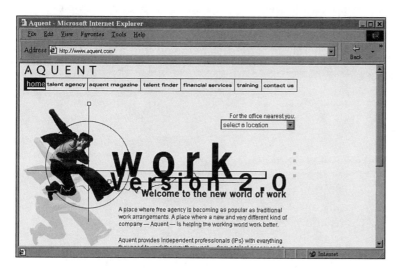

Figure 21.2

*Aquent's (*www.aquent.com*) talent-match service connects employers in need of short-term talent for project work or special projects. It's predicted that in the next 10 years, more than half the work force will work under contract or project assignments.*

In these days of job insecurity, losing your job is "business as usual." Try to stay positive and learn from the experience, and use the time off to examine your skills and interests. And if necessary, take comfort in knowing that temporary work options are available, and that you will find a new job. Your job right now is to do just that!

The Least You Need to Know

➤ Life in the working world is less secure than ever before—losing your job is not the end of the world.

➤ Use your downtime to take a self-inventory and refocus your career objectives and restrategize your job-hunting strategy.

➤ Tap into the Web for advice and support from career experts to help you stay focused in recovering from a job loss.

➤ Don't draw attention to your job loss on your résumé or during interviews, but do prepare appropriate responses to questions from potential employers.

➤ Get the word out to your networking community that you're looking for work, but don't desperately rely on others to help you find a new job.

Diversity in the Workplace

As if looking for a job isn't tough enough, discrimination and gender bias can pose even more problems for the minority job seeker. Although a significant sector of the workforce is made up of minorities and soon minorities will be the majority in both population and in the work world, racism and unfair hiring and promotion practices still pervade many companies today.

Maybe you're thinking to yourself: "But I work harder than most people in my company. Shouldn't I be recognized and rewarded on the basis of merit alone?" In a perfect world, yes. In the real world, it isn't always that way. Racism, sexual orientation discrimination, and gender bias are more covert than during the days of segregation and blatant harassment, and even though there are laws to protect you, discrimination can stall a career or make for really horrible working conditions.

But there is good news. If you're a member of a protected class—women, minorities, gays, people with disabilities, and people over the age of 45—there are plenty of companies that have declared diversity a priority and are celebrating individuality as not only an asset, but as a crucial element to staying competitive in today's global marketplace. As you guessed, these same forward-thinking companies are wired and ready to attract talent through the online medium, so look to the Web as an important resource for minority job seekers.

Finding the jobs is one thing, but other career development issues deserve your attention as well. And there are numerous online resources to help you deal with the issues you face as a job seeker and member of a protected class. This chapter points you in the direction of those resources and offers some pointers on dealing with the issue head-on, before you go about the task of looking for a company that values you as an individual.

Diversity in the Workplace

If you're a minority job seeker concerned about locating companies that support diversity in the workplace, or if you're considering leaving a job because you sense discrimination, isolation, or outright racism, don't despair. There are things you can do to identify and combat discrimination in the workplace, and there are plenty of Web sites devoted to the issue of diversity in the workplace and other concerns for minority job seekers.

I talked with Chandra Prasad, diversity editor at Vault.com and a freelance writer, and she offers these suggestions and insights for dealing with the diversity issue when it's time to look for a new job.

Be Sure Your Job-Hunting Materials Are in Tip-Top Shape

Say you've been actively seeking a job, and you know the market is hungry for people with your skill set, but you're just not getting any calls for interviews. Before you jump to the conclusion that you're being discriminated against, take a critical look at your résumé and cover letter. Are there typos or grammatical errors? Is it a solid, well-written résumé with keywords and a stop-them-dead-in-their-tracks skills summary? Is the résumé formatted properly, both for the electronic medium or print form?

Have a friend or colleague (not someone you work with now) review your application materials—they speak volumes about your attention to detail, accuracy, and general communication skills—things that nearly every employer values. Have your materials checked, rechecked, and checked again by friends, and proofread it yourself several times. Don't forget to use the spell checker, even though a passthrough with that tool isn't completely foolproof.

Thanks for the Tip

Excuse Me, Ma'am, Your Minority Status Is Showing

The question of whether or not to include items on your résumé that reveal your minority status is a sticky issue. Ask any human resource person and they'll say, "No way!" due to the legal issues surrounding Equal Opportunity and Affirmative Action. But from a résumé point of view, if you headed the Black Student Coalition, by all means enter it on your résumé. It lets employers know you've had responsibilities that require leadership, management, and communication skills.

If you think you need professional help with your materials, go online and make use of the many, many résumé help sites. One site to check out is the Resume Expert section at Monster.com. Kim Isaacs, moderator of the résumé message board (see Figure 22.1) will review résumés as long as they're embedded in your posting to the board.

It helps to include specific questions, too, such as, "I'm not sure this is the best objective statement, and I think the grammar is weak," or, "The document is longer than one page. Is that okay?" Kim will review your résumé for free, and post her comments in reply to your original message. Don't worry—there are plenty of examples of what Kim needs in order to critique your résumé, so spend some time reading through other people's postings before you post.

To take advantage of this free online service, you do have to be a registered member of Monster.com, but the process is quick and painless. You'll be issued a username and password to use the message board system, as well as take advantage of the numerous résumé (and other career issues) resources.

Be sure to read the chapters in Part 2 of this book, which deals entirely with résumés and cover letters, as well as privacy and access issues related to online job sites.

Use Identity-Specific Job Banks and Networks

If newspaper ads and general online job banks (such as Monster.com or CareerPath.com) aren't working for you, try employment agencies, job banks, and recruitment services that specialize in minority placement. Identity-specific job banks such as Minorities' Job Bank (www.minorities-jb.com) offer a job bank, résumé posting option, employer and member profiles, career development resources, and feature articles dealing with minority job issues.

Figure 22.1

The Resume Expert at Monster.com reviews résumés posted to the message board and responds with specific tips and pointers.

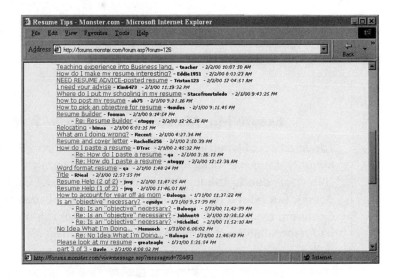

Also worth checking out are the "Villages" or communities specific to African-Americans, Asian-Americans, Native Americans, Hispanics, women, and a Minorities Global Village. Another valuable source is the Minorities News Headlines feature, which tracks minority issues in the news. Minorities' Job Bank has also been named a "Select Site" by the Dow Jones Business Directory.

For networking online, be sure to check out these sites:

➤ The National Society of Hispanic MBAs (www.nshmba.org)

➤ The National Society of Black Engineers (www.nsbe.org)

➤ The National Association of Asian-American Professionals (www.naaap.org)

If you don't find what you're looking for in the preceding sites, another good starting point is the Multicultural Advantage Online Networking Center (members.aol.com/multnet/netcenter.htm), which features online discussion forums on "The Multicultural Advantage Business Exchange," "The Diversity Recruitment Online Networking Forum," "Power Moves for People of Color Networking Forum," and "Leaders of Color Online Networking Forum." There's also a section on "The Online Guide to Networking with Recruiters." Or, you can take part in an opinion poll or read job postings in several industries.

Site for Sore Eyes

Have a Favorite Diversity Magazine?

The Equal Opportunity Publications Web site (www.eop.com) features information on its magazines and publications, including classified advertising found in said rags—"Equal Opportunity," "Woman Engineer," "Minority Engineer," "Careers & the Disabled," and "Workforce Diversity for Engineering and IT Professionals." This site also enables you to post your résumé or view job listings.

And at the end of this chapter, you'll find diversity resource and job sites for minorities, women, gays, and people with disabilities. Read on!

Present Your Background As an Asset

Are you bilingual? Have you impacted an employer's bottom line by working with minority clients who feel more comfortable dealing with a member of their own community? Then, let potential employers know this! It's also important to ask questions in the interview about diversity policies and to take note of things when you're visiting a company Web site or interviewing at the office, such as the names on the doors of executive offices, and who's doing which jobs. If a company claims to have a diverse workforce, but all of the management positions are filled by nonminorities, the company might not be truly interested in a diverse leadership.

Overachieve

Regardless of a person's background, if you work hard, maintain a professional attitude, and contribute to the success of the team and the company, you leave no room for question as to your abilities to do the job. Don't let discrimination enter into the formula—go above and beyond the call of duty. When you work twice as hard as anyone else, your performance will bring the greatest success.

Thanks for the Tip

The Seven Signs of Commitment to Diversity

David Clark, vice president in charge of diversity management and training at Federated Department Stores, offers advice for minority job seekers in a keynote address that you can read online at *Career Magazine* (www.careermag.com/newsarts/diversity/fed.html). Clark says to test a company's commitment to diversity, look for these seven signs: broad-based thinking, leadership from the top, active recruiting of diversity, an emphasis on training and development, written policies and guidelines, the extension of diversity to community and vendors, and constant communication and reinforcement of the company's diversity policies and practices.

The Extra Mile

Keep a Cool Head

Even if you work in a company that embraces diversity, there's the chance that you'll run into discrimination or bias when dealing with customers or clients. Although there might be a temptation to strike back, remember you represent your company. Try to keep your head together, refute the comment politely and professionally, and you'll walk away the winner.

Reach Out to Mentors and Networking Contacts

People you admire—at work or otherwise—can offer guidance, advice, and wisdom by sharing their life and work experiences with you. Look for someone with plenty of experience who's willing to help out younger or less-experienced workers. Learning from someone who's been there, done that, can bring clarity and focus to problems and challenges you face in life or on the job.

Women in the Workplace

I remember sitting in a weekly meeting at a former job and one of the account execs updating the team on a hot, new client prospect. He mentioned the names of the two key people, describing "Lisa" as "a real nice girl, brown hair." He told us "Brian" was "a real sharp thinker, the point man." I asked, "What color is *his* hair?" No one got it. The account exec just looked at me, puzzled, and kept talking.

Disgruntled? Join the Club

Feeling like there's no where to turn or that you need to blow off some steam? Check out Disgruntled (www.disgruntled.com), the "business magazine for people who work for a living." There's a lengthy list of resources and contact information for civil rights and discrimination, employment law, general information for employees, government, rights of groups, pension information, rights of union members, sex discrimination, sexual harassment, and women's issues, as well as information on whistle blowing.

Sure, it's not a huge deal. Referring to a woman's physical features rather than her intellect or skill set is just one of those sneaky little ways sexism and gender bias creep into the workplace, oftentimes without a second thought.

If you're a femme job seeker and want to look at companies that have proven track records in the area of equal opportunity and related gender-in-the-workplace issues, log on to these specialty sites for advice, guidance, information, company profiles, job listings, and more.

➤ **Advancing Women** (www.advancingwomen.com)

My favorite women's career site (see Figure 22.2), Advancing Women, is a network for women to share career strategies and provide employment opportunities and cutting-edge resources that power women's success.

According to its Web site, Advancing Women was "the first women's community and Web site to fuse the power of the Net as a communication, networking, and information tool, with the compelling agenda of women seeking the most effective means of advancing their career and business goals."

The Career Center section can help level the playing field for you in your job search to give you the tools, strategy, and a network of contacts with human resource professionals worldwide. One of these highlights of this must-see site for women professionals is the technology news section, which can help you use the Web to network and gather advice, tools, and information to overcome the challenges that women face in their careers.

➤ **Ka-Ching.com** (`www.ka-ching.com`)

That Oprah Winfrey sure has some great ideas. Besides the fabulously popular talk show, she's behind the production of a very smart collection of Web sites for women—the Oxygen Media network (`www.oxygen.com`). The Ka-Ching.com site focuses specifically on business and career-related issues and covers everything from the job hunt to thriving on the job, plus balancing work and life. Career information includes résumé and cover letter writing tips, negotiating the best salary, job profiles, plus a battery of online calculators to help you figure out such things as whether to lease or buy a car, how much your 401(k) will be worth, and how much debt is costing you, as well as provide you with a variety of small business spreadsheets and a slew of other money-related topics. The site also features message boards and chat rooms, electronic newsletters, and advice from experts and information on continuing education. A must-see site!

➤ **Women's Wire** (`www.womenswire.com`)

Women's Wire work section includes Career Coach expert advice, plus free and up-to-date job listings, stress-fighting tips, and tools and advice on hitting the fast track to management. A must-see is the Best Companies for Women channel (`www.womenswire.com/work/work.html`) where you can find out how employers fare when it comes to salary, advancement opportunities, childcare, and benefits. Frivolous features in this otherwise on-target women's resource include work horoscopes and fashion advice.

➤ **Career Women** (`www.careerwomen.net`)

A comprehensive online resource for career women. Post your résumé, view job openings, and read company profiles (direct links to sponsoring company human resource sites and job postings). Other features include career women news, resources, and advice. Worth checking out.

Figure 22.2

Advancing Women's career network is an excellent resource for women professionals, especially when it comes to the power of networking.

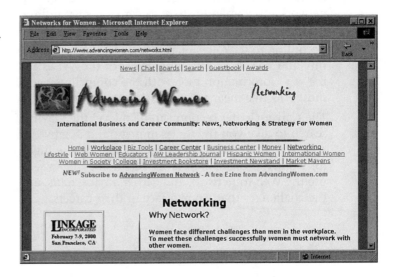

People with Disabilities

The Americans with Disabilities Act (ADA) has opened a lot of doors when it comes to finding workplaces that are physically and environmentally suited for workers with disabilities. ADA has also helped to facilitate the communication and promotion of public and private efforts that empower people with disabilities with the tools and information necessary for career development.

Below are some Web sites dedicated to helping people with disabilities find work, re-enter the workforce, and locate online job resources.

➤ **Ability Magazine** (www.abilitymagazine.com)

The content at the online version of this notable publication focusing on disabilities provides information on technology, the Americans with Disability Act, job opportunities for people with disabilities, human interest stories, national and local resource centers, and more. An extensive collection of links and online resources will point you in the right direction. A good starting point.

➤ **Job Seeking Skills for People with Disabilities** (www.csun.edu/~sp20558/dis/sh.html)

Before you start your job search, be sure to log on to this comprehensive primer for workers with disabilities. Provided by California State Northridge, this resource guide provides information such as identifying occupations, completing job applications, developing résumés, writing cover letters, interviewing skills, locating internships, and personal marketing skills. You can also get the employer's insider perspective in the section that deals with employee/employer expectations.

➤ **Independence Bank** (www.ind-bank.org)

The Independence Bank is a résumé bank and job site with an easy-to-use résumé entry form and a searchable directory of employers that recruit people with disabilities. A links page contains other notable sites of interest to the disabled job seeker.

➤ **Challenge 2000** (www2.interaccess.com/netown/)

Challenge 2000 is the online extension of Job Resources for the Disabled, a non-profit, Chicago-based organization. It's an informative site for persons with developmental disabilities, and covers issues such as community resources, job-searching information, EEO employers, and family support resources.

➤ **Careers On-Line** (disserv3.stu.umn.edu/COL/)

This site provides job search and employment information to people with disabilities, broken down by discipline; regional, national, and international job listings; job hotlines; and links to other disability and employment programs.

Diversity Sites and Resources

There are many sites devoted to the issue of diversity in the workplace. If you don't find what you're looking for at these sites, go to your favorite search engine and use keywords specific to the information you're looking for. You might even find more specific information in the links pages at the following sites:

➤ **Career Exposure Diversity Links** (**www.careerexposure.com/diversity.html**)

An awesome and extensive list of links to the best of the best diversity sites. An excellent starting point for interesting facts and statistics on diversity issues, plus specific categories with resources and links to general sites, organization links, multicultural organizations, women's resources, minority career resources, and government links.

➤ **Diversity Forum** (**www.diversityforum.com**)

Be sure to head over to www.diversityforum.com for a "massive directory" of information on affirmative action and equal employment opportunity data, information, resources, and events. Plus, you'll find links to every significant public, private, and nonprofit civil rights organization in the field. You can also peruse more than 30,000 job listings from more than 1,200 companies. Not a bad starting point, eh?

➤ **Black Collegian** (**www.blackcollegian.com**)

The online version (see Figure 22.3) of the much-heralded print publication for African-American college students and degreed professionals includes job resources and job listings, résumé advice and posting, career guidance, and a plethora of other great articles, news and resources, plus a special section on "X-tra Curricular" activities. After all, there is more to life than just work!

➤ **DiversiLink** (**www.diversilink.com**)

Although you don't have to be a card-carrying member of the Society for Hispanic Professional Engineers (or even an engineer), you can view job listings, get career advice, or post your résumé in a private job résumé database. You can also get help preparing your job hunting materials, and visit virtual job fairs to "meet" employers and find out about current openings. If you need guidance in the area of career development, be sure to visit the Career Center, which takes you to Todo Latino (www.todolatino.com) where you can get coaching and interviewing and negotiating tips, or "Ask El Consejero" questions. You can also take a "Character and Temperament Quiz" which is cited as "The most popular and useful personality assessment tool ever devised. Online test can be administered in Spanish."

➤ **Diversity Employment** (**www.diversityemployment.com**)

Featuring the standard job site contents and search tools, you can scan job postings by title or region. This site is a a multicultural employment job and résumé database. All listings are dated, although my observation has been a good number of the listings are from third-party recruiters such as Olsten Staffing. Be sure to read Chapter 17, "Headhunters and Third-Party Recruiters," if you haven't dealt with this aspect of the job hunt before. Many experts say there are other ways to approach a situation, and getting around the recruiter can increase your chances of getting an offer, as the employer can skip the sometimes hefty placement fee paid to third-party recruiters.

➤ **Diversity Link** (www.diversitylink.com)

A well-rounded Web site that "links females, minorities, and other diversity professionals with proactive employers and search firms offering outstanding career opportunities." Employer postings include U.S. Department of Energy and Barnes & Noble, as well as Fortune 1000 companies such as GE, Ingersoll-Rand, and Sony.

➤ **Gaywork** (www.gaywork.com)

Regardless of your sexual orientation, if you want to connect with "truly equal opportunity employers," this diversity site is definitely worth checking out. The up-to-date job database is a cinch to search and is filled with a variety of interesting positions. If you want to post your résumé for employers to see, it stays on display for two months, and it's easy to update, revise, or delete. To reach employers that offer domestic partner benefits, for example, this is a must-see site. The site also links to Gay.com (www.gay.com), which features lifestyle, entertainment, news, discussion forums, advice, issues, and other pertinent information.

➤ **MinorityCareer** (www.minoritycareer.com)

Featuring job postings from corporate giants such as Ernst & Young, Pitney Bowes, and Southwest Airlines, this site is the online extension of Minority Employment magazine. Besides the résumé upload feature, you can view job postings and get the latest scoop on minority career fairs, expos, and events.

➤ **Saludos** (www.saludos.com)

A Web site dedicated exclusively to promoting Hispanic careers and education, supported by Saludos Hispanos magazine. In the Career Center, you can explore career fields, learn about mentoring programs and read profiles, post your résumé, view job listings, read company profiles, and get current information on job fairs and scholarship opportunities. You can also check out articles from Saludos Hispanos magazine, the sponsor of the site.

➤ **Yahoo! Professional Associations Directory** (dir.yahoo.com/Society_and_Culture/Organizations/Professional/)

Professional groups and associations offer more than just networking opportunities and industry reports and news. If you don't already belong to a professional association, perhaps now is the time to sign up. Through Yahoo!'s mega directory, you can connect with groups such as Women in Communications or the Asian American Journalists Association to get the inside scoop on job opportunities, events, and news in your profession, or find out about meetings or charters in your area.

Figure 22.3

The Black Collegian offers resources, advice, and news on diversity issues—both at work and in life.

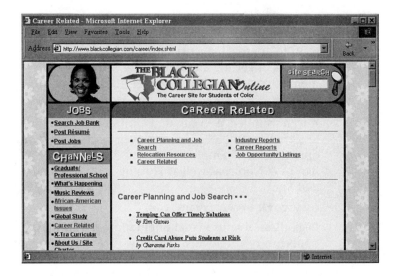

As minorities become the majority of the workforce in the new millennium, tapping into the vast resources on the Web can help you advance your career, overcome obstacles, and equip yourself with the knowledge, information, tools, and resources you need to succeed.

The Least You Need to Know

➤ Identity-specific job sites and diversity Web sites can help you locate diversity-friendly employers.

➤ Minority sites can you connect you with networking and mentoring opportunities—two essential tools in your job-hunting arsenal.

➤ You can gather legal information, news, and events online regarding discrimination, equal opportunity employers, affirmative action, and equal-pay-for-equal-work issues.

Chapter 23

Just for Executives, High Rollers, and Those in High Demand

In This Chapter

➤ A Web guide that's done all the thinking and link collecting for you—a one-stop site for the busy executive

➤ Go online to get company and industry profiles, plus insider advice and opinions on what it's really like to work in profiled companies

➤ Skip the association meetings—go online to network and hob-nob with other high-level execs

➤ Use free and fee-based executive job-posting sites to look for your next high-level position

➤ Learn how to work with recruiters and headhunters and how to find them if they haven't already tracked you down

Executives and professionals in high-demand positions are busy people. You barely have enough time to do the things you enjoy outside of work, so how are you supposed to find time to look for a new job? Job hunting can be time-consuming, but thanks to the increase of career Web sites for executives, you can save time, gain access to a wider pool of job openings, and quickly and easily do research to gather the information you need to succeed in landing your next dream job.

Although many people think that most high-rolling execs don't have to look for a job—headhunters and recruiters come to you whether you're in the market for a new position or not—the fact is, if you've decided it's time to move on to greener pastures, you can't sit around and wait for a new job to fall into your lap. You have to go find it.

This chapter shows you how the online executive job hunt works, and what you can do to get your résumé to the right people at the right time. You'll learn how and where to look for jobs, how to network online, and how to do in-depth company or industry research to knock 'em dead in the interview. If it's executive recruiters you're after, you'll learn where to go to locate these people, who more and more are turning to the Web to attract and hire high-level players.

You don't need to be an Internet expert to tap into these resources, either. A strong understanding of your business or industry and some general logic skills are all you need to get you started on productive online research sessions. Plus, you'll find that there are plenty of job site guides and search engine directories to point you in the direction of the Web's most powerful research sources. To learn more about online researching, be sure to read Chapters 10, 11, and 12.

CEO Express: The Executive's Toolbox (`www.ceoexpress.com`)

I've seen plenty of "good" Web sites in my years on the Web, but I am truly amazed at the scope of this one-stop, businessperson's Web guide. CEO and Editor Patricia Pomerleau, a self-described busy executive and accomplished businesswoman, has collected links to the most popular and useful online news and information sources to create a fully customizable guide to sites of interest to other busy executives. Simply put, it is a businessperson's dream site, and particularly helpful to execs who are new to the Web.

CEO Express features an unprecedented tool called "passive customization,"—*passive* meaning the information and resources you need given your interests as a busy CEO have already been collected for you, and *customization* meaning you can add or delete links based on your very specific interests. For example, you can add a link to your company intranet or links to your favorite Web sites.

A Customizable Desktop and User-Friendly Interface

After becoming a CEO Express member, which takes about one minute and asks for standard information such as your name, title, company size, and where you live, you'll see edit icons next to each of the categories, as shown in Figure 23.1, including categories provided by the editor and personal categories of your favorite links or bookmarks. Just click any of those icons to get an edit page where you can add or delete links. The edit system is incredibly easy to use, and allows you to go back at any time and add or delete links based on your current Web-surfing trends and interests.

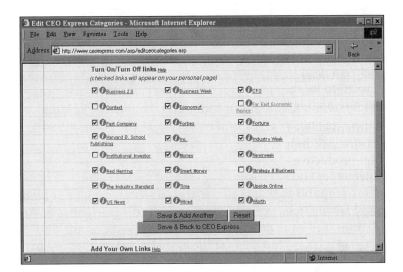

Figure 23.1

Edit tools in each CEO Express category let you add or delete links and resources. This figure shows the edit page, where you simply click links to delete, or type Web addresses or file-names of links you want to add.

Categories of links provided by CEO Express, as well as other site highlights, include the following executive-level Web resources and interests, and more. Be sure to visit the site at www.ceoexpress.com for full category contents.

Daily News and Information

From your personal page on CEO Express, you'll be able to access breaking news that's updated several times daily. Reach the most updated happenings around the nation and across the world with the click of a button.

Link categories include news sites for daily, business, international, and online TV news; business magazines such as Fast Company and Fortune; tech magazines such as C|NET and ZDNet; and online magazines such as Salon and Slate; time and weather reports; newsfeeds from sources such as AP Wire, Bloomberg, and Business News; Internet search tool links to the most popular and powerful search engines, including tips on how to conduct effective searches; Web site locators, including Dot Com Locator and InterNIC; and health-related sites such as Dr.Koop and WebMD.

Business Research

Link categories in the business research section include financial markets; SEC; U.S. and government agencies such as the IRS, U.S. Trademarks, and World Bank; Internet research and surveys, including the Electronic Commerce Guide, Internet business surveys, and WWW User Survey; Quotes and Market News, such as BigCharts, CBS Marketwatch, Yahoo! Finance, and Money Central; Banking and Finance sites such as Rate Monitor and Federal Reserve; Company research sources such as Annual Reports,

Company Sleuth, Hoover's, Peerscape, Thomas Register, Wall Street Research, and professional and trade association sites, plus tips on conducting online research (a must-read).

You also get links to International Business resources, including the Global Business Centre and Emerging Markets; Investing and IPO Research sources include the CDA Insider Watch, Morningstar, Motley Fool, IPO Central, and IPO Lockup. For bankruptcy information, links include American Bankruptcy Institute and the Internet Bankruptcy Library; and finally, cutting-edge links take you to sites such as MIT's Media Lab, eBay, and Strategic Enterprise Knowledge Centers.

Private Email Account

Having a Web-based email account offers convenience and privacy, and allows access from any Web-connected computer, anywhere in the world. Sure beats the pants off Telnetting or forwarding your email from your work or home account when you're on the road! To set up your CEO Express email account, just click on the email button on the CEO Express home page taskbar after registering as a member. That button will take you to a setup page where you can select an email address at *yourname@expressmailbox.com*.

CEO Express Email also features these convenient tools:

➤ Forward other email accounts to your CEO Express account.

➤ Upload contacts into the Express Mailbox system from applications such as Outlook98/2000, Netscape Messenger, and Outlook Express.

➤ Establish filters and folders that let you organize and screen incoming email.

➤ Utilize advance-editing features that allow different backgrounds, fonts, festive greetings, and other bells and whistles.

➤ Send files as attachments to email.

➤ Add additional "VIP" features such as email by phone, voice mail, and fax to email, pager notification, extra disk storage space, and the ability to forward CEO Express email to other accounts or import all your email accounts to your CEO Express email.

Telnet Email Access

If you're on the road or away from the office and need to check your email, Telnet is an "old-fashioned" way of connecting to your email account by calling into a local Internet service provider and using an online mail reader such as elm to access your messages. Sounds complicated, eh? It is. Get a Web-based email account for your personal or business email, including your job-hunting email needs!

Network at CEO Express Forums and Roundtables

CEO Express offers forums on various business issues. Expert speakers on various business issues host roundtable discussions, surveys, and other discussions on topics relevant to CEO members.

Better Networking

Compared to mining newsgroups for pertinent discussions in your area of expertise, monitored or hosted online discussions like the ones found at CEO Express are usually more interesting, informative, intelligent, and focused. To find hosted or monitored online forums, be sure to check out Yack! at www.yack.com. This directory of online chat sessions and other forums covers everything from sports and entertainment to finance and business.

CEO Express Career Center

As if the busy executive's online business resource guide isn't enough, the good folks at CEO Express also provide links to online career sites, including general and niche job banks, recruiter and headhunter directories, and a guide to career resources such as Ask the Headhunter and Wall Street Journal's Careers magazine.

If this is your first time going online to look for a job, this is a good starting point. Be sure to check out the Career Resources center for links to Career Magazine, HeadHunter.net, Hoover's, Monster.com's Career Center, National Association for Female Execs, and Wall Street Journal Careers (www.careers.wsj.com), which features extensive reporting and advice from executive-level career experts, as seen in Figure 23.2.

Figure 23.2

Career experts at Careers.wsj.com offer straightforward advice on a variety of issues affecting executive-level job seekers, with an emphasis on the online job hunt.

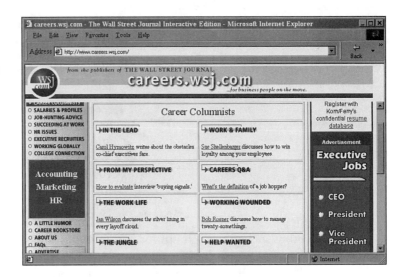

Company and Industry Research Sites

High-level execs know that without detailed knowledge of a target company, its competitors, and the industry, it's hard to convince a prospective employer that you're deserving of an executive-level salary, and that you can actually do the job. But traditional methods of gathering the information you need to succeed in the job search are tedious and time-consuming. Not anymore—going online to do company or industry research is simply the smartest way to go. Not only will you save time, but you'll be able to access just about any business information resource imaginable, and you'll be able to do it from the comfort of your desktop computer.

You can gather information or data about your industry, your competitors, product offerings, new services, market forecasts and conditions, stock information, daily news, trade publication features, and news on the other movers and shakers in your business community. Here are some of the most popular and comprehensive resources for conducting industry or business research online.

Hoover's Online

Hoover's Business Network (www.hoovers.com) was built to "serve the needs of people behind desks." Content is hand-picked by a team of editors and represents the best the Web has to offer to busy professionals. Hoover's content is developed from a business-oriented perspective and also covers topics such as money management, career development, news, and business travel.

At the core of Hoover's Online is the proprietary company and industry information, known for its quality, accuracy, and reliability. The profiles cover the largest and most influential public and private companies around the world to give you a more complete understanding of a company's personality, history and strategy, market position, officers, competition, and financial health.

Besides providing detailed financial and corporate information on thousands of U.S. and international companies, a little icing on the cake is Hoover's "List of Lists," which points you in the direction of polls, surveys, rankings, and top performers in a variety of categories. Companies includes lists such as the "Top 50 Companies with the Best Diversity Records" and Fortune's "100 Best Companies to Work For." Brands and Products lists include "Top 10 Advertising Slogans of the Century" and Newsweek's "Guide to the Web." People lists include "Businessmen of the Century," "Unsung Heroes of Business," and "America's Top 100 Asian Entrepreneurs." Locations lists link you to sites and articles covering the best places to live or work. Access the "List of Lists" at www.hoovers.com/company/lists_best/.

Vault.com

Vault.com (www.vault.com) is another top-notch resource for career information that brings job seekers accurate and timely information from independent research and company insiders. Vault researchers interview and survey thousands of insiders in 3,000 top companies to bring you the inside scoop on how companies operate and how they fare in their given industries. Vault.com's channels (see Figure 23.3) cover industries such as law, aerospace, accounting, advertising, investment banking, Internet and new media, and every other major industry sector.

Reports help you catch up on the latest news and research, and gather quick information through insider Company Snapshots. After you've located your target companies, be sure to visit the message boards, where you can post questions or read postings from people who actually work at the company. The message boards are moderated, so if you have a question not covered already, pose a question to a channel expert.

Vault.com also offers 12 free weekly email newsletters packed with current industry trends and news, interviews with industry insiders, career guidance, and more.

Another value-add is Vault.com's Vaultmatch, a free service that matches job seekers with positions that meet your qualifications and interests. Vault.com's job board is a popular, free listing site with more than 100,000 top jobs in an easy-to-search format. Be sure to read Chapter 14 for a detailed review of Vault.com's job-search tool.

Other Vault.com features include information and links to career books and guides, leading trade publications and magazines, online courses, and other tools to help you manage and advance your career.

Figure 23.3

*Vault.com channels pro-
vide insider reports and
detailed industry and
company information in
a wide variety of profes-
sions.*

EDGAR

EDGAR-Online (www.edgar-online.com) is the leading commercial provider of free
access to U.S. Securities & Exchange Commission (SEC) filings and related business
intelligence on the Internet. Other services include functions such as EDGAR-Online
People (www.edgar-online.com/people/), a new service that allows users to search the
SEC filings by an executive's name. See who's who and whose ears are ringing. Maybe
yours?

A variety of free and paid subscriber services are available from EDGAR Online. At no
cost, customers can access far more information than can be found on the Securities
and Exchange Commission's own 24-hour delayed Web site. This includes "packaged"
and advanced searching by filing type, industry, location by city and state, and other
search criteria.

Fee services allow you to quickly dig up the Management's Discussion section of a
10-Q or 10-K from a document with the EDGAR Online "Glimpse" function, or the
Financial Data Schedule of a 10-Q or 10-K from a document using "FDS" function.
EDGAR makes it easy to gather even more information by providing access to third-
party research from companies as PC Quote, Big Charts, Hoover's, News Alert, Zacks
Investment Research, Wall Street Research Net, and Company Link.

Networking on the Big Network

Wouldn't it be great if you could stay active in your professional associations without
having to attend all those darned meetings? What if you could stay in touch with

associates and business contacts without having to pick up the phone? When it comes to networking, there's no easier place to do it than on the Web.

Although Chapter 11, "It's Who You Know," covers the online networking scene—how to find and use newsgroups and other online forums related to your career interests—this section offers executive-level starting points, so take a look to see what the online world can do to help you network effectively, whether you're doing job-related networking or not. After all, the best time to make "friends" is when you don't need anything from them!

Newsgroups

One good starting point for finding and using newsgroups is Deja.com (www.deja.com), a directory of thousands and thousands of newsgroups on the Web. If you've never visited or participated in a newsgroup or other online community, take a quick run through the New User tour at www.deja.com/help/newusers.shtml.

Newsgroups offer more than the opportunity to meet fellow executives—you can participate by offering advice, expertise, or otherwise demonstrate your knowledge on a particular subject. For example, engaging in "virtual conversations" on a topic that demonstrates a certain skill set or knowledge base is a good way to get attention from Web-savvy recruiters and headhunters who mine newsgroups to find high-demand and hard-to-find experts.

Newsgroups and discussion forums are also good places to scout out information or discussions on your target companies.

Virtual Community of Associations

The Virtual Community of Associations (www.vcanet.org) is a service of the Greater Washington Society of Association Executives (GWSAE), the country's largest regional association for association executives, with 3,500 members representing more than 1,000 national and international associations in the greater Washington, D.C. area (read "special interest" groups).

The VCA Member Directory provides a resource to association members and the general public for locating associations and their Web sites. The VCA Member Directory contains a master listing of all VCA member association names and Web-site addresses or URLs.

Yahoo! Directory of Professional Associations

For a lengthy list of links to professional associations in every imaginable industry, be sure to check out Yahoo!'s directory of professional associations at dir.yahoo.com/Business_and_Economy/Organizations/Professional/. Or, do a keyword search at any search engine to find your professional association if it's not listed here.

Advancing Women

Advancing Women (www.advancingwomen.com) is a network for women to share career strategies, provide employment opportunities, and cutting-edge resources that power women in advancing their career and business goals. This professional women's network came about in response to the lack of networks for and by women—where professionals make the best contacts, do business, forge alliances, learn about career opportunities, and get job offers.

Look for Jobs

Somewhere, sometime, someone started a rumor that all those positions posted at online job sites are just for entry- and midlevel professionals. Although "traditional" executive recruiters have been a little slow to come around to the online recruiting scene, there are plenty of executive-level job-posting sites, and plenty of online recruiters and executive headhunters who use the Web to find new talent. General job sites such as Monster.com and CareerMosaic list upper-level positions, too, so don't rule them out as sources for executive-level job postings.

Using General Job Sites

Many of the national, general job sites don't have special job sections just for executive positions, so when you do a search, use keywords such as executive, CIO, COO, CEO, CFO, vice president, president, or an exact job title to make sure you get listings that match your experience level.

Many executive job-posting sites charge a fee to access job listings. But when you consider the salary levels of available jobs, it's probably worth the investment. If you've never gone online to job hunt before, be sure to have an electronic version of your résumé on hand before you set out on your search. If you need help getting your résumé ready for the Web, be sure to read through Chapter 5, "Understanding the Electronic Résumé," before you begin your search.

You should also spend some time reading through the search tips at any job site you visit so you know how to best pinpoint job postings. Online job searching isn't complicated, but taking a few minutes to understand how a site's search engine works can yield better results, and save time.

Careers.wsj.com

This is an excellent source of free career news and great job leads, including openings posted in *The Wall Street Journal*. Pick an employer, an industry, a job function, or a location, and then read over a brief summary of all listings matching your criteria. Full job announcements include brief company information taken from Hoover's Online. To access the jobs section, click the **Jobseek** button on the main page at `www.careers.wsj.com`.

Exec-U-Net (`www.execunet.com`)

For a fee, you can access the Exec-U-Net Job Opportunities Report, which lists about 700 jobs per issue (twice a month) in the fields of general management, finance, sales, marketing, human resources, operations management, research and development, engineering, and MIS opportunities. They have several levels of membership, offering varying levels of access to career information and services. Full membership is required for the Job Opportunities Report. It'll cost you between $195 and $325, depending on how long you subscribe. There's a money-back guarantee, so try it out for ten days, and if you don't think you're getting your money's worth, cancel your subscription.

Executive Job Hunting (`zoomjobs.com`)

This one-stop job-hunting site boasts access to more than 1.7 million positions in the $40K to $750K range, offering search capabilities of job databases, trade publications, newspaper ads, newsgroup postings, and postings in the site's own recruiting division. Although I had a hard time figuring out who and what's behind this site, I did a little digging and discovered that the site is put together by Career Advisory Network, a biggie in the recruiting scene. Why they didn't just come out and say who and what the site is all about is a mystery to me, but nonethelesss you can access a wealth of online job-hunting resources and tools from this site. Figure 23.4 shows some of the resources available at this mega job site.

Figure 23.4

Executive Job Hunting, also known as zoomjobs.com, *provides access to online job openings as seen at job sites, newsgroups, newspapers, and company listings at Fortune 500 companies.*

The registration process is time-consuming and requires you to provide a good deal of personal information, plus they ask a lot of questions about your career objectives that are probably used by their own recruiting team to target candidates to fill their clients' open positions. But given the huge number of job postings, it's worth the time. Plus, it's good practice if you plan to apply directly for available positions, as opposed to going through recruiters or headhunters.

6FigureJobs.com

Although anyone can view job postings for free at 6FigureJobs.com (www.6figure-jobs.com), only qualified candidates will be admitted into the "Network of Experienced Professionals" database, which is accessible to executive recruiters and employers. Acceptance to this elite group of job seekers provides access to jobs not posted in the public-access section of the site, and also gives you options in terms of level of confidentiality, location, salary requirements, and how you want to be notified of jobs that match your preferences and requirements.

Before you throw your hat into the ring, be sure you have a 25-word skills or experience summary to add during the registration process. This is the first thing employers and recruiters see when scanning for qualified candidates, so spend some time thinking about what sets you apart from the rest of the pack before you submit your application.

The online application takes about five minutes to fill out, assuming you have an electronic résumé to copy and paste into the résumé input field. A plain-text–formatted résumé is a safe bet in any online résumé submission—read Chapter 5 if you need help getting your résumé ready for online job hunting.

If you've never applied for a job online before, my advice to you is to visit the site, search the public-access job postings, which include contract, full-time, and positions at startups, and review the Executive Center application form to find out what you'll need to be considered for acceptance into the database.

Working with Online Headhunters and Recruiters

Although you can apply directly to your target companies, more often than not you'll be dealing with an intermediary for your executive-level job hunt. These middlemen, also known as executive search consultants, recruiters, and headhunters, are the folks deployed by employers to attract and retain hard-to-find or high-in-demand professionals. Here are some virtual recruiting services, as well as ways to get your résumé to the go-betweens to get started on your job hunt.

Career Central

Career Central (www.careercentral.com) is the first email-based recruitment service designed to meet the needs of high-demand professionals and MBA-level-and-up job seekers who are actively looking, and those who are "just thinking." All you need to do to become a member is register and provide background information, interests, and the type of job position you're looking for.

When Career Central has a job that meets your criteria, they notify you instantly via JobCast email. Members who are interested send Career Central a résumé tailored to the job, and within five days, the recruiting services team reviews the résumés and forwards those that meet our clients' search specifications. Hiring managers receive résumés only from our exclusive database of qualified and interested candidates. No other service is able to provide this level of focus and confidentiality to the job-matching process.

Be Your Own Headhunter

Forget recruiters and executive-search consultants. You can become your very own headhunter! Learn from a wildly successful headhunter and career consultant how headhunters work the system to find the right people for the right jobs. Visit Ask the Headhunter at www.asktheheadhunter.com.

Besides the completely confidential job-hunting opportunities, there are wonderful articles and columns by respected career experts such as Dr. Mark Albion, which you can access in the Members Resources section.

Association of Executive Search Consultants

Even if you don't access the member listing of The Association of Executive Search Consultants, which represents retained executive search consulting firms, be sure to read "Guidelines for Selecting an Executive Search Consulting Firm" at www.aesc.org/selecting.html. Before you start your job search, know how the industry operates, and how to spot the good, the bad, and the ugly in the recruiting game. It's written for employers, but it still provides insight as to the makings of a reputable recruiting agency.

Other valuable career resources for executives include the AESC Directory of Members, AESC Professional Practice Standards, links to useful Web sites, useful products, publications, and services such as online research services, recruiting industry publishers, career services, and executive networks.

The Member Listings provide contact information as well as links to available recruiter Web sites, both U.S. and international.

Futurestep

Futurestep (www.futurestep.com) is an executive online recruitment service from Korn/Ferry International and *The Wall Street Journal*. Although there are no job postings on the site, simply complete a few simple assessment tools to be considered for top-notch unadvertised positions.

Besides executive recruiting, qualified candidates can also tap into a host of personalized career services, such as Salary Feedback. Based on the information you provide in your registration, Futurestep will estimate your salary market value and provide you estimates based on your desired position, geographical preference, and your current industry. The Career Style Feedback report summarizes your style of decision making, problem solving, and communicating with other people. The report will also display your satisfaction with different kinds of career tracks and career experiences. The Desired Job Characteristics chart will summarize what you seek in terms of an ideal job, with the most important characteristics higher in the chart.

LeadersOnline (www.leadersonline.com)

LeadersOnline is an Internet-based recruiting service for technology professionals, and focuses on matching emerging leaders with high-caliber IT positions in the $75,000 to $150,000 salary range. Backed by Heidrick & Struggles, a well-known executive search firm, this site offers options in terms of who sees your résumé, when and to whom you release your personal information, and how many "hits" you receive. Near the top of your career page (which is the first page you will see when you log in), there is a counter which shows the number of times your profile has been viewed by a potential employer.

Go with an Expert

Regardless of how or where you find recruiters, or how they find you, be certain to work with agencies and consultants that specialize in placing candidates in your field of expertise. You don't want to trust someone who doesn't understand the needs of employers, or job seekers, trying to put you in a position. Ask for credentials, a client list, and for the names of two or three satisfied customers for a reference check. Be picky!

Now that you're familiar with the specialty sites designed to put high-level execs in high-paying and hard-to-fill positions, go online to explore the growing number of career sites and resources just for the busy executive. After all, your spare time should be spent enjoying life, not pounding the pavement for another job.

The Least You Need to Know

➤ Tackle all your online executive needs with personalized Web guides that provide links to news, business research tools, and career information.

➤ Company and industry research sources are accessible online, and provide valuable information to help you target companies and research prospective employers.

➤ Newsgroups, discussion forums, and professional association Web sites are great places to network and rub shoulders with other high rollers.

➤ Recruiters and headhunters are ready and waiting to see what you're made of—find them online, or let them find you.

➤ Executive-level job sites save time by cutting out job postings that don't meet your requirements and interests.

Chapter 24

Just for Entrepreneurs and Free Agents

In This Chapter

➤ Sites that take you step-by-step on starting a new business

➤ How to own your very own McDonald's restaurant

➤ What to know before you make the leap to becoming an independent professional

➤ Where to go online to get gigs, find health insurance, and get advice and tips on marketing yourself as a free agent

➤ Online resources and tips on how to locate or negotiate alternative work arrangements, such as telecommuting, compressed work week, and job sharing

Thinking about chucking the daily grind and becoming a free agent or starting your own business? You're not the only one. Free agents, entrepreneurs, and telecommuters make up a significant portion of the workforce, and the numbers are growing at a breakneck speed. With the Internet fueling this change in the way we work and where we work, more and more people are starting a business, building home offices, building a clientele, and otherwise finding interesting, challenging work to do—on their terms, not the "Boss Man's."

Why should you waste your time and talent at the same company, doing the same or similar work all the time? And how many times have you thought to yourself: "Why is my boss making 10 times as much money as I? I do all the work. If it weren't for my talent and expertise, he'd lose all his clients." Ego aside, you might be right. But going solo is a serious endeavor. Just like anyone who starts a business, setting up a free agent network is challenging, and it takes a certain kind of person to pull it off.

This chapter covers online resources to help you decide whether free agency or life as an entrepreneur is the right move for you. I also highlight Web sites that connect you with other free agents and with the clients looking for a hired gun to come in, do a project, shake hands, and say goodbye.

And for those who can't sever the tie to a big company and a steady paycheck, telecommuting and work-at-home arrangements are becoming more attractive to both employers and professionals. Why clog up the roadways and take up valuable office space when all you need is a PC, a fax machine, and a filing cabinet to do your work at home?

This chapter covers Web resources on everything from starting a franchise to landing projects and where to go to get advice on taxes, health insurance, marketing your services, getting paid and how much to charge, and everything else you need to know before you make the leap.

Starting Your Own Business

It's the American Dream, isn't it, to run your own business? No more workin' for The Man—you want to work for yourself, and reap all the profits and glory that come with a successful business venture. Well, before you give your two-week notice, take some time to investigate what it takes to start a business, and figure out whether you've got the "right stuff."

As you might have guessed, going online is an excellent way to research small business ownership and to get advice and information to develop a sound business plan before you take the plunge. Here are some of the best resources for small business owner wannabes—from getting started to staying afloat.

Entrepreneur Magazine Online

Entrepreneur Magazine (www.entrepreneurmag.com), the popular print publication, offers an equally compelling and content-rich online resource for all you people itching to start your own business. Millions of Americans—and more and more all the time, thanks in part to the Web and the opportunities it presents—own their own companies. If you've got a bright idea for a new business, or are curious how people actually go about managing this shift in career direction, this is the online magazine for you.

It's a huge site, though, so be sure to browse the content areas from the main page before you jump in. Some golden nuggets, though, are the magazine's feature articles and the Small Business Resource Center. Here, you can search through an extensive archive of small business information in the Small Business Library, a collection of more than 2,000 articles from back issues of *Entrepreneur, New Business Opportunities, Business Start-Ups,* and *Entrepreneurial Woman.*

For startup businesses, there's a complete step-by-step guide for starting a business—the Starting Smart tool, seen in Figure 24.1. If that's not enough, download small business forms from FormNET, a collection of more than 350 forms that deal with everything from starting a business to international trade. You can also browse through an index of small business Web sites or access the Infoseek search engine to scour the Web for other helpful small business tools and information.

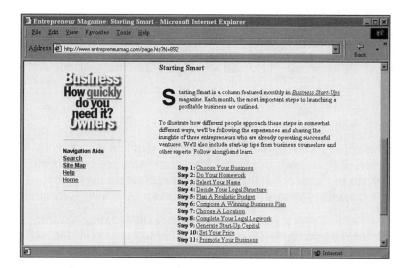

Figure 24.1

The Starting Smart Tool helps you plan, organize, and develop a business plan before you take the plunge into owning your own business.

You can also access a variety of databases of franchise and business opportunities, or search for financing sources through the Guide to Raising Money. If you need suppliers, visit the Thomas Register of American Manufacturers. You'll also find summaries of the top businesses you can start today in the Toolkit area.

The Small Business Forum has chat rooms where you can log on to participate in online seminars with successful entrepreneurs and small business experts, or meet and greet other entrepreneurs. There are also tools to help you create your own Web page, or schedule meetings in the Small Business Forum. With specialty message boards that include Hot Opportunities, Starting Out, Marketing Smarts, Management Issues, Franchising, International Marketing, Homebased Business, and Network Marketing, you're sure to find the information you need.

SmallBizSearch

The Small Biz Search (www.smallbizsearch.com) engine specializes in finding Web content specific to the information needs of small business owners. If you're going online to research your startup options and gather information, make this search engine a part of your toolbox.

The Small Business Advisor

Wow. If you're only thinking about starting your own business, the first glimpse at this Web site is an indication of just how much thinkin' you need to do before you set up shop. Jam-packed with advice and information for starting a business, the Small Business Advisor (www.isquare.com) covers everything under the sun from business news, tax advice, a glossary of terms, and tips for marketing, accounting, stress management, and running your business.

Be sure to check out the Checklists feature—things to do to get your business up and running, such as choosing a partner, working with your attorney and insurance agent, choosing a bank, setting up a customer satisfaction program, and working with employees.

BigStep.com

After careful research and planning, you're ready to take the big step and launch your business. A great way to market your goods or services is with an e-commerce Web site. One site you'll definitely want to check out is Bigstep.com (www.bigstep.com)—an online destination where small businesses can create and maintain their own Web sites.

WYSIWYG

What you see is what you get. This type of site builder lets you point-and-click, add text and pictures, and choose a site color and design menu without having to know a stitch of programming code.

Using a Web-based WYSIWYG site-building wizard, you can build pages, create a catalog or portfolio, sell goods or services, build and maintain a database of customers and contacts, send email newsletters, and more—all without having to learn HTML or buy any packaged software. Better yet, because the site-building tools are Web-based, you can make changes or add to your site from any computer, anywhere in the world.

The basic service is absolutely free, and the cost to set up a merchant account is unbelievably affordable. Besides a low monthly fee, you pay on a per-transaction basis, so the cost is relative to how much business you do, versus paying big bucks just to have an e-commerce site.

Each of Bigstep.com's six sections (Site Building, Communication, Commerce, Catalog, Marketing, and Reporting) includes "tasks"—simple, self-guided activities to help you build and manage your online business and tips on what you need to do to prepare for launching your e-business. If you're new to the Web, a little hand-holding can offer great peace of mind. Figure 24.2 shows the Web-site-building wizard design section.

Here are the main services of BigStep.com:

➤ **Site Building**—Build, edit, and publish the core pages of your Web site using an HTML wizard in the basic or advanced mode. I used this service myself, and must say it's incredibly easy to use, and the design templates are actually very attractive.

➤ **Communication**—Use your customer database and newsletters to build relationships with the people who use your business—online and offline.

➤ **Catalog**—Create an online catalog or portfolio that displays your goods and services. Connect this catalog to your commerce system to start selling online.

➤ **Commerce**—Set up secure online transactions and create a checkout process for your Web site.

➤ **Marketing**—Promote your Web site to increase your business and reach new customers, online and offline. This section helps you submit your site to search engines, Web guides, and directories to help new and existing customers find you. Then, you can create and customize email newsletters to target customers with specific interests.

➤ **Reporting**—View reports about the number of visitors to your site, analyze your site's success, and learn how your customers find your site so you know where to focus your future marketing efforts.

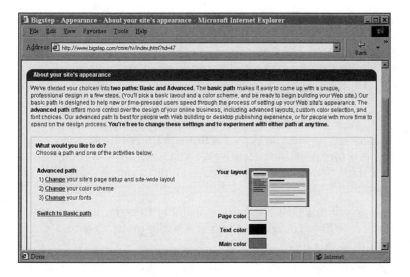

Figure 24.2

BigStep.com takes you step-by-step through building your own e-commerce Web site with an easy-to-use WYSIWYG HTML editor.

Franchise Opportunities

Maybe you've already invested a small fortune in your favorite chain restaurant by eating there on a regular basis, and you're thinking you might as well plop down the cash and buy into the franchise. Not a bad idea, and plenty of folks do it—just take a look down Restaurant Row in any town in America.

Franchising isn't just for the restaurant business, though. Sectors that offer franchise opportunities include business services (Mail Boxes, Etc. and Kinko's), cleaning services (Maid Brigade, Steamatic), food (McDonald's, Subway, Mr. Goodcents Subs & Pasta), home services (Lawn Doctor, Certa ProPainters, Floor Coverings International), personal care (Fantastic Sams hair care, Pressed4Time dry cleaning), professional services (Pacific Medical claims processing and billing, Travel Service Network, ACTION International sales and marketing consulting), retail (GNC, AAMCO Transmissions, 7-Eleven), and specialty products (Crown Trophy, Ashley Avery's Collectables, Northern Greeting Card distributor).

But a lot of people go into franchising with the wrong expectations and end up working more hours than they ever imagined a human being could or should work. It's not easy work, but it is a popular way of "owning" your own business while riding on the coattails of a recognized brand with strong marketing campaigns to support your flow of business.

To learn more about franchise business opportunities, be sure to check out *Entrepreneur* Magazine's Franchise channel at www.entrepreneurmag.com/franchise/.

The New Economy: It's a Different Ballgame These Days

It's the end of the working world as we know it. The era of daily commutes, cubicles, and navy blue suits is slowly coming to an end. As a staggering number of professionals throw in the towel on the 9-to-5 grind and proclaim themselves free agents, it's predicted that within the next ten years, about 50% of the workforce will be self-employed. Working solo. Independent contractors. Project gurus. Free agents. Solo practitioners. E-lancers.

And, thanks largely to the Web, you'll find free agents in nearly every industry that needs talented gurus to perform specific tasks over a finite period of time. There's even an increase in the need for "portable executives"—CEOs, CFOs, and high-rolling chiefs who come in for a short period to fix a problem, roll out a new product, or fill in during a transition period.

The Internet has made much of this possible. With the ability to communicate, negotiate, and share information online, going free agent is actually pretty easy to do, after you've got all your ducks in a row.

But going solo isn't something you just do on a whim. Ease into it gradually. Take a small assignment and work at nights or on the weekends for a while to build up your clientele and get your feet wet. Or go online and test the waters by meeting or getting advice from established free agents. Here are some exceptional starting points if you're considering going solo as your next career move.

FreeAgentNation

Besides his witty commentary and superbly written articles that you'll find at many other free agent Web sites, Dan Pink has put together a top-notch information hub and gathering place for the many millions of people who work as freelancers, self-employeds, independent professionals, temps, consultants, and contractors.

At FreeAgentNation (www.freeagentnation.com), you'll find lots of helpful tools and tips at "Free Agent University" and "Gas-Food-Lodging." You can read about free agency in the "Newsstand," or connect with other free agents in the "Town Hall." And you can sign up for the Free Agent Nation e-newsletter, which chronicles life in this new world of work.

Monster.com Free Agent Guide

After again, this larger-than-life career site hits a grand-slam home run and delivers a smart, comprehensive guide to life as a free agent. And seeing as how I'm a free agent myself, you can bet I've scoured the Web for tips, advice, and resources to make the transition to free agency life a little smoother. If only Monster.com could get my cats to talk to me...

Oh, yeah. Monster.com would like you to use the Free Agent Auction, but more on that later. If you're curious about what it's like to be a free agent and what you need to know before you make the leap, be sure to check out Monster.com's Free Agent Guide at content.talentmarket.monster.com/contractor/freeagentguide/index.stm.

Site for Sore Eyes

Aquent Magazine

For a sassy, smart, and irreverent view of life as a hired gun, be sure to check out Aquent Magazine at www.aquentmagazine.com. Articles such as "Bearing Your First Web Child" and "Beating the Night Terrors" will touch the hearts and tickle the funny bones of any independent professional. The magazine's not all laughs, though. You'll find tips and information on getting work, doing work, getting paid, how to deal with taxes, and how to stay (in)sane.

Working Today

Working Today is the "national voice for America's independent workforce." This nonprofit membership organization promotes the interests of freelancers, independent contractors, temps, part-timers, and contingent workers by providing access to group-rate health insurance, free legal and financial advice, tax information, referrals to resources for independent workers, and a voice in the political arena.

For a directory of online resources and links to sites of interest to free agents and independent workers, be sure to check out the Directory of Resources (www.workingtoday.org/other/toolkit1.html). There's not a link in here that isn't worthy of inclusion. Topics cover Small Business and Contractor Resources, Temp Resources, Job and Project Search Tools, Salary Information, Tax Advice, Health and Disability Insurance, Investing and Retirement Planning, Family and Personal Support, Online Communities That Care About Work, Politics, and General Information.

Working Solo

Another great resource for independent professionals, Terri Lonier's Working Solo (www.workingsolo.com), has a slew of resources, information, products, and services to help you grow your small business or get started as a free agent. Sign up for the free monthly newsletter, or read expert advice and gain insight on key small business topics such as "Six Ways to Test Your Business Idea," "The Name Game: Naming Your Business," "Make the Telephone a Power Tool," "Lifelong Learning," "How to Survive an Audit," and "Ten Ways to Fund Your Business."

Bartering—No Doh!

As a free agent or small business owner, you might need the services of other professionals such as accountants, lawyers, computer technicians, marketers, or designers. Forget forking out the cold, hard cash—it's time to barter! Be sure to check out these Web sites: www.BarterTrust.com, www.Barter.com, www.Targetbarter.com, www.barternews.com, www.nate.org, and www.irta.net.

Project Marketplace: Going Once, Going Twice

Looking for projects? Well, people looking for experts need a place to find you, too. The following sites make this possible by providing a forum for you to present your skills and services, and to hook up with companies in need of your expertise. Here are a handful of the most popular free agent exchange and project auction sites on the Web.

➤ *Guru.com.*   Guru.com (www.guru.com) is a site that helps independent professionals by providing a free gig-matching service for gurus to find contract or ongoing freelance assignments. Gurus can browse an extensive contract job directory or use the smart and savvy gig search engine to find the ideal assignment. Or, let employers find you by creating a Guru profile—an online portfolio that tells potential clients about your professional, educational, and personal background. Figure 24.3 shows my personal profile overview at Guru.com.

Be sure to check out the informative and engaging advice and information sections or tool around the professional community to meet and get advice from other free agents. The site also offers Web-based business-management tools and special discounts on goods and services, including health insurance.

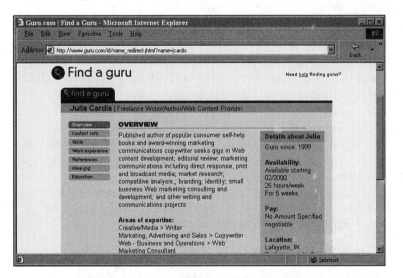

Figure 24.3

My free agent profile—this gives employers a quick overview of my expertise, experience, availability, and willingness to work on- or off-site.

➤ *eLance.com.*   eLance.com (www.elance.com) is an up-and-coming free agent project exchange forum where companies post projects and solicit bids from free agents. The best-qualified or the nicest price wins. Or, if you're not into the bidding war, for standardized services, buyers can browse the descriptions and place orders for fixed-price services posted by the experts on eLance. Both buyers and sellers use eLance tools such as the Work Space—a shared file system for exchanging and viewing files—and private message boards to get the job done across the digital domain.

➤ *FreeAgent.com.* FreeAgent.com (www.freeagent.com) offers a project exchange where you look for projects and employers look for you. The system works just like any other contract exchange site—you set up an e-portfolio for employers to review your credentials, or you can view the project postings and apply for projects of interest.

The site also offers the e-office for-fee service in which FreeAgent.com helps review the contract and helps get you the best possible terms after you find the client and negotiate the billing rate. After you start or complete the project, you submit your timesheets to FreeAgent.com, which in turn invoices the client. When payment is received, FreeAgent.com handles the nitty-gritty payroll service, deducting authorized insurance, payroll taxes, membership fees, 401(k), and other withholdings.

➤ *Monster.com Free Agent Auction.* Taking a slightly different twist on the talent auction concept, instead of free agents bidding for work or responding to RFPs (request for proposal), here the employers bid against one another for talent. The highest price gets the free agent, and the work begins. Just like the other free agent sites, you'll have to complete a profile, so be sure to read the FAQs to make sure you stand out from the competition and get the highest bidding price. Take a spin at talentmarket.monster.com.

➤ *WorkExchange.* Employers post projects to the WorkExchange (www.workexchange.com) database by filling out specification forms, including the type of work, completion date, and work location, and after submitted, the project is posted on the site by WorkExchange's support staff. As freelancers see the projects and bid, WorkExchange relays the bids to employers who then accept or decline offers.

A large network of partner sites such as Lycos, Iwon.com, WetFeet.com, and other Web portals promise a larger number of projects. An interesting feature is the Community Reputation, a member rating system that allows free agents and employers to fill out a virtual "report card" on one another to let other members or employers know what it was like working with one another—such as whether the work got done on time, and whether payment was received as promised. Check them out at www.workexchange.com.

Talent Brokers and Executive Contract Work

Say you're a contract worker or free agent, but you don't want to "mess" with finding new projects, taxes, or the other operational issues that go along with contract work. Talent brokers and project agencies are here to help. A major step beyond the traditional temporary agency, these folks don't place just anyone in temporary positions. Rigorous testing and rounds and rounds of interviews are required for placement by a talent agency.

And if you're a high-level executive verging on major burnout from working the same high-stress job, or if you've just been "right-sized" out of a job, consider an interim assignment.

➤ *Aquent.* Formerly MacTemps. Aquent (www.aquent.com) is a specialized talent agency providing both contract and permanent experts in the areas of Creative and Design, Production and Presentations, Web Applications and Development, and Systems Administration and Technical Support. Aquent provides a range of personal and business insurance products geared toward the special needs of free agents, and steps up to the plate when it comes to cash-flow issues, such as getting paid on a regular basis versus having to track down delinquent accounts or risk nonpayment—pitfalls of life as a free agent. The agency also provides ongoing training and other support services for the independent professional.

➤ *IMCOR.* IMCOR (www.imcor.com) is a broker of "Portable Executives"—industry experts, project managers, and line managers available to work on a flexible basis to manage a specific project, fill a sudden management vacancy, roll out a new product or lead a project, or to try out for a permanent position. Assignments usually require a full-time commitment, and usually on very short notice.

Project assignments last on average six months, with roughly 40% converting to permanent positions. Some assignments, however, can be as short as one week or as long as 18 months. The "tryout" assignments usually convert to permanent positions.

Jobs for Open-Collar and Bathrobe Professionals

With office space costs on the rise and unemployment at an all-time low (at least for now), the concept of telecommuting is becoming quite attractive to employers and employees alike. Not only does telecommuting save costs across the board (less money spent on commuting, less time in the car/more time on the job, increased productivity, and so on), it's a darned good way to attract and retain today's active professional.

If your company doesn't offer telecommuting, compressed workweek, job share, or other perks and you're considering approaching your boss about these options, you can go online to get advice and facts to prove it's a good idea. And if your boss won't bend at all or not far enough, you can even find telecommuter-friendly employers online.

Here are some excellent starting points for exploring telecommuting, work-at-home opportunities, and other work style arrangements.

➤ *About.com Telecommuting Guide.* About.com has a Telecommuting section (telecommuting.about.com) that is a one-stop resource for open-collar workers and bathrobe professionals. Follow this Web guide to a plethora of sites and online experts offering good reasons to work from home, as well as common pitfalls to avoid when it comes to flex time and other alternative work arrangements.

➤ *Home-Based Working Moms.* Home-Based Working Moms (www.hbwm.com) is a national association of parents who work at home. HBWM provides its members with support, networking, information, a monthly (print) newsletter, email discussion list, panel of experts, publicity opportunities, online membership directory, and member discounts on computers, office supplies, and travel. Be sure to read the articles on how to avoid scams and spot a reputable work-at-home opportunity.

➤ *Moneymakin' Mommies.* This clever and resource-packed site (see Figure 24.4) helps stay-at-home parents (not just mommies) find legitimate work-at-home jobs, freelance opportunities, tips on how to run a successful business, a barter exchange for goods and services, and other ways to make money at home. Check out this family-friendly site at www.moneymakingmommy.com.

Figure 24.4

Looking for work that lets you be a stay-at-home mom? Be sure to visit Moneymakin' Mommies for tips, job leads, and advice on how to be a super parent.

For those job seekers who are coming to the realization that working for one company just isn't going to satisfy, there are options, and plenty of employers are happy to work with you on an as-needed basis.

Be sure to investigate this opportunity, though, before you throw in the towel on your regular-paying job. The last thing you want is to mess up your life by making a hasty decision about going solo. It's a liberating experience, but don't paint yourself into a corner just for that fleeting feeling of freedom. It's hard work, so be sure you've got your ducks in a row before you declare yourself an independent professional.

A Final Word to Job Hunters

We can all thank our lucky stars that the Web is here to guide us as we go about managing our careers and looking for the dream job we all deserve.

I hope this book and the information and advice you find online help you land a dream job. At the very least, I hope the Web helps you take charge of your career so that *every* job you land is a dream job—always better than the one before.

Happy hunting, and best of luck managing your career.

The Least You Need to Know

➤ Starting a business is a complicated matter—go online to get the information and advice you need to succeed.

➤ Learn about franchising opportunities online and what it takes to get started in the business.

➤ The world of work is a-changin' from full-time positions to contract positions and freelance assignments.

➤ Going online is the fastest and smartest way to launch your free agent career, and find out what it takes to make it as a hired gun.

➤ Telecommuting, work-at-home, and flexible work arrangements are appealing to both employees and employers, so find out how to negotiate these terms or find employers that will work with you to meet your alternative work-style needs.

Glossary

Active job seeker   Someone who is sending out résumés, networking, and otherwise actively trying to find a new job. See *Passive job seeker*.

ASCII   The American Standard Code for Information Interchange. Also known as *plain-text* that can be read and understood by most computers.

Background check   An investigation into your past, including your credit history, employment record, driving record, and just about anything else an employer wants to know before making the offer.

Bathrobe professionals   People who work from home in a more casual atmosphere.

BBS   See *Bulletin Board System*.

Blind ad   A job posting that doesn't specify the employer, often placed by *third-party recruiters*; also known as a *vaporous ad*.

Browser   A software application that allows you to view Web documents and manage your online activity through the use of a *history* folder, favorites folder (or bookmarks), and other tools you need to navigate the Web.

Bulletin Board System (BBS)   An online posting system where users can ask questions and post replies.

Candidate-controlled résumé posting site   A *résumé database* that allows you to deny or allow access to your résumé.

Chat   A real-time, virtual dialogue/typing session between participants of a chat room.

Chronological résumé (also reverse chronological) A résumé that outlines your work experience on a timeline basis.

Cobranding Alliances between different Web sites to share information, content, and market share. Check job sites for cobranding agreements to find out whether your information is shared, and to save time visiting the same site twice. (Also known as partnerships, alliances, and network affiliates.)

Cold call See *Cold letter.*

Cold email See *Cold letter.*

Cold letter Cold letters, emails, and *calls* are unsolicited attempts at landing a job—the equivalent to junk mail. They are all attempts to make contacts with a company you'd like to work for but are not responses to specific ads or openings.

Company insiders Someone who works at a company and is willing to provide information or opinions on what it's like to work at the company.

Company profile An overview of a company's products, services, clients, location, and work environment.

Contractor A self-employed expert who works for a company on a finite project. Usually involves the signing of a contractual agreement to ensure work is done on time and on budget, and to protect the expert's interests as well. See *Freelancer.*

Cover letter A letter that accompanies your *résumé* to introduce the résumé and highlight your skills and selling points; it should contain the job title and where you saw the posting.

Criteria Necessary things such as a geographic location, a salary requirement, job title, keywords, or other information that indicates your preferences in terms of what you're looking for in a job.

Curriculum Vitae A résumé for people in academia, or the European term for résumé.

Database Also *résumé database.* A computer-based storage system for vast amounts of data and information. You can upload your résumé to a database that employers use to search for résumés.

Discussion forum An online meeting place where users post messages and read responses.

Distance learning Advanced training or college-level courses that you take online.

Diversity The initiative to employ people of nonmajority ethnicities, lifestyles, and gender. Diversity provides a broad spectrum of ideas and attitudes that benefit companies in an increasingly global economy.

Download   To transfer a file from a server to your computer's desktop or other file location. The opposite of *upload*.

Downsize   A reduction in a company's workforce to reduce overhead and create a leaner, meaner machine.

EEO   Equal employment opportunity. See *Diversity*.

E-lancer   Similar to a *freelancer*, an e-lancer obtains and manages projects online. E-lancers have a broader geographic range in terms of where they find clients and how their work is exchanged with clients.

Email   Electronic mail is used in the job search as a means of transmitting your résumé and cover letter, or for networking or communicating with career-related resources.

Email monitoring   The act of viewing or reading employees' sent and received email messages on work-owned computers.

Employee salvaging   An attempt on the part of an employer to find out who's looking for a job in order to keep the good people from leaving.

Employment agency   A business that helps job seekers find jobs, and helps employers find candidates. See *Headhunter*.

Executive search firms   Agencies that place high-level executives and other hard-to-fill positions. Often confused with *headhunters*.

FAQ   Frequently Asked Questions. A list of commonly asked questions or general information for new site visitors.

Filter   A keyword, location, job title, or other requirement used to limit results based on specified criteria.

Fired   Canned, let go, booted, or otherwise dismissed from a position due to inability to perform the job or due to wrongdoing, such as looking for a job on company time.

Flex time   A work arrangement that allows flexibility on start and stop times, telecommuting arrangements, job sharing, and condensed workweeks, as opposed to a strict Monday through Friday, 8-to-5 routine.

Forum   An online *discussion board, bulletin board, message board,* or *newsgroup*.

Franchise   A privately owned small business authorized to sell or distribute a nationally advertised company's product or service. McDonald's is an example of a franchise. The owner benefits from advertising, brand recognition, and other services such as training support provided by the franchise grantor.

Free agent   See *Freelancer*.

Freelancer   A self-employed person who works on a per-project basis or short-term assignment for a company; an e-lancer is a person who primarily gets projects using the Web or uses the Web to communicate and deliver the final product. See also *Free agent, E-lancer, Independent professional, Contractor.*

Functional résumé   A résumé that highlights your skills and experience, rather than your work history. It should include somewhere the places and dates you've worked, even if you have a bumpy past.

Gateway site   A starting point or Web guide that deals with a specific topic or category of interest.

Generic résumé   A résumé that contains no identifying information, such as your full name, address, or the companies you've worked for.

Hacker   A computer expert known for legally or illegally invading the systems of other companies or individuals and creating uses for computer equipment and software other than those uses originally intended.

Headhunter   A talent scout hired by one company to locate a high-level executive for a specific position. Often involves recruiting an employee away from another company, often a competitor.

Hidden jobs   Jobs that employers don't want you to find. Ha! Jobs that aren't advertised to the general public or that haven't been created yet.

History list   A list of Web documents that you've visited in an online session. You can erase your history list to keep prying eyes from seeing where you've gone online.

Home page   The opening or welcome page of a Web site.

Hot jobs   New or developing career fields that promise employability and well-paying jobs for people with the required skills.

HTML (Hypertext Markup Language)   The basic coding system used to create Web documents.

HTTP (Hypertext Transfer Protocol)   The data-transmission protocol used to transfer Web documents across the Internet. Often seen preceding a Web address, as in `http://www.somewebsite.com`.

Hyperlinks   Highlighted text or graphics that you can click on to access a linked Web page.

Independent professional   See *Freelancer.*

Industry profile   An overview of what it's like to work in a given field or profession, like accounting or manufacturing, and what skills and education are required for various positions in that field.

Industry-specific job sites   See *Niche job sites.*

Informational interview   An information-gathering meeting with a seasoned professional in which you ask about career opportunities, challenges, and advice on how to succeed in a given industry.

Inhouse recruiter   See *Recruiter*.

Interface   The way something is set up to operate. With computers, interface consists of operating system commands, display formats, and other devices that allow the user to communicate and operate the program or computer. For example, the Windows operating system interface consists of pull-down menus, clickable icons, and other standard features that are found on any computer running a Windows operating system.

Internet service provider (ISP)   A company that provides you with access to the Internet, usually for a monthly fee. Might (should) also provide hosting of your personal or résumé Web site.

Intranet   An internal network within a company, or used by a group of free agents to communicate in a centralized network from remote locations.

Job agent   A robot that scours new job postings and sends you an email letting you know a match has been found. Uses *push* technology.

Job search engine   A search engine that searches job-posting sites for matches based on your *keywords* and other *criteria*.

Job sharing   An alternative work arrangement in which two part-time employees share the duties and responsibilities of a full-time position.

Keyword summary   A brief paragraph of keywords on a résumé that summarizes skills, software or hardware, industry buzzwords, or other important terminology that an employer might use to search for candidates.

Lay off   To dismiss an employee due to production slowdowns, *downsizing*, or other reasons not related to job performance.

Link   See *Hyperlink*.

Log in/on   The procedure of entering your username and password to gain access to a members-only area of a Web site.

Log off/out   The procedure of terminating your session or disconnecting from a Web site.

Lurking   The act of reading newsgroup or discussion messages without posting or otherwise participating in the forum. No one knows you're there.

Mega job site   A darned big job site. A national, general job site that has lots of job postings, plenty of user services, and other content to guide you in your career search. Monster.com is an example of a mega job site.

Meta search engine   A search engine that deploys numerous search engines at the same time to bring back the highest number of search results. DogPile.com and Google.com are examples of meta search engines.

Minimum/Maximum salary requirements   The least or most money you're willing to accept.

Modem   A peripheral device that enables your computer to utilize regular phone lines to call your ISP, which, in turn, provides access to the Internet.

Netiquette   Proper online behavior.

Networking   For job hunters, career networking is the building of contacts to learn about job opportunities or otherwise get your foot in the door.

New Economy   A term given to the current economy, fueled by technology and the quest for information, skills, and speed. It's similar to the industrial age, the agrarian age, and other revolutions spurred by technological advancements. The new economy is concerned with the global economy and the information revolution.

Newsgroup   An online *forum* or posting *discussion* that follows a specific topic or discussion.

Niche job sites   Job sites that have postings and information for a certain industry or field. See also *Industry-specific job sites.*

No-collar workers   *Telecommuters, free agents,* and other workers not restricted by the routines of office or on-location work.

One-page fact sheet   A summary sheet you give to references that contains dates of employment, job titles, and attributes you'd like your references to mention.

Outplacement service   A service sometimes provided to terminated or laid-off employees to assist in the finding of a new job, to provide additional training or counseling.

Passive job seeker   Someone who has a job, but might consider other options if the right offer came along.

Password-protected résumé   A résumé that requires a username and password to access.

Plain-text résumé   A no-frills, ASCII-formatted résumé that transfers nicely via email and online job application forms. No bold, italic, bullets, frilly fonts, or underlines can be used.

Portable executive   A high-level executive who works on a temporary basis, usually from a week to 18 months, during a transition period or for a new product launch or other specialty project.

Portfolio (online portfolio)   A Web site that showcases your samples or illustrates your professional achievements.

Positioning   The act of presenting yourself in the most favorable light to a potential employer.

Prescreening   Questions or requested information that weeds out unqualified applicants.

Proactive   Acting or preparing to deal with anticipated problems or opportunities. A proactive professional knows that a certain skill or experience will be outdated in two years, and therefore seeks training to stay competitive.

Profile   A summary of your skills, experience, and desired work projects. Used as an overview of your résumé or a highlight of your expertise.

Push   This kind of technology retrieves data from the Web and pushes it to users who have requested that additional information be supplied, as in job agents that update you with new job postings.

Query   To submit a request to a search engine that includes keywords or other criteria.

RealAudio   A popular audio format that allows you to listen to sound files on the Web.

Recruiter   A person who finds and screens job candidates. An *inhouse recruiter* works on staff for one employer. A *third-party recruiter* works on behalf of several companies at any given time.

Reference check   When a potential employer calls on your former employers or personal references to check you out and get an endorsement or denial of your ability to do the job.

Regional job guides   Job listings that are specific to a certain region or city.

Relocate   To pick up and move for a job.

Relocation expenses   When an employer is willing to pick up the costs of moving.

Résumé   A career document that outlines and highlights your skills, work experience, education, and your qualifications to do the job.

Résumé database (bank)   Where you upload your résumé.

Right-sizing   When a company trims its workforce until it's just the right size for the operating budget.

Salary history   A summary of where you've worked and how much you earned.

Salary survey   A report on the average salary for a given profession, broken down by geographic locations and years of experience.

Screening tool   See *Prescreening*.

Search engine   A technology that searches the Web for documents that match a keyword query.

Skills and Interest assessments   Tools or quizzes to help you decide what you're good at and what you want to do in your career.

Spam   Unsolicited email sent to large groups of recipients. Usually advertising for an online service.

Spider technology   Software that scours the Web or databases to retrieve information or résumés.

Target employer   The employer you're trying to get a job from.

Telecommuting   A work arrangement in which an employee works from home or another remote location and communicates with the home office via fax, Internet, cell phone, or overnighted documents.

Telnet   A program that lets Internet users log in to email from computers other than their own.

Third-party recruiter   See *Recruiter*.

Transferable skills   Skills that describe a function you can perform that can be used in a variety of job situations. They typically describe how you work with data, things, and people.

Upload   Transferring a file from your computer to another. For example, putting your résumé on a Web site. The opposite of downloading.

Vapor job ads   Bogus job ads placed by slimy recruiters to get you to send your résumé to sell to another recruiter, or to keep on file in case a real position opens up someday.

Virtual job fair   An online gathering of employers or recruiters designed to attract a large number of candidates for the purpose of screening applicants and filling positions.

Virus   A program that duplicates itself and travels between computers. Employers frown upon résumés as attachments, as viruses can be transmitted this way.

Web Form   A Web form is an interactive document that contains fields for you to input information, such as your name, résumé, skills summary, or objective statement.

Websumé   An HTML-formatted version of your résumé.

Wizard   A magical program that takes you step-by-step through the building of a document, such as a résumé or Web page.

WYSIWYG (What You See Is What You Get)   An HTML editor program that requires no knowledge of code, and lets users point-and-click, select from design templates, or otherwise use a wizard to build a Web site.

Index

347

X-Z